DATE DUE NOV 0 6 2018

LET'S GO

(SO WE CAN GET BACK)

JEFF TWEEDY

DUTTON

LET'S GO

(SO WE CAN GET BACK)

A MEMOIR OF RECORDING

AND DISCORDING WITH

WILCO, ETC.

DUTTON

An imprint of Penguin Random House LLC
375 Hudson Street
New York, NY 10014

Song lyrics © Words Ampersand Music, administered by BMG Rights Management.

Comic on pages 134–139 © 2018 George Eckart

DUTTON and the D colophon are registered
trademarks of Penguin Random House LLC.

LIBRARY OF CONGRESS CATALOGING-IN-PUBLICATION DATA
Names: Tweedy, Jeff, 1967– author.
Title: Let's go (so we can get back) : a memoir of recording and
discording with Wilco, etc. / Jeff Tweedy.
Description: New York, NY : Dutton, [2018]
Identifiers: LCCN 2018040327 (print) | LCCN 2018042754 (ebook) |
ISBN 9781101985281 (ebook) | ISBN 9781101985267 (hc)
Subjects: LCSH: Tweedy, Jeff, 1967– | Alternative rock musicians—United
States—Biography. | Alternative country musicians—United States—Biography. |
Wilco (Musical group) | LCGFT: Autobiographies.
Classification: LCC ML420.T954 (ebook) | LCC ML420.T954 A3
2018 (print) | DDC 782.42166092 [B]—dc23
LC record available at https://lccn.loc.gov/2018040327

Printed in the United States of America
1   3   5   7   9   10   8   6   4   2

BOOK DESIGN BY KATY RIEGEL

TO SUSIE, SPENCER, AND SAMMY

CONTENTS

LET'S GO

(SO WE CAN GET BACK)

INTRODUCTION

NOBODY WANTS TO eat the cat's eyes.

I'm not an especially superstitious person by nature, but I get it. If a red velvet cake with a cat's portrait in icing just mysteriously shows up backstage during a tour, and then it inexplicably reappears the next night, and five days and two cities later the cake is still there, with a slice or two cut out but the cat's face and the eyes are mostly unscathed, I don't think it's unreasonable to be cautious. What if it's a demon cat cake? It probably isn't, but nobody in the band is taking responsibility for the cake, or has any explanation for how it's followed us this far, so I can't automatically discount the possibility that it's some sort of supernatural sweet.

I'm in the dressing room of Kings Theatre in Brooklyn, sitting on a couch and mindlessly strumming my guitar and trying to avoid eye contact with the cat cake. Nels Cline, the guitarist for my band Wilco, has boldly volunteered to be the first among us to try a bite.

"It tastes nothing like the record," he announces.

I find this reassuring.

The cat on the cake is the same white Persian cat featured on the cover of our 2015 album, *Star Wars*. Or maybe it's a British longhair. I don't know nearly enough about cats. It's also the same cat from a painting that hangs in the kitchen at the Loft, the Chicago studio that's been our second home since 2000. It's a pretty fascinating painting. The cat is sitting on a black velvet cushion, in front of a vase filled with pale roses. Who poses a cat like that? It's ridiculous. The cat's expression isn't the usual feline sneer of bored indifference. This cat has an expression that's more like "I am Coconut. I am your new god." All cats are arrogant, but I find this one to be exceptionally so.

Since releasing the album, we've come to discover that there are reproductions of this exact painting hung on the walls in some of our followers' parents' and grandparents' homes. So that was an unintentional though satisfying freak-out we were able to deliver as a bonus for a few lucky fans. We've tried tracking down the artist (and by "we" I mean Mark, my close friend and studio manager, who also did the initial mock-up of the cover). It's signed by somebody named Tamara Barett, but nobody by that name claims responsibility for the cat portrait. We reached out to a half dozen Tamara Baretts, hoping one of them would take credit, but they've all claimed ignorance. We even exchanged emails with Tamara Burnett, a pet portraitist whose style is almost identical to Tamara Barett. Burnett told us we had the wrong Tamara, but admitted, "It looks like something I would have done."

I guess we were hoping that putting the painting on a record cover would get her attention—the real Tamara—at least enough for her to call a lawyer and threaten us with a lawsuit for using her art without permission. So we could pay her. But it didn't work. We heard nothing, not even a peep. (We didn't even hear from George Lucas, and I was sure we'd at least get a cease-and-desist letter for naming our album *Star Wars*. We even had backup artwork done so we could change the name of the record to *Cease and Desist* in the event he went after us. Nope. No such luck.)

At this point you're probably wondering, "Is this whole book going to be like this? Is he going to spend almost three hundred pages overexplaining kitschy cat art?" Maybe. It's too soon to say, really. Sorry if that isn't what you were expecting. (If that is what you were expecting, well . . . kudos, that's impressive.)

You might also be thinking, "Speaking of cats, I bet there is a really elaborate and interesting explanation for why Wilco put a Persian or possibly British longhair cat on an album cover." First of all, thank you for assuming that. Let me answer your question by not really answering it. The cat painting, as I mentioned, is on display at the Loft, where I and the other Wilco members go to play and sometimes record music, so it's something we see every, or almost every, day.

But the Loft is a big space with a lot of art. The cat painting is in the kitchen, so we only see it during lunch and snack breaks, in between jamming. (Yes, that is how professional musicians talk. "Would anyone care to do some jamming?" "Why, yes, let's jam." "Then jam we shall!") In the recording space, mounted on the console, are framed and signed black-and-white photographs of Bob Newhart and Don Rickles. They're the centerpieces of the room. Both of them are signed *To Wilco*, but only Don's signature is still visible. Newhart's signature has disappeared. I don't mean faded. It's gone. Vanished. His handwriting has been eradicated by the power of sad mid-tempo rock. I know that's not a satisfactory explanation, but that's the best I can do.

Between the Newhart and Rickles portraits is an equally amazing photo (also signed) of Rich Kelly & Friendship. If you're unfamiliar with this New Jersey ensemble, I want you to do something for me. Put down this book, go to the nearest device with Internet connectivity, direct your browser to YouTube, and search for "Rich Kelly & Friendship" and "I'd Like to Teach the World to Sing." Then watch it. In its entirety. But if you're in a hurry, fast-forward to the 1:35 mark, when the bassist breaks into a happy foot solo. Everything about this video, but especially the dancing, makes me happy. I love how the guitarist moves his microphone stand out of the way, suggesting that the bassist's happy-feet freak-out is entirely expected. I love how they shout his name after it's over—"Tom Sullivan!"—confirming yet again that, yes, *this was a "solo,"* and not just the exact moment when Tom Sullivan's diet pills kicked in. This isn't just a grainy video of the best lounge act you never knew existed until right now. It's nothing short of magical realism. I never studied art theory, so I don't know if this is technically accurate. But it certainly seems like magical realism to me, as it's something that really happened, and it's fucking magical.

That framed photo of Rich Kelly & Friendship in matching tuxedos, along with the portraits of Don Rickles and Bob Newhart it's sandwiched between, is a defining tableaux at the Loft. You might even call it the holy trinity of our recording space. You can't ignore it or pretend it isn't there, not with all those sets of eyes following you. It'd be like walking into Italy's Basilica of St. Clare church and *not* noticing the San Damiano Cross. Of course you notice it. It's a huge, historically significant crucifix on the wall! That's the same feeling we want people to have when they enter the Loft. You stare at Bob, Don, and Rich like you might gaze up at the San Damiano Cross, with hushed reverence and mouth agape in wonderment at the awesome, unknowable infinitude of the universe.

That's what we were looking at when we made the *Star Wars* album. Every song, every note, was created under their collective benevolent gaze. I remember singing the lyrics "Orchestrate the shallow pink refrigerator drone" and looking up and thinking Don Rickles was glaring back at me like he was saying, "Pink refrigerator drone? Boy, are you a hockey puck!"

My point is, there isn't a fascinating or aesthetically complicated reason for why we put a cat on the cover of our album and called it *Star Wars*. The album needed a name and a cover. The cat painting could just as easily have been Don Rickles. And instead of *Star Wars*, we could have named it *Jerry Maguire* or *E.T.* and it would have made just as much sense. I'm just trying to put it in the right context for you. It's entirely plausible that Wilco could've made a record called *Wrath of Khan* with an album cover that's just an old black-and-white head shot of Don Rickles in a tux.

It could still happen.

It's hard for me to not be self-conscious for lots of reasons I hope to illuminate for you later, but it's even worse writing a book about yourself. You're basically the lead character in your own narrative. How do you not constantly worry, "Who do I think I am?" and "Look at you, writing a book, aren't you special." It's nonfiction, so I guess my only obligation is to tell the truth. But I'm also acutely aware that

I can't be entirely objective. It's not like I can give the main character a fatal flaw that we all know is going to be the source of his undoing in the final chapter. I mean, hopefully, anyway. Maybe there is a fatal flaw and I'm the only one who isn't seeing it. Maybe I'm writing myself toward an emotional breakdown and I'm the last one to realize it. That actually sounds like a pretty great book.

But if you're me, which I am, it's hard not to assume that some of you are just skimming the first few pages, trying to decide if this book is worth your money. Are you sure you want to fork over $28 for a bunch of chapters on "Here's what was going through my head during the three-and-a-half-minute guitar solo on 'At Least That's What You Said'"? Like Tuli Kupferberg from the Fugs said when I met him and told him that he was my hero, "Oy, times are tough all over." Nobody has the disposable income to splurge on a memoir by a moderately successful indie rock "stalwart" if it's not going to deliver something pretty entertaining.

Let's reveal some spoilers right up front before we waste anybody's time.

1. There are two different guys named Jay covered in this book.
You're going to need to stay on your toes to keep up. They both get written about pretty extensively and sometimes they even appear in the same section. I've done my best to make it clear who I'm talking about when I write "Jay," but, like I said, heads up. Be alert.

2. There will be no mention of prescription painkillers.
If you picked this book up looking for wild, druggy stories about my addiction to opiates, you're out of luck. I want to put those years

behind me. And frankly, there really isn't much to tell. When you take a lot of Vicodin, your life is not a nonstop Algonquin Round Table. There's a lot of being numb, and a lot of being sad that you're not numb. That's it.

Let's leave it at this: I had some addiction problems, and then I got better. We're all good now. Thanks for asking! Oh, and the songs I wrote during that time period are just musical explorations of how happy I was at the time. Sorry if there was any misunderstanding.

3. That last part was a joke.

Jesus, of *course* I'm going to write about the drugs. I'm pulling your leg. Would you have believed Keith Richards if he'd started his memoir with "Listen, guys, the less said about my experiences with heroin, the better. I'd rather just write about what it's like to be a grandfather"?

4. I wish this book was about the Raccoonists.

If you're not familiar with the Raccoonists, I'm not sure where you get the nerve calling yourself a fan. How have you not heard of the band I started with my kids, Spencer and Sammy? We have just one officially released song, "Own It." It was included as the B-side on a Deerhoof split 7-inch. We also recorded a full album's worth of material, including some of the best covers of George Harrison, Teenage Fanclub, and Skip Spence ever sung by a fifteen-year-old. (I personally feel that a lyric like "A severed eye would gratify my soul, I must confess" sounds more convincing when it's coming from a guy with unfinished algebra homework.) We haven't released any of it yet, because the musical mission of the Raccoonists is to be as enigmatic as possible. It's like those lines from the Wilco song "The

Late Greats": "So good you won't ever know / You'll never hear it on the radio." That could be about the Raccoonists. It isn't. Not even slightly. But it *could* be, that's what I'm saying.

The only reason I wrote this book is because I wanted to finally tell the story of the greatest rock trio, featuring me on guitar with a teenage drummer and a barely teenage lead vocalist, that never officially released an album, or went on tour, or was ever heard outside of a basement and that the world is mostly unaware of. I intended this to be like that Michael Azerrad book *Our Band Could Be Your Life*, but less about bands like Black Flag and Minutemen, and entirely about the Raccoonists. I would've shared all of the scandalous details, like how the band's original name was the Rockingest, but I misunderstood Spencer and thought he said the Raccoonists, and I said, "That's the greatest band name I've ever heard," and he didn't fight me on it, so we went with the Raccoonists, even though the Rockingest is arguably a better name.

I would have liked to be able to share the story about the time we almost broke up because it was a school night, and Susie was like, "You have to stop now. Don't make me be the dick here. Jeff, tell them to get in their pj's." And I intended to tell you all about how the Raccoonists actually broke up, because Spencer told us, "I'm going to college," and Sammy and I were like, "Seriously? This is how it ends? Et tu, Spencer?" But then the band Tweedy was born from its ashes, like a phoenix rising, and then we went on tour in Japan, and Sammy came along, and we convinced him to sing "Thirteen" during the Tokyo and Osaka shows, and it was like a mini Raccoonists reunion, except nobody knew it was significant, because other than that 7-inch

B-side, nobody knew the Raccoonists had ever been a real band. Which just made it more "Late Great"–ish, even though that song (I can't emphasize this enough) isn't at all about the Raccoonists.

Anyway, that's what I wanted to write about. But my publisher kept editing it out and I kept slipping it back in, and then they started using words like "actionable" if I persisted in writing about my band with my kids to the exclusion of the other bands I'm in or was in.

FIFTEEN MINUTES BEFORE the show at the Kings, the mood backstage is like a summer picnic. All the civilians and guests have been ushered out, and it's just the guys and me, making small talk, nibbling on snacks, and fiddling with our instruments. I've still got David Bowie on my mind, so I see if I can figure how to play "Space Oddity." Slowly, the other guys start joining in, grabbing their guitars and calling out chord changes to one another, singing harmony, or just drumming along on the nearest flat surface. Anything to contribute. It's that organic and natural. Nobody says, "Let's play some Bowie." It starts with a note, which blindly stumbles into a recognizable melody, and then, piece by piece, it transforms into a song. It's like the cafeteria scene from *Fame*. The David Bowie Hot Lunch just kind of happens.

Those are the best moments on the road with Wilco. What we do onstage means a lot to all of us, but when it's just the band in a room, with no audience besides the six of us, and we rediscover a song together, for no other reason than to see if we can do it, that's when we're the most grateful we get to do what we do. Those moments are pure reminders of what made us want to play music in the first place. Music is magic.

1

THE WORLD'S LONGEST MAIN STREET

I GREW UP IN a place called Belleville, a town of about forty thousand in Southern Illinois, a half-hour drive outside of St. Louis. It's the "stove capital of the world," or at least it was at the turn of the century. That's what we were told, anyway. It's also the home of Jimmy Connors and Buddy Ebsen (Uncle Jed from *The Beverly Hillbillies*), and when I was growing up they made Stag Beer there. So as you can imagine, my childhood was pretty magical.

In reality it was pretty depressing. Depressing and depressed in all of the familiar ways common to dying midwestern manufacturing hubs: a lot of old empty buildings and a lot of occupied barstools. The things that made our town unique and special were hard to get super excited about. Belleville has (purportedly) the longest Main Street in the U.S., spanning 9.2 miles and ending somewhere around East St. Louis. One stretch of road and so many opportunities to get loaded and almost zero chance of getting lost. I don't know how many bars were on Main Street, but there must've been a lot, because Belleville's other claim to fame was having the most taverns per capita. I found out later that wasn't true, which was kind of a relief, because it never felt like something worth bragging about. As if day drinking was a commodity we could have exported and sold to the rest of the world.

I lived just a half block off the Main Street with too many bars, on a tree-lined street with a name like something out of a Norman Rockwell painting: Fortieth. Our small single-family wood-framed house with a porch and a swing ended up being the last home my folks would ever own after my mother impulsively paid $16,000 for it at an auction in the early spring of 1967. Apparently she knew she was pregnant with me but hadn't told my dad. I was the card up her proverbial sleeve to ease his expected top-blowing at her fiscal irresponsibility. The previous owner had died in that house, which creeped me out as a kid, and as it turned out, both of my parents ended up dying there as well. So everyone who ever owned the house I grew up in died there.

Which is, I think, the main reason my siblings and I weren't overly sentimental about hanging on to it after we buried my dad in 2017. Aside from all of that backstory, the place was fairly nondescript. The one word I think would be most useful in setting the scene of my childhood? Mauve. There was a lot of mauve. Mauve carpets, mauve wallpaper, mauve furniture. Everything was mauve. Think of a smaller me, and then picture the color mauve, and you've conjured my childhood in a nutshell.

I'm not sure if my parents intended to have me. I've heard different accounts. The popular story is that I was an accident. Regardless,

I was late to the family party. My older sister, Debbie, who's fifteen years my senior, was born when my dad was just eighteen. They had two more kids, Steve and Greg, and by the time I showed up, my dad was in his midthirties, an age that most men of his generation considered well past prime baby-making years. My dad changed his story over time. He once told me, "I remember your mother called me at work and said, 'I want another one,' and I was home before she hung up the phone." I don't know if that's true. He always told that version with at least a six-pack under his belt, so I can't vouch for its veracity. It's possible he was trying to spare my feelings. Who wants to be an accident? That's a hard way to come into the world, created just because the responsible parties weren't paying attention. On the other hand, aren't we all accidents? Sorry, moving on . . .

My dad—his name was Bob, but for the purposes of this narrative, let's stick with Dad—worked on the railroad (yes, all the livelong day). He dropped out of high school after he got my mom pregnant when she was fifteen and got a job as a diesel mechanic for the Alton and Southern Railway. In the early 1960s, some higher-up figured out that Dad was way smarter than his lack of a high school diploma would indicate, so they sent him to Arizona to study computers and learn how to program with punch cards, and eventually he got promoted to superintendent of the switching yard. That's almost the extent of what I know about what my dad did all day. I only went down to the railroad to see him once, as far as I can remember. I never had much curiosity about his job. For his part, he didn't seem that curious about me, either, and I never felt much pressure from him to care about trains. Which is odd, because what kid doesn't like trains?

However, my dad did have a record I was fascinated by, *Sounds of Steam Locomotives*. It was a collection of recordings of train engines. That's all it was, the rhythmic clanging of steel wheels on steel tracks, the heavy chuff of heated steam being pushed through a locomotive's smokestack, a train's moaning whistle that always sounded to me like voices. It was a weird record, even more so because it was owned by my dad, who spent the vast majority of his waking hours around trains. Wouldn't that be the last thing he'd want to hear after coming home? Was there a time before I was born when, after work, he would sit with a beer next to the hi-fi, listening to tracks like "2–8–2 No. 2599, Chicago Northwestern" and "4–8–4 No. 801, Union Pacific" and nodding along like they were pop songs?

I guess when I think back on it, it makes total sense how I developed a fondness for almost any recorded sound. Maybe indirectly (because my dad and I never openly discussed it), I learned from him how you could find music in just about anything.

I WASN'T AN ONLY child, but I grew up like one. Since my sister and brothers were so much older, most of the time it was just my parents and me. My dad was on call at the railroad twenty-four hours a day, so he'd always be gone or in bed early. It got pretty lonely in my house growing up.

Most nights I'd stay close to my mother, who was born JoAnn Werkmeister, as she watched TV and smoked cigarettes on the couch. It was the best she could do. She'd been a mother for so much of her life that by the time I came around, she'd kind of given up on parenting. Well, maybe not given up, but she wasn't interested in being an authority figure. I wasn't given a lot of boundaries or rules. I didn't have a bedtime. If I made it to bed at all, it was usually my decision.

She was a night owl—she took occasional naps throughout the day, like a house cat—so she always stayed up late, and she'd let me stay up with her. We'd watch Johnny Carson, and then later, on channel 4's late-night *Bijou Picture Show*—the Turner Classic Movies of its day—old movies my mom would tell me she'd seen in theaters when they were brand-new. She adored Judy Garland, so I especially have memories of watching movies like *Presenting Lily Mars*, *Meet Me in St. Louis*, *For Me and My Gal*, *Strike Up the Band*, *Babes in Arms* with her. Sometimes I'd drift off—it's hard to stay awake at 3:00 a.m. when you're a little kid—and sometimes she'd fall asleep. With a lit cigarette still dangling in her mouth. I'd watch mesmerized as it slowly burned down to the filter and hold my breath in suspense as an ash the length of an entire cigarette would somehow balance itself against her breathing for whole minutes before plopping onto the lap of her robe. That might sound like really irresponsible and dangerous parenting, I know, but it's a memory that evokes nothing but warm feelings for me. The smell of the cigarettes and the black-and-white TV flickering in the dark, the only sounds being Judy Garland's familiar voice—"Psychologically, I'm very confused, but personally I feel just wonderful"—and my mom's gentle breathing nearby. I never felt so content.

Almost every night we'd wake up my dad, who was trying to sleep in the next room. We had a small house, so the master bedroom was inconveniently located right next to the living room. There was just a wall—not even a particularly thick wall—separating him and whatever we were blaring on the TV.

He'd burst out of the bedroom in his saggy white briefs and start screaming, "Goddammit, shut this place down, JoAnn!"

"Go back to bed, Bob!" she'd scream right back at him.

"Do you know what time it is? It's two o'clock in the goddamn morning! I have to be up before you even know what day it is!"

He'd slam the door shut and my mom would light another cigarette. "Mom," I'd whisper, trying to be conciliatory. "Maybe the TV is a little bit loud."

"Don't let him tell you what to do," she'd say.

I'd turn the volume down anyway, at least until we heard snoring coming from the next room and we knew he was asleep again, and then the volume would go right back up. It was a nightly battle of wills, and my mother always won.

I tried to be the arbitrator between my parents, the neutral voice of reason, but they both knew I was on her side. My mom was very permissive with me about a lot of things, because she was more interested in having me as a friend and an ally than being my parent. We were a unified front against an unfair and unreasonable world (i.e., my dad and his demands for a quiet home after midnight). She took great strides to keep me by her side. If I ever said, "I'm lonely," she wouldn't suggest something rational like "Why don't you call that kid who lives down the block and go play with him?" She'd teach me how to play solitaire. That was her solution to my loneliness. "Here, I'll get you some cards." Because she wanted me there.

My parents did the best they could without a lot of role models in terms of making good boundaries and healthy decisions for their children. My mom's dad, the cabbie/pimp and career alcoholic, left emotional scars she never outgrew. When she was nine years old, she got a pair of pink cowboy boots for her birthday. It was the only gift she'd asked for, and for a girl not accustomed to getting what she wanted, it was a glorious surprise. She couldn't remember herself ever being that happy. But then she went outside to play, still wearing the boots, and she got hit by a car. It was pretty horrific. They took her to the hospital, and she was so severely injured that they had to cut her brand-new pink cowboy boots off her body. She ended up being in traction for more than a month. Her dad only came to visit her once that entire time, drunk and causing such an awful scene that he had to be forcibly removed by the police.

It's hard for me to even imagine my mom at that age, feeling the world fall apart all around her. Barely nine years old, run over by a car, with her cherished pink cowboy boots destroyed, and then her dad finally shows up for a visit, weeks later, wasted, and has to be dragged from her room, kicking and screaming, "I'm here to see my little girl. Let go of me, you cocksuckers!" It's just sadness piled on top of more sadness.

I felt bad for my mom and dad. Not at the time. At the time, I felt closer to my mom, I needed her more, and I loved that I was her confidant and best friend. I was the uncontested oedipal victor, a psychiatrist once told me. I really didn't like the sound of that. It was only later, when I was old enough to think about their relationship, that I could recognize how my father could legitimately claim he was being treated unfairly. He was getting up at four o'clock in the morning, sometimes earlier, to drive down to the railroad and work a twelve-hour shift. On top of that, he was always on call. The phone could ring at any hour of the night or day and he would be expected to deliver himself to the railroad's needs above all other concerns. It wasn't easy for him to get eight hours of rest even without us almost intentionally ruining whatever sleep he could manage. There's no reason we couldn't have watched TV in the kitchen or even gone to bed ourselves. But Mom wasn't interested.

"Turn that shit down!" he'd scream from behind the bedroom wall.

"Put a pillow over your head," my mom would shout back, and we'd both giggle like preteen bullies.

I think my dad genuinely loved my mom. And she loved him, too, but maybe not as much. When I was a kid, I thought that she wasn't getting what she needed emotionally from him. But in hindsight, it was probably the other way around. It was my dad who had no chance. She wasn't going to trust a man with her happiness. Not after her father made it so abundantly clear what could happen when you trusted a man. She trusted me, but I was her perennial baby, fostered to be her bringer of happiness. But with her husband, they were roommates, at best. She wasn't going to leave him, but she wasn't going to let him get too close, either.

WHILE I WAS never groomed for the railroad, my brothers did end up going into the family business. Greg was in track maintenance, and Steve was a brakeman. I also had several uncles and cousins who worked on the railroad. Anytime I would express an openness to the idea of working around trains, my mother would say firmly, "You're never going to go work on the goddamn railroad." She was hell-bent against it. I don't know if she just wanted better for me, or if she worried it was too dangerous. I never quite figured out why it was okay for my brothers but not for me. Maybe it wasn't, but she knew she had already lost those battles and wasn't focusing on their futures anymore. Just mine.

I suppose that's why my mother wouldn't even allow my dad's railroad friends in the house. When they'd come over, they'd sit in the backyard and drink and smoke pipes and tell awful stories. They had amazing names, like Skip Pratt and Lee Goldschmidt and Jack Stufflebeam. I remember them being unbelievably filthy and foul-mouthed. Every story was the dirtiest thing you'd ever heard in your life. Skip Pratt had the lowest TPH (teeth per head) ratio of the bunch, was a section gang leader—he was in charge of the workers who maintained a certain section of track—and I could never understand a word he said, but I could tell he wasn't talking about his job. He was my brother Greg's boss. All I ever heard Greg say about him was that he pissed on people's lunches if they left them unattended. That was it. If you brought a sandwich to work, you better hide it from Skip or he'd piss all over it. I knew that Jack S. seemed like the nice guy, but his wife, Sharon, was prone to drinking way too much at social gatherings and would end up grinding on strangers. I saw her with her boobs hanging out more often than I saw her fully dressed. At weddings it was strange *not* to see her boobs, which is confusing for a child. I was happy not to see her unsolicited tits, but still . . . Was she feeling okay?

Nothing about that world was appealing to me, so I was fine with keeping my distance. But I did appreciate that the railroad kept a roof over our heads and food in our refrigerator. The railroad was also how I got my first record player. Not because my dad used his salary to buy me a record player. He just came home with one. It was a little Fisher turntable and receiver, with a few dents and scratches in the faux wood chassis because it had "fallen off a train." That was my dad's code for "This is stolen merchandise." If he brought home anything from work for our family, it had "fallen off the train." We once ate Cheez-Its with our dinner for an entire year because a couple of cases of Cheez-Its had "fallen off a train."

Before I got my own records and my own stereo, I would listen to whatever records my parents had in the cabinet underneath their hi-fi. It wasn't all locomotive sounds. I can remember my parents' record collection vividly, and not always for the music. There was a Marty Robbins record cover with a little bit of side boob on it. That was pretty amazing. Come for the rustic ballads and stay for the winking cowgirl slinging guns, naked from the waist up. If you're ten years old and you see that image, it gets burned into your subconscious.

My dad had a monogamous relationship with music. By that I mean he consumed one song at a time. That was enough for him. There was a six- or seven-month period when the only song he played was Mac Davis's "It's Hard to Be Humble." That's a long time for one song. Maybe it's from being born during the Depression, but anything more than one song felt like too much to him. Why did anybody need more than that? It was just greedy.

I have no idea where my dad would find these songs, because they weren't exactly the hits of the day. It's still a mystery. There was the summer when Leo Sayer's "Long Tall Glasses (I Can Dance)" was nailed to the turntable. I must've heard it a few hundred times. And then the next summer, it was Glen Campbell's "Southern Nights."

Every night and all day long on the weekends, it was "Free as a breeze / Not to mention the trees / Whistling tunes that you know and love so." I spent most of the first half of my life thinking I hated "Southern Nights," because it was inflicted on me. I didn't choose it, it was chosen *for* me, and it was unrelenting. The thought of it made my skin crawl. At some point I figured out that the song was written by Allen Toussaint, and I adore him, so its stock shot up with that knowledge alone. His version is murky and mysterious, pretty incredible, but kind of demo-ish. Hearing it really made me appreciate the meticulous pop craft of Glen Campbell's version, but I still felt a little queasy whenever I stumbled upon it.

When my dad died we put together a playlist of all of "his" songs to play at the funeral home before and after the service. My sons, Spencer and Sammy, fell in love with "Southern Nights" in particular, so after the funeral we drove back to Chicago listening to Glen Campbell in the car. It was beautiful to hear that song through their ears and feel it being liberated from its past, transforming into something with powerful personal meaning for all of us. We just opened the windows and let it blare. And then we got home and learned that Glen Campbell had died. I'm pretty sure we killed Glen Campbell.

My dad was the same about the music I made. He listened to everything by Uncle Tupelo and Wilco, but he enjoyed certain songs more than others, like his favorite, "Casino Queen." But that may have only been because I wrote it for him. I'd taken him to one of those riverboat casinos on the Mississippi, and he said, "You should write a song about this." So I did. I'm glad I wasn't living at home when he played "Casino Queen" into the ground. I don't think I would have ever recovered.

He also loved "Hummingbird." He loved it so much that for years he'd ask me, "Why don't you write more songs like 'Hummingbird'?" I'd tell him, "I have no idea. I can't. I'm not even sure how I wrote 'Hummingbird.'" But I think he was onto something. I probably would have been more successful if I had carved out a niche for myself. People used to do that. You know how Chubby Checker had a hit with "The Twist" in 1960, and then he came out with "Let's Twist Again" and then "Slow Twistin'" and "Twist It Up"? They were all huge hits. That's how a lot of successful artists used to do it—find a formula that works and drive it into the ground on the way to the bank. After "Hummingbird," I should have just continued that theme. "Mottled Duck." "I'm the Man Who Loves Coots." "Impossible Warblers (Unlikely Bananaquits)."

My dad was smart, but he wasn't often right when it came to career advice. He might have been right about "Hummingbird," though.

THE FIRST RECORDS I remember buying with my own money were 45s. It was 1974 or thereabout, so I was maybe eight at the time. My sister, Debbie, was home from college, and she took me to a Record Bar. I bought "Dream On" by Aerosmith and "Magic" by Pilot because I'd heard both songs on the radio and I couldn't believe my ears. The radio was my only source of new music at the time, and I was still trying to piece together what I was hearing. Peter Frampton was on the radio so much that I thought he was the DJ. I honestly thought that was the name of a DJ. I had no idea he played music.

Debbie and my aunt Gail went to school together all the way through high school, and my sister was the older of the two. (My mother and maternal grandmother were pregnant at the same time with their first and last children, respectively. Make sense? That's the way we do it in Southern Illinois. So Aunt Gail functions as a sort of utility relative in our family: extra sister, bonus mom, and of course straight-up aunt all in one package.) The two of them gave me a crate of 45s, which they'd collected as teenagers. They had singles by the Beatles, Herman's Hermits, the Monkees, Sonny and Cher, lots of Motown stuff. It was a very pop-heavy record collection for the time, just not *my* time. I was about ten years late. Though it was very contemporary for the mid-sixties, when they were in high school.

Because I was still pretty unsophisticated about records, I didn't know the difference between an A-side and a B-side on a 45, so sometimes I'd fall in love with the wrong song. My sister had a 45 of the Monkees' "Daydream Believer" but I listened to the flip side first, "(I'm Not Your) Steppin' Stone," so that's the one I listened to over and over. Not a bad song but it took months before I finally heard "Daydream Believer," which is probably the greatest thing the Monkees ever recorded.

My favorite was "Turn! Turn! Turn!" by the Byrds. I felt genuine love for that song. Maybe my first feelings of love toward a piece of music. It seemed to exist in its own sonic universe, unlike anything I'd heard before. It was one of the first times I thought about the shape of a song. Even to my untrained ears it felt like it followed its own set of rules, like it had an internal logic all its own. Most of the other pop songs in my inherited collection had an easily identifiable verse/chorus structure, but this was different. I guess technically

"Turn! Turn! Turn!" has verses and a chorus, but it always hit me more like a living organism than the sturdily crafted repetition typical of hit singles. More like a tree than a table.

The first LP I ever bought was also with my own money—money I had managed to scrape together from a paper route and cash stuffed into birthday cards. My mother flew us out to visit Debbie in Tucson, Arizona, where she was living at the time. We took a day trip to Mexico, and my mother bought some Kahlúa and an onyx chess set and I bought a Spanish copy of *Parallel Lines* by Blondie. I'd heard "Heart of Glass" on the radio, and I'd seen them on Wolfman Jack's *Midnight Special*. The songs were in English, but the sleeve was written in Spanish. And it was a very, very, very cheap pressing. Like flimsy, 50-gram vinyl. It was almost see-through. It was the same quality as those flexi discs that used to come in magazines. Now that I think about it, it might not have been entirely legit.

But the bulk of my early music education, and the albums and songs that changed and formed my musical perspective, mostly came from my brother Steve. Once, when he was home from college when I was very young, probably around eight or nine, he walked in on me in the kitchen, filling out a Columbia House record club mail-order form. I was just semi-randomly checking off records, picking names I remembered from the radio and album covers that looked cool. Kansas, Foreigner, Billy Joel . . . My brother sat there watching me, wincing. Eventually he couldn't stand it anymore, and he snatched the form from my hands.

"What are you doing?" he asked me. "I can't let you do this."

"What?" I said. "They're offering twelve records for a penny. A *penny!*"

"It's a scam," he told me.

"You don't know that," I insisted.

He was right, of course. The fine print was a Faustian bargain I'm sure some people my age are still working to get out from under. Basically, you were signing your life away to a record company, and all for the illusion of getting a Kiss record for a fraction of the price. I was too high on savings to be reasoned with. "Where else am I going to get twelve records for that kind of money?" I asked my brother. "*Twelve* records."

"You want records?" he said. "You can have mine."

He was true to his word. He gave me everything. And he didn't have a casual collection. It wasn't like my aunt's and my sister's 45s of sixties bubblegum pop hits. My brother had the musical taste and ambition of a somewhat pretentious yet serious 1970s college pseudointellectual. His records ran the gamut from Harry Chapin to Kraftwerk to Frank Zappa to Amon Düül. I went from not being entirely clear on the difference between the Beatles and the Monkees to spending entire weekends listening to the electronic space music of Isao Tomita and losing my grip on reality to Edgar Froese, Atomic Rooster, and Hawkwind. I would stay up all night listening to Aphrodite's Child's *666 (The Apocalypse of John, 13/18)*, a concept album about the Book of Revelation, and being terrified by it. It was so over the top and dramatic, and it made me want to crawl under my bed and hide, but I couldn't stop listening. My brother also had a copy of Manfred Mann's Earth Band's *The Good Earth* record, which came with a coupon you could send in to claim ownership of one square foot of the Scottish countryside. On the cover, there was a picture of what you could theoretically own, an incredibly lush piece of sod with snails and mushrooms and wildflowers growing on it. We never sent in our coupon, so we never owned a tiny patch of the Scottish countryside. Still, we had the record, with its synthesized rooster sounds, and that ain't nothing.

It was around this time that I started dreaming about songs. Not my own songs—I was still a long way away from creating anything resembling a song—but the songs I would read about in rock magazines and put together in my imagination. When I was nine or ten, my mother would bring me to the grocery store with her, and if I complained enough about how bored I was, she would let me hang out by the magazine stand and flip through copies of *Rolling Stone* and *Creem* while she shopped. I'd read them cover to cover, and I especially loved record reviews.

Ironic, right? Almost every musician I've ever met hates to be reviewed, but I try to take reviews with a grain of salt, because I feel so indebted to the practice. I will say that today, reviews aren't quite the same as they were back in the early ages of rock journalism. Reviews back then devoted way more ink to trying to describe what music *sounded* like. That was their main purpose. It's why people read them, because it was the only way to decide if you wanted to spend your money on a particular record. There were no streaming services where you could hear any song ever created practically for free. In the late seventies/early eighties, you judged an album by its cover art, word of mouth from your friends, or if you were a nine-year-old without a lot of musically adventurous peers, you based your record-buying decisions on what you read in rock magazines while your mother was buying groceries.

That's how I learned about the Clash, months before I'd heard even a single note of any of their songs. At that time they didn't play the Clash on any local radio stations. KSHE, the station that most kids my age listened to, stuck with mainstream stuff like Bob Seger, Journey, and REO Speedwagon. I'm pretty sure they used the same exact playlist for the entire time I lived in Belleville. So when I saw the Clash mentioned in *Rolling Stone*, there was no name recognition. The only thing that registered was how incredible they looked. As I stood there reading Tom Carson's review of *London Calling* I was transported. It gave me chills. He was describing music that made you feel "exalted and triumphantly alive," while the only danger imminent in my world was being bumped into by a cart pushed by a distracted shopper. It went on, saying that *London Calling* was "like a series of insistent messages sent to the scattered armies of the night, proffering warnings and comfort, good cheer and exhortations to keep moving." I was sold. The Clash really gave romantics something to sink their teeth into, and however I feel about them today, I still don't think any band ever generated better rock journalism.

Take for instance Lester Bangs's essay about the Clash, "Six Days on the Road to the Promised Land," which was published in *New Musical Express* the year I turned ten (although I didn't read it until years later when I started loitering in record stores). It may be the single best piece of writing about rock music ever. Because it's not just about the music, but how music itself can be a "scalding propulsion." Watching the Clash perform, Bangs wrote, was like wishing for a night we can "pretend is the rest of [our] lives." It's about the power of personal liberation, and even if tomorrow you go back to your boring existence, at least you had that one night when "you were blasted outside of yourself and the monotony which defines most life anywhere at any time . . . when you supped on lightning and nothing else in the realms of the living or dead mattered at all." That's really powerful stuff. You should read the whole thing. No, seriously, read it now. I'll wait. If you're like me, it might make you cry in spite of yourself knowing better. At this point in my life I find it hard to suspend disbelief when it comes to test-marketed revolutionary rhetoric and slathered-on romantic hyperbole, but it still makes me cry every time I read it. I've read it out loud to my kids, and I've never been able to get through it without choking up. It means that much to me. Which is weird, because, like I said, it's not really who I am, but when I read it as a kid, and even when I read it again as an adult, there's something about it that feels like the keys to a cage for me. Every time I go back to Bangs's text—and I return to it the way some people refer back to their favorite Bible passages—it feels liberating.

To some extent, even then I knew it didn't have anything to do with me. I was a ten-year-old living in Southern Illinois. I was never going to get to see a band like the Clash. I'd be lucky to find one of their records. Punk rock was an exotic event happening somewhere else in the world. It was like reading about a civil war, or a revolution happening in some other country. Still, it resonated with me, maybe because it had nothing to do with my small and uneventful world. Maybe it was so foreign it allowed me to fantasize about a world I would want to be a part of. That's what I assume happens when someone is radicalized and joins a militia or some cult. Your life feels empty and worthless and small, and then you find this thing that feels special, and it speaks to you in ways nothing else has, and it becomes a way forward. You feel like you have a purpose, and you're part of a global community even if you never set foot outside of your tiny corner of the world. I read the Lester Bangs essay with the kind of focus I could never muster in school, and when I was finished, I was different. It changed me. I remember thinking, "It doesn't have to be like this." I didn't have to pretend everything was okay. When David Bowie died, I read a lot of beautiful tributes to him with the consistent theme that his work acted as an affirmation of worth to so many people who felt like oddballs and misfits. Through him they gained the strength to be themselves and, not only that, to be proud of who they are. I've always related to that on a very inward level. I'm a pretty normal-looking straight white dude with all of the general societal acceptance that status entails, and yet I am still grateful to have found some encouragement to resist conformity in the way I look at and think about the world.

I mean, maybe. I wasn't sure yet, having not *technically* heard the album. For the moment, it was enough just to daydream about the Clash's epic grandeur. Who cares if it might not be true?

I eventually found the album, in a Target of all places. I was there with my mom—as with her grocery store outings, I was a constant companion—and I'd flip through records while she did her shopping. They had a copy of *London Calling*, with a big sticker on the front that read PARENTAL ADVISORY: EXPLICIT CONTENT, STRONG LANGUAGE, or something to that effect. This was before Tipper Gore and the PMRC, so I don't know if it was the label or the store that put it on there. Either way, I had to get it off. In reality, my mom probably would have bought me a record with an EXPLICIT CONTENT warning on the front, but I wasn't going to push my luck.

I tried scratching off the sticker with my fingernail. It didn't go so well. I only got about a third of it off. And then we had to leave. So I hid the record in a different section and hoped it would be there the next time we came back.

We returned two weeks later, and *London Calling* was still there. I went to work on it, holding it under my arm and casually peeling off tiny pieces with my thumbnail while I flipped through records real casual-like. This time, I got another third of it off before we had to go. Those stickers were surprisingly resilient.

A month or two passed before we returned. I was convinced my copy of *London Calling* would be gone, but there it was where I had left it, behind the card divider for Z. This time I finally got all of the sticker off. I took the record up to my mom and asked her, as nonchalantly as I could manage, "Hey, can I please get this?"

She shrugged. "Sure, fine." Without even a glance.

I threw it in the cart, amazed that I was somehow getting away with the perfect crime.

I still have that record. You can distinctly see my fingernail imprints on the jacket, from where I dug into the shrink-wrap, scratching at the EXPLICIT CONTENT sticker. I like that those gouges are still there. It's evidence that this record didn't come easy. I was like that clichéd prisoner, slowly digging his way to freedom with a spoon, slowly scraping away at a wall, and whistling like everything's normal when the warden walks by.

As it turns out, *London Calling* is a pretty conventional rock album for the most part, and I hated it the first few times I listened to it. I felt obligated to honor my investment, though, and kept listening to it. I'm not sure if it was because of the feeling that I had sunk value into it already—like Vietnam—or if it was just one of those records that takes a while for you to wrap your head around, but I kept coming back to it. Eventually I learned to accept it on its own terms. *London Calling* wasn't a dangerous attempt to burn everything down that had come before. If it was dangerous at all, it was because it dared to have ambition. It wasn't nihilistic at all. In fact, it was daring in how sincerely and unabashedly it was begging everyone to care more, not less. If "punk" music was going to be "my" music, this was an important lesson. Labels are not to be trusted.

Somewhere around this time, there was a nightly news segment about the punk rock happenings in England and how it was coming to America. They talked about it with the same fearful, ominous tone a TV anchor would use when warning about killer bees or swine flu. It was that level of alarm. They showed footage of kids in London with Mohawks and safety pins through their cheeks, spitting in each other's faces and looking disaffected and dangerous, while a stern adult voice explained the punk scene with *Reefer Madness* hyperbole like "Its hallmarks are violence and destruction." I remember watching it with my parents and trying to appear disinterested while still registering the intensity of their disapproval.

My mom turned to me and said, "I don't care what you listen to, as long as it's not punk rock."

I smiled at her and nodded. "Got it. I thought I wasn't supposed to listen to acid rock?"

That got a slight chuckle, and with that I had successfully changed the subject.

A few weeks later, she overheard "Death or Glory" blaring from my bedroom and somehow managed to make out Joe Strummer singing, "He who fucks nuns will later join the church." She called me downstairs. "Jeffrey Scot!" You know it's never good when they use your middle name. Even serial killers get the middle name treatment. "Are you trying to kill me, Jeff?"

I had no idea how to respond, I had no idea what she was talking about. Eventually she was forced to repeat the lyric she had overheard. In an angry whisper she repeated the offending line. To which I replied, "Oh my god, I had no idea that's what they were saying! What does that even mean?" And that was that. She waved me back to my room. I wasn't lying, either, I still don't know what it means.

THE CLASH TURNED out to be a gateway drug. Like weed leads to sniffing glue, the Clash led to the Sex Pistols and the Ramones and so on and so on.

By some stroke of luck, I found a radio station that played new wave and punk rock from midnight to 2:00 a.m. every Sunday. KWUR was out of Washington University in St. Louis, and it was nothing short of divine providence that an iffy college radio signal made it all the way to Belleville, twenty-five miles away. I was already a pretty intense listener—it's not like I was taking notes, trying to build up a reference level to impress my friends—but it started to seep into my brain in ways I hadn't expected. During one weekend, my brother Steve was visiting, and I was making him listen *with* me. About midway through a song, which I'd never heard before, I said to him, "This sounds like Gang of Four." Then the song ended and the DJ came back on and announced, "That was Gang of Four."

My brother was genuinely perplexed. "How the hell did you know that?" I didn't know. At that point, I had read enough rock magazines without paying for them and listened to enough college radio that I was able to make musical assumptions. The song seemed like it was about Marxism, and there was clanging metal drumming, which I'd read about in *Creem* reviews. I started to get pretty good at identifying music by artists I barely knew.

When I was twelve, I went to live with my sister in Arizona for a few months. The reasons are still unclear to me. I was told it was so I could play baseball during the winter, which I guess made sense. I had family in Arizona, I loved baseball, and my skills weren't going to blossom in Southern Illinois, where they only play baseball one season per year. But I don't remember baseball being so important to me that I was begging for an intensive year-round training schedule.

Part of the deal was that I had to enroll in junior high, which is where I met a kid named Boots McCormick. I swear I didn't make that up. That was his actual, family-given name, Boots McCormick. And he was not, as far as I could tell, a Chicago gangster from the twenties. He was a big guy, with the body square-footage of a football player, but sweet and kind. I met him in art class, and we probably wouldn't have talked to each other at all—I was the new kid, and everybody knew I wasn't staying for long—but then he noticed me finishing an assignment where we were asked to illustrate a word and I had chosen, wait for it, the word . . . *PUNK*. And yes, I did incorporate safety pins in my design.

"You like punk?" he asked.

I eyed him suspiciously. At that time, it could've easily been a trick question, with an answer in the affirmative being more likely to invite ridicule and bodily harm than create a budding friendship. "Yeah, I guess," I said noncommittally.

"You like the Sex Pistols?" he asked.

"Oh yeah," I said, feeling weirdly optimistic.

"How about Dead Kennedys? Minor Threat? Circle Jerks?" He kept listing off names of bands, some of which I recognized and others I'd never heard of.

"Black Flag?" Boots said with a broad smile. "They're my favorite."

"Wow." I felt like I was on another planet. All I could think was "How did I miss this? What the fuck is going on? I need to find some Black Flag records immediately."

Back in Belleville, I was starting to get more adventurous not just with what I listened to but where I found it. The main record store in town was called Lame Duck Records. It was part of a regional chain, located in an old shopping plaza, and it's where you went for all the new Top 40 releases. If you were looking for the new Bruce Springsteen or Fleetwood Mac, they would for sure have it. They might have one or two copies of a new Ramones or Clash release by chance, but asking for the latest Black Flag would get you a blank stare from any of the clerks. On the plus side, it was well lit and run by professionals, and you knew you could walk in and buy a copy of Styx's *Paradise Theatre* and leave without ever feeling like you were in physical danger.

That was option A. Option B was Record Works, a hole-in-the-wall record store about the size of a walk-in closet located next to a dog-grooming place that was conveniently located just three blocks from my house. It was owned by a guy named Dave Reeves, whose parents owned a Tastee Freez in one of the nearby smaller towns. Legend has it that he had a comic book collection that he sold and parlayed into his own business, an independent record store that specialized in imported new wave and punk rock. He was also terrifying. Dave looked a little bit like Baby Huey—the cartoon duck in diapers, not Baby Huey the soul singer. He had a mullet, smoked Kool cigarettes, and had a body that was way too big for his head. It was disconcertingly out of proportion. Dave's shirt never quite fit and was always unbuttoned or bursting at the seams. He was a strange mix of goofy and legitimately dangerous. He never threatened me, but I always had a sense of stranger danger with him, like it wouldn't have been all that surprising if he stabbed somebody randomly just to see the look on their face.

Despite this compelling evidence to stay away, I would go to Record Works pretty much every day, because it was the only place that had the records I cared about, and it was close enough I could ride my bike there without having to tell my mom. The selection was small, but it was almost entirely imports or releases on smaller labels. It was the kind of store you visited if you wanted to discover, say, X's *Wild Gift*. It was the opposite of Lame Duck. If you were looking for Bruce Springsteen's *The River*, Dave had maybe one copy, but he didn't know where he'd seen it last, so go ahead and look for it, if that's what you're into.

One of my friends from grade school and I would steal mason jars filled with quarters from his grandmother's porch to buy records from Dave. I still don't know why she had mason jars filled with quarters. Maybe she was filling them up to bury them in the backyard like some kind of proto–doomsday prepper counting on there being plenty of well-stocked vending machines after the apocalypse. We never asked. But we'd take a handful out of a few jars, just enough so it wouldn't look like anything was missing, but enough to buy three or four records each. We did that over the span of a few months until we finally got caught. While it worked, we managed to buy a lot of great records. The only problem was, to get the best stuff, you had to talk to Dave Reeves. For a guy in his twenties who'd spent all of his life in Belleville and socialized almost entirely with bikers and prepubescents looking for cool records, he had amazing taste in music and somehow knew everything cool happening in the world. But to find out what he knew, to get the real gems he was hiding in that store, you had to spend time with a socially awkward man-mutant.

Dave liked to hold his hand over a candle, just to prove to you how long he could do it. Which is a creepy thing to do anyway, but especially when you're an adult trying to show off to teenagers. His skin would start to smolder, and we'd watch him try not to seem alarmed, and we would wonder to ourselves, "What kind of reaction is he looking for here? What positive reinforcement can I give him so he'll stop this?" But if you could get past those feelings of dread, eventually he'd say, "Hey, have you checked out this?" And he'd hand you a record that would change your life.

The one thing Dave hated more than anything in the world was Lame Duck Records. Never mind that they weren't his competition at all. Nobody in Belleville was thinking, "I want the new Wire album. I better try Lame Duck first." The only ones looking for Wire records were the people already at his store, and they just wanted him to stop burning his hand with candles long enough so they could buy it. But he still seethed at the idea that Lame Duck existed at all. He would send us over on our bikes to do reconnaissance for him. "Were there a lot of people in there?" he'd ask. He wanted reports that they were struggling, that record buyers were finally waking up and rejecting the mainstream mediocrity. Of course, none of that was true.

But we kept coming back to the store, kept vying for Dave's attention. We never confused him with somebody we wanted to emulate. He was a cautionary tale more than a real mentor. But musically, he was important to us. He was the only adult who cared about the things we cared about, who innately understood our longing for music that made us feel special.

Everybody wants meaning in their life, and we all find it in different ways. For me it was buying records. There are some unhealthy aspects of forming an identity based on the things you buy, but I would argue that at least there is an artistic consciousness on the other end of the bargain you make with a record. I paid for it, but I stumbled on true inspiration that transcended commerce. I wasn't collecting these records and singles and cassettes because I thought they made me cooler. In Belleville in the late seventies and early eighties, being a fan of the Rezillos or the Cramps didn't make you cooler. The music didn't make much of a difference to my exterior world.

The difference was when I was alone, in my attic bedroom, sweating in the summer heat—we didn't have air-conditioning in our house, and in the attic we had slatted windows that provided not even the hint of a breeze—daydreaming in the dark about what it would feel like to be Joe Strummer or D. Boon or Paul Westerberg, that's where I discovered a secret self. A better self than the one I was stuck with.

2

GALOSHES

NOT MANY OF the musicians I know can tell you exactly when they decided to become a musician. This fact has led me to some fairly untenable theories about whether it's something you can actually decide. At one point I used to say it's kind of like having straight or curly hair. You don't really choose which you're born with, you just decide how you're going to deal with it. That analogy falls apart pretty fast when I factor in the ready availability of home-perm kits, curling irons, and relaxing agents. It's really just an even more obnoxious way of saying musicians aren't made, they're born. Blech. I don't have a clue. So I'll speak for myself: I don't remember deciding anything.

You could make an argument that my path to musicianhood likely began when I received my first guitar. This would, however, be incorrect.

My mom bought me a guitar when I was six years old because I had begged for it. I was eager to be a guitarist. I was already motivated to rock. Okay, now, let me just say, I know good carpenters aren't supposed to blame their tools, but I would argue carpenters also aren't often handed cheese graters when reaching for hammers. What I'm trying to say is, this guitar, ordered by my dear mother, from a JCPenney Christmas catalog, was, in fact, a colossal piece of shit. Also, going back to my carpenter analogy, I hadn't even learned the trade yet, so this was closer to handing a carpenter's apprentice a guitar. Anyway . . . it was a real setback.

I think about this a lot: How often is the beginning and end of musical ambition a shiny new sadistic dog turd like my first guitar? I suppose it can be a rite of passage to wrestle a shoddy instrument into submission, and maybe some degree of challenge can create some steely resolve in heartier souls, but for me it was doom. I just could not overcome the finger-mangling pain of strings more suited to slicing eggs than a lilting "Mary Had a Little Lamb." Oh, and I did give it an honest effort. I even took lessons. From a guy who taught in a studio space over a storefront in downtown Belleville, heated year-round by blistering-heat-radiating steam pipes.

Every week for an hour I'd sit in a balmy room with peeling paint, listening to a teacher with a gray ponytail lead me through basic guitar chords straight from a Mel Bay book. I'd clumsily attempt to re-create his fingerings while ignoring the moat of ass sweat pooling in the seat of my corduroy pants. After five lessons I was begging my mom to let me quit. She begrudgingly said yes, I put the guitar in my closet, and forgot all about it.

The first actual real hint that I might have a future in music was a little more auspicious. It happened in 1975 when I was eight years old.

I walked into my third-grade class with a portable cassette player—one of those handheld Panasonic things, small enough to carry in a backpack—and a single cassette on which I'd recorded a radio broadcast of Bruce Springsteen's *Born to Run* album in its entirety. During recess, I played it for some classmates and told them that the voice they were hearing on that tiny, tinny speaker belonged to me.

"Wait, you *made* this?" one of them asked as a husky and clearly adult voice started pleading about screen doors slamming and Mary's dress swaying.

"Yep," I said. I explained to them that I'd written every song, played every instrument, and recorded all the vocals. It was all me, every last note on that TDK cassette with *Born to Run* and *Jeff Tweedy* written in blue pen on the front.

"I think I've heard this on the radio," a kid protested.

"Probably," I said. "It is pretty popular."

"Are you sure this is you?" another kid asked. "It doesn't sound anything like you."

I just shrugged. "Don't know what to tell you."

I had no interest in trying to convince them. My lie wasn't contingent on their believing me. I didn't care if they did or didn't, because *I* believed it. I wasn't embarrassed when they pointed out the abundant evidence that I was full of shit. It was probably an error in judgment to take credit for literally the most popular mainstream rock in the world at that moment. Why couldn't I have gone for something a little more obscure? For example, if I'd recorded a Byrds B-side from my sister's 45s on a cassette, I'd at least have had a fighting chance. Still, they couldn't penetrate my fantasy. I was immune to it. I know that sounds like the unhinged ramblings of an insane person, but I wasn't completely disconnected from reality. It was just playacting. I didn't go home later and demand that my mom start calling me "The Boss." I was just trying on a new identity, wearing somebody else's skin to see how it felt.

That moment was just as important as the day I finally pulled the neglected guitar out of the closet and forced myself to figure out how chords worked, or found the courage to walk onstage and sing in front of a basement full of strangers, or put words and notes together to make a song that hadn't existed before. For any of that to happen, I had to envision what it would feel like to be that person, to be somebody who had accomplished all of these things already.

There was something else happening, too, something just as important as musical self-actualizing. It wasn't that I wished I'd written a song like "Thunder Road." I just liked the idea of being a guy singing a melodramatic ballad about leaving a town full of losers to an audience made up of the *very town full of losers* he's pulling out of there to get the hell away from. So he can "win." I didn't want to be Bruce Springsteen. I wanted to be me, punishing the popular kids with music. I wanted to publicly shame them, to shout at them in a song, "How did you not realize when you looked down on me in school that I would become this famous and celebrated, singing songs about how this small town couldn't appreciate me and that's why I left? Don't you feel stupid now?"

It was a comforting fantasy as a preteen, but I've been disabused of the notion countless times over the years that music is in any way an effective means of revenge. The people in the crosshairs of my scorn, which I expected to respond with full-on biblical weeping and gnashing of teeth, didn't care. Not only did they not feel punished by the song's awesome and unforgiving power, they refused to recognize that my musical chastisement had been directed at them. They didn't care in my third-grade class, and they didn't care forty years later when we were all grown-ups and I had maybe accomplished enough to deserve a reaction beyond "Oh, you were that guy in French class that I never talked to."

Back in 2005, Susie and I and the boys took a weekend trip to Belleville to visit my parents. We all went out to eat at a local restaurant, and right in the middle of dinner, I noticed two middle-aged blond women staring at us from across the room. It was hard to miss them; they gestured and pointed with all the subtlety of vaudeville actors. I kept looking over my shoulder to see if the people in the booth behind us were paying attention. After several minutes of this strange sideshow, they slid out of their chairs and walked straight toward us with scary determination.

I remember thinking, "Who are these people? What do they want from us? Are we about to get murdered?" My hand drifted toward a fork, in case I'd have to use it as a makeshift weapon to protect my family. But when they reached our table, they were all smiles, touching shoulders and laughing like we were old friends, and wasn't it just hilarious that we'd all come to the same restaurant and hadn't even texted one another beforehand, I mean what are the odds?

"Are you here for the reunion?" one of them chirped. "Of course you are. It's crazy, everyone looks so old."

"The what?" I asked.

"I can't even," the second one said, laughing. "Weren't we all just kids, like, five seconds ago?"

In an instant, the years disappeared from their faces, and I realized they weren't my mom's friends, which up until that moment would have been my best guess. I wasn't 100 percent sure of their names, but I knew them from high school. We didn't run in the same social circles. They were rich kids to me. I was socially adjacent to them, though. That's where I most often found myself during high school. I was never an outright enemy of any clique, nor was I ever fully absorbed and identified as a part of any distinct group. I was a misfit, but I was aware I had it better than the true outcasts. That didn't stop me from feeling alienated and irrationally repulsed by most of my classmates.

By sheer coincidence, I had come to town over the exact weekend of my twentieth high school reunion.

"No, I'm not . . . I can't make it," I told them. "We're heading home tonight."

They pretend-pouted. "That's so sad," one of them complained. "It would've been so great to catch up."

"Oh yeah," I said with a straight face, even though the very idea was hilarious. I needed to "catch up" with her like I needed to sit down with Madonna and reminisce about all the times I watched the "Lucky Star" video on MTV as a teen.

"Are you still in that thing?" the other one asked.

I waited for clarification that never came. "What thing?" I finally asked.

"That little band you were in," she said. "Weren't you in a band or something?"

I just blinked, waiting to see where they were going with this.

"Are you still in that little band? Are you still together?"

It was sublime poetry, the way they danced between foggy memory and under-the-radar insult. They didn't remember much about my band, other than that it was definitely "little."

"Yep," I said. "Still in a band."

They smiled and nodded, but like you do when somebody tells you they've been living in their parents' basement and sleeping on a beanbag chair.

My son Spencer, who was ten at the time, was old enough to be indignant about this drive-by dismissal of his dad's work. The rest of us were content just to remain motionless and quiet like we were hiding from predators. Spencer wasn't having it. "Wilco just won a Grammy," he blurted out.

The women turned to him, beaming. "A Grammy?" one of them exclaimed. "Well, good for you!"

"Now, isn't that neat."

Midwestern sarcasm, when it's done correctly, can be a thing of rare beauty. It's like performance art. Everywhere else in the world, you can identify sarcasm if you're paying attention. Even if the hostility isn't overt, you can read the signs. There'll be slightly elongated syllables or a pitch that's just a little off. It's like a trombone player with a plunger head. There's that slight "wah-wah" tone-bending to let you know not to take this too seriously. Midwestern sarcasm plays it straight and makes you listen more closely. You have to treat every conversation like a safecracker. Unless your ears have been trained to recognize it, you'll miss the hint of a minor key. Sometimes you don't realize what's happened until hours later, when it's 3:00 a.m. and you're half-asleep, and it suddenly hits you. "Aw, crap, they didn't mean any of that, did they?"

Midwestern sarcasm becomes even more deadly when it's combined with small-town isolationism. These women had been cheerleaders at our high school, they weren't indie rock aficionados, and Wilco isn't exactly a household name. So on the one hand, it wasn't surprising that they hadn't followed every turn in my career. It's shocking that they even remembered I played music at all.

Then again, we're all from Belleville, which has never been a hotbed of cultural activity. This is a town where everybody knows who's cheating on who, and who's been out of work, and whose kids have DUIs. Anybody from a small town knows what this is like. Your business is everybody else's business. If you leave for a while and come back even for a short visit, the never-left locals will ask you, "What have you been up to?" But, of course, they already know. It's been discussed and debated from the moment you first crossed the river. Not being around to defend yourself means you're fair game for gossip. It's how small-town bonding works. Having a third party on which to focus judgment and scorn is the number one survival strategy. The only question is whether your departure was a bad idea or the *worst* idea. Still, the question gets asked, just so you have to scramble to come up with a satisfying answer, and they can weigh in, underwhelmed. "Oh . . . good for you!" Which is midwestern sarcasm for "Your dreams remain unattainable, but how adorable, you keep trying."

I WAS IN FRESHMAN English class at Belleville West High School when something incredibly important happened, although I didn't realize the significance at the time. We had an assignment where we were paired up with another student and interviewed them to find out about their life. I don't know what we were supposed to be learning from this, other than confirming that high school kids in rural midwestern towns rarely have personal identities that hold up to journalistic scrutiny. I tried, I honestly did. But I couldn't tell you a single thing about the person I interviewed. I don't remember anything we learned about any of the kids in that class. Other than one.

We all stood up and read aloud from the dossiers we'd created. The kid who interviewed me went through the bullet points of my personality, announcing to the class that my favorite band was the Ramones. Crickets. Not even a murmured, "Who?" Um . . . okay. More kids stood up, rattling off the likes and dislikes of their peers, and it all started to blend into a big goulash of sports and obviousness. Then a girl on the other side of the classroom introduced a kid named Jay—he was easy not to notice, with his hair always covering his face and his gaze always directed at the floor—and she said, "Jay's favorite band is the Sex Pistols."

I feel like we might've made eye contact at that moment, but it probably wasn't that cinematically perfect. At the very least, I perked up and made a mental note to introduce myself.

After class, I walked over to him and said, "Hey, man, that's cool that you like the Sex Pistols." And he said, "Yeah." Then we just stood there for a minute—very likely an *entire* minute—not saying anything. And then I was like, "You want to hang out sometime?" And he said, "Yeah." That was it.

I'm sure anybody watching was probably thinking, "Those two are going to start a band that plays a punk-country hybrid that a smattering of critics and punk-country-hybrid loyalists will blow way out of proportion."

From the very beginning, Jay had a tough time reciprocating warmth. I slowly but surely learned the rules, that you don't express too much excitement or emotion around him. You're calmly bemused at best, and if you must communicate any feelings of earnest enthusiasm with "words" or "outward expressions of your internal life," it's safest to provide a disclaimer or caveat. Like "The new Adam and the Ants album is awesome . . . I love . . . I mean it's okay. They look so stupid." Nothing about that was natural to me. But I wanted to be friends with Jay, if only because I was so amazed that somebody else existed— someone my age, who lived in Belleville and went to my school—who felt the same way about this music that I did. The odds against that happening seemed astronomical, like finding a message in a bottle.

Our entire relationship, in the beginning, revolved around listening to music. We were the guys who would take records to parties and then inevitably end up in a room by ourselves listening to those records. The musical tastes of our classmates were predominantly classic rock—although I guess at the time it was just called "rock." If Styx played in St. Louis, at least two hundred of my classmates would be wearing Styx T-shirts the next day. (If you wore a Stray Cats T-shirt, you'd get pizza thrown at you, and you'd be called a faggot.) There was a jukebox in our cafeteria, and if you played anything other than the 1978 Trooper song "Raise a Little Hell," somebody would walk over and kick the jukebox repeatedly until it stopped. And then they'd call you (and probably the jukebox) a faggot.

Because of Jay, I was drawn into a social circle that didn't care about popular culture, but was so passionate about music that it bordered on cultish. The entire Farrar family was intimidating in their musicality. Jay was in a band called the Plebes with his older brothers,

Wade and Dade. Everybody in his family played an instrument. They would have bona fide hootenannies. I think even their dogs were proficient on the banjo. My family, by contrast, was not in any way musical. I had a cousin once removed who had become a country music performer—Herb Henson, or "Cousin Herb"—but he died before I was born.

My cousins—my dad's brother's children—all played instruments, and they would bring acoustic guitars to family gatherings. Songs were played, and the guitars were passed around, but it wasn't anything like the Carter Family sing-alongs I assumed were happening at the Farrar house. My first exposure to Woody Guthrie and Bachman-Turner Overdrive all happened on the same guitar. It wasn't until my late teens that I realized "Takin' Care of Business" wasn't a Lead Belly song.

My earliest live music memories involved my cousin David Tweedy, who had an electric guitar and just enough of those Tweedy clan demons—alcoholism, drug use—to self-sabotage any potential he might've had. He was truly virtuosic. During one of our visits to Uncle Bill's house, I remember David forcing me and a few other neighborhood kids to sit on the front lawn while he pointed his giant stereo speakers out his bedroom window, cranked the volume all the way up, climbed atop his orange-and-pink-sunset-muraled custom van, undid his ponytail and shook his hair down to his ass, called out to his mom to drop the needle, and proceeded to shred along to every single acid-tinged note on Alice Cooper's "Welcome to My Nightmare." It was pretty fucking hot, I have to say. *Majestic* is the word. It was that delicious combination of terrifying and scintillating; one of the great recipes for rock and roll.

Becoming friends with Jay meant upping my game. It wasn't enough just to find records that I'd never heard of. I needed to find records that Jay and his brothers didn't know about yet. It was a healthy competition. We all wanted to be the guy to turn everybody on to the next thing that we all had to hear. Everybody wanted that feather in their cap, to be the one who found the next Flying Burrito Brothers that blew everybody's mind. There were so many things working against us, like the fact that the next band to blow everybody's mind would probably have a fucking stupid name like the Flying Burrito Brothers. Seriously, who picks up an album by a band called the Flying Burrito Brothers and thinks, "I bet this is good"? I sometimes wonder how many amazing records I ignored because I could never get past the band's name. What if Black Sabbath had stuck with the Polka Tulk Blues Band?

But competition gets old, and you eventually figure out that it makes more sense to combine your resources and become a hive mind. That way you cover more ground and discover more music. We became so devoted to this hunting-and-gathering approach that we wouldn't even buy the same records. It wasn't just about what you were buying, but what the other guy was buying. "Okay, if you get the Green on Red record, I'll get the Dream Syndicate record." You still wanted to find that new band that would blow everybody away. There was a lot of fanzine reading and grilling of record store clerks—"What is this? Have you heard this?"—but only if it didn't interfere with the greater good. We were a small group with the collective record-buying budget of a train hobo, so we had to be resourceful.

We made trips to St. Louis to buy records. Which never failed to confuse our parents. "We have record stores here!" they'd yell at us. Yes, we'd tell them, but they don't have the records we *want*. St. Louis was like another planet, and getting there was about as practical as leaving the earth's atmosphere. Driving to St. Louis took about thirty minutes—geographically, it was nothing. But to get to St. Louis proper from Belleville, you had to go through East St. Louis. This was the same place where John Carpenter shot *Escape from New York* because he was looking for something even more depressing and crime-ridden than the real New York City. This was during the *early eighties*, when New York was still a festering cesspool of homicide and police corruption and crack babies. But I guess Carpenter wasn't impressed. He was like, "Nah, not bleak and dismal enough. Let's go to East St. Louis."

Those harrowing car trips were always worth it. We discovered record stores like Vintage Vinyl and Euclid Records, the latter of which I'd soon be working at as a clerk. My future manager Tony Margherita was already working there at the time, and he made an impression on us almost immediately. He was so much more together than what we were used to from a record store employee. He wasn't hungry for the attention or admiration of teenage boys—he was seven years older than Jay and me, so he was like a cool older brother. He was a large and imposing figure, but not in a Dave Reeves "I've made some bad choices" sort of way. He had the wingspan of a basketball player and the calm confidence of somebody who couldn't care less if you liked him. I remember once showing up to the store five minutes before it closed, and seeing Tony standing in the window and shaking his head, just wagging a finger at us. I'm sure he recognized us as the kids who'd come by the store a few times a month, but he didn't care. We kept banging on the glass door. "Come on, man! Just let us look at the new releases. We'll be quick!" But he wasn't having any of it.

We were also regularly driving to St. Louis for shows. A lot of the bands we wanted to see would end up at Mississippi Nights, a club right off the river. Our parents weren't as concerned as they probably should've been, I guess because the club was in the touristy Laclede's Landing part of town, with its cobblestone streets and the Gateway Arch just a few blocks away. It seemed harmless enough from a distance, and that's how we tried to keep it for them. When we had plans to be at Mississippi Nights, we always tried to keep it vague. We'd say, "Just going to the Landing tonight," and not "Seeing Jodie Foster's Army tonight, don't wait up."

My first concert, the one that counts (not the Sing Along with Mitch Miller show my mom made me go to once) was the Stray Cats at Mississippi Nights. I was fourteen, and Jay and I went with my brother. The band was pretty unknown at that point; they weren't being played on MTV yet. Their U.S. record, *Built for Speed*, had just come out a month before, but I knew about them because of an import copy of their first record I'd managed to find. They were fantastic—I remember they put their guitars in trash cans instead of using stands, which was just ridiculous—but bragging to classmates that I'd seen a Long Island rockabilly band that was big in Britain didn't do much to elevate my social status.

Jay and I and a few others tried to see the Ramones at Mississippi Nights, even though it was an over-twenty-one show. The record store guy who sold us the tickets told us not to worry about it. "Just show up, and they'll figure it out when you get there," he said. That didn't work out so well. The door people took one look at us and turned us away. There was a whole group of us—maybe twenty kids or more—milling in the back parking lot, clinging to worthless tickets, but refusing to go home.

We chose that spot because it's where the Ramones tour bus was parked, just a few yards from a staircase leading up to the stage. We waited until somebody emerged from the bus. The first to come out was Dee Dee, surrounded by a gaggle of radio promoters. Somebody in our group shouted at him, "Hey, Dee Dee, what's going on?"

He turned to us. We had his attention! It was our chance to plead our case, make him understand why we belonged inside that club, maybe even sidestage.

"Why are you singing all these songs about teenage this and teenage that but we can't get into your show?" somebody yelled. Yes, perfect. Appeal to his sense of artistic integrity.

He paused, considering our airing of grievances, and decided he was unmoved. "What, are you giving me shit?" he shouted back at us.

"Don't let them give you shit, Dee Dee," one of the radio promoters said, egging him on.

"You guys giving me shit?" Dee Dee shouted a little louder.

"No, we're not giving you shit," we shouted back. "But they won't let us in!"

"You what?"

"We have tickets, but they won't let us in!"

"That's bullshit!"

"We just want to see the show!" we pleaded with him.

"We're not fucking playing!" he told us. "That's bullshit! I'll get you in. We're going to get you guys in."

We cheered for him as he disappeared into the club. And then we waited. Because, obviously, he was coming back for us. Dee Dee Ramone had made a promise. He had given us his *word*. It would only be a matter of time before he kicked opened the doors and beckoned for us to join him inside. He would be our Moses parting the Red Sea—the Red Sea in this metaphor being the Mississippi Nights staff just trying to do their jobs—and leading us to the Promised Land (i.e., the front of the stage, with the perfect vantage of the band). He wasn't just going to get us inside; he was going to parade us past the adults who had tried to keep us out. "Who's responsible for this outrage? Look what you've done!" How could the band that wrote "Teenage Lobotomy" abide actual teenagers being turned away from their show? It was an abomination!

We waited. The minutes turned into hours, and then it started to rain. But we didn't budge, because we knew justice was coming. Then the tour bus door opened and Joey Ramone burst out in all his gangly glory, like a praying mantis/human hybrid, walking carefully down the stairs. I pushed my way to the front of the crowd of kids and yelled out to him, "What's going on, Joey?"

He wasn't listening, so I shouted louder. "Are you guys still playing?! Are you still going to play the show?!"

He turned to me and said, "What, because it's raining? Uh . . . No, kid, I forgot my galoshes."

Then he walked into the club, and the door slammed hard behind him.

A few minutes later, we heard Dee Dee count in the first song. "One two three four!" And then the sound of muffled bedlam. We still didn't leave, because even hearing the Ramones play behind

concrete while getting soaked by a driving rain was better than driving back to Belleville and listening to their records in our bedrooms.
Every once in a while, somebody would open the backstage door for
a precious few seconds, and we'd catch a glimpse of the band onstage, silhouetted by smoke, green-and-purple-lit black leather jack-
ets, guitar necks, and cymbals. The music would burst out like a
sonic boom, catching us by surprise, sometimes literally knocking
us backward. And then the door would slam shut again. But for at
least a couple of seconds, we were part of it, enthralled just to be
there, grateful for even a few stolen notes.

WE GOT INTO more shows at Mississippi Nights than we were
barred from, and every one felt transformative. Some more than others. A lot of times we just left with ringing ears and big, exhausted
smiles, and that was enough. But sometimes going to shows felt like
gathering evidence. Here was proof, right in front of our own eyes,
that a life where all you did was play music was possible.

I had a girlfriend in high school who dragged me to big arena rock
shows. I went to see Bruce Springsteen and John Cougar and the
Who's first "farewell" tour in '82 at the Ralston Purina Checker-
dome in St. Louis. It all sounded so bad to me. I wasn't just bored; I
hated those shows. I felt sad afterward. Nothing about the experience was exciting to me. Something always seemed overly macho
about how bands postured themselves on those enormous stages. It
was just a giant muddy-sounding spectacle. I'm not sure why the
macho-ness bothered me, I loved Black Flag, and there was nothing

more macho than Henry Rollins at that time. Actually, that was my least favorite part of Black Flag, but it was a different type of macho, or at least it was to me. The Who were larger-than-life rock deities demonstrating a power that was monolithic, distant, and authoritative. Henry Rollins was just a guy yelling onstage a few feet away. You could run over and give him a head butt (if you were into that kind of thing). He'd kill you, but nobody would stop you. He was just a super-jacked guy who declined to wear a shirt. Springsteen, on the other hand, was going to save us all whether we wanted to be saved or not.

That probably seems counterintuitive. How does a guy go from insisting to his friends that Bruce Springsteen's *Born to Run* was all his doing to recoiling at the same guy singing "Born to Run" onstage? I don't know. It would've been easier to imagine exacting revenge on the popular kids with Springsteen bombast, which was at least a form of idol worship they respected, than by creating a musical identity around the Replacements—a band that embraced fallibility as an aesthetic and meant next to nothing to most of my classmates—but that's where my heart landed.

I got to see the Replacements at Mississippi Nights in 1982. They were opening for X, who were on their *Under the Big Black Sun* tour, and somehow, miraculously, it was an all-ages show. Which meant we got to watch from inside this time, but it wasn't necessarily a better view. The underage kids at Mississippi Nights were confined to something called the "kiddie corral," a small fenced-in section to the side of the stage. The back bar and the entire dance floor were open only to customers old enough to drink legally, the adults.

When the Replacements came out, the kiddie corral was packed.

We were standing shoulder to shoulder, craning for a better view, elbows shoving to protect our slim cut of real estate. The dance floor, however, was empty. The older patrons had either not shown up yet or were drinking at the bar, completely ignoring the racket onstage. Some of them managed to sneer at the band or offer up a few boos, but for the most part, they treated the opening act like an intrusion into their conversations.

They opened up with "God Damn Job," and Paul Westerberg immediately fell forward off the front of the stage, landing hard on the concrete floor, where he stayed to finish the song because nobody came over to help him stand back up. It was a beautiful moment, a guy playing guitar and singing facedown into a microphone, lying on an empty dance floor, while a corral filled with disaffected sweaty teenagers watched from a dark corner.

At some point, Exene Cervenka from X wandered out through the audience in a children's Halloween devil costume and stood right at the front of the stage, enthusiastically nodding along. I remember Bob Stinson tearing off his pink housecoat and playing a nude guitar solo, or maybe it was a pink bathrobe; it's a little hazy after all these years. Either way, it was a speculator mess, which only seemed to gain power the more it was ignored by the over-twenty-one set at the bar. Their indifference made it more momentous, it felt private, like a secret that belonged to us, not them. We eventually stomped our feet so hard in the kiddie corral, we broke a sizable hole in the floor.

I hesitate to be too over the top with rock show mythologizing, but this was a night that lived up to the fantasies of empowerment I would often indulge in when I listened to records. When I'd lie in my dark bedroom listening to the Clash, I could picture how terribly ashamed everybody would be if that were me onstage, and I was punishing them for something . . . For not being nicer to me? Or just for being "okay" with themselves? I was never sure exactly why I thought they deserved to be punished. Maybe it was just for liking stupid bullshit like Black Oak Arkansas. Anyway, this show perfectly manifested that fantasy for me. It was a living incarnation of how I expected rock and roll revenge to play out. It put all the jive assholes in their place. But these assholes were so dead they didn't even notice.

The Replacements' bassist, Tommy Stinson, was fifteen years old when I saw him play at Mississippi Nights. I was fourteen, just a month away from my fifteenth birthday. Could that be me up there? The only difference between us was that he had a big amp and a bass, and he learned how to plug it in and play, and he joined a band, and they booked this gig and somehow got here from Minneapolis; maybe they stole a car, I don't know. Okay, there were a *lot* of mysteries still. But the line between Tommy Stinson and me was shorter than the one between me and Bruce Springsteen.

When X came out to play, and the "grown-ups" finally crowded onto the dance floor, Exene scolded them for not paying attention to "one of the best bands in the world." Then, during "We're Desperate," she climbed over the adults and into the kiddie corral and sang it with us. We screamed along and held her up, halfway convinced that this meant we were de facto members of X now.

It was a big moment for me. This was more than just "I think I should give this a go." It was "Oh, now I know I'm not crazy for wanting to be a part of this so badly." It was like finding out Santa Claus is real. I felt validated. This thing that I thought I was imagining, in fact, exists. My dad always used to say, "If you know better, you can do better." I don't think I ever understood what he meant until that night.

I got so swept up in that moment I completely forgot we'd created a sizable and ominous hole in the floor, about a yard in either direction, where you could see down to the foundation and the dirt underneath the building. It wasn't that deep, maybe a few feet, but in the dark of the theater, it might as well have been a black hole, sucking lost souls into an abyss.

I fell backward and almost tumbled into a darkness that, as far as I could tell, didn't have a bottom, and that would be the end of me. Thankfully, I was caught and pulled back from oblivion by the anonymous arms of some conscientious thrashers.

Had I been spared an untimely demise for some higher purpose? Not at all. I was just a drunk teenager who almost fell in a hole, which would have been momentarily embarrassing and then quickly forgotten. But in my head, my brush with death had significance. You figure life out just at the precipice of it ending. How fucking typical! I could imagine people at my school talking about it. "Did you hear about the Tweedy kid? Yeah, the guy who told everyone he made *Born to Run* back in third grade. He had a moment of self-discovery at a punk show in St. Louis, and then he fell into an enormous hole in the floor and died. He just vanished." I would've gotten their attention then. Not exactly the punishing attention I was hoping for, but whatever.

ALL OF THE ways I am exactly like Bob Dylan is, one time a biking accident changed my life.

Not a motorcycle accident, like in 1966 when Dylan crashed his Triumph Tiger on a mountain road in upstate New York, broke some bones, and went into seclusion. I was on a Schwinn Stingray, so I wasn't "riding" in the classic sense; I was pedaling.

I was twelve when it happened. It was the last day of school before summer vacation. My best friend and I were killing time waiting for my mom to come pick me up by racing his and his little brother's bikes down a steep hill in front of his parents' house on a dead-end street.

It had been raining, and the freshly blacktopped roads were slick, but we were both young and brazen enough to think we were indestructible. We may have even been shouting taunts at each other as we hurled toward the cul-de-sac. Fear was just an adrenaline high, not an overt warning from our brains that we were doing something profoundly stupid and potentially fatal. The game was to hit the brakes just as we reached the bottom and skid to a stop without wiping out. On our last run of the day I mistimed my braking and sailed off the end of his street into a drainage ditch, where I landed on some concrete reinforcement rebar poking out of the crumbling edges of an old culvert. Three rusty rods went right into my leg, puncturing it like a carving fork in a roast. When I pulled myself off, a big chunk of my upper thigh was missing. It was surreal. I looked up and bloody globs of my flesh were dangling off the bent metal. As I lay there staring at the mangled wads of tissue that just a few seconds ago had been inside my body, I refused to process the scene as something actually happening. It was more like "Whoa. Leg stuff is gross."

I didn't lose the leg—which, as I was passing out in the ditch, hearing my friend's laughing stop abruptly and seeing his face empty itself of blood as he got a clearer look at it, seemed like a very real possibility—but it was a serious injury. In the ER, they made my mom and dad sit down before they would allow them to see the wound. It was almost down to the bone and took hundreds of stitches to repair, but I was able to go home that night. By the end of the next day I had a high fever, which put me back in the hospital with an infection from the ditch water I had landed in. The stitches were removed and weren't replaced until the wound had been left open and cleaned with hydrogen peroxide and alcohol three times a day for two weeks. After that, I'd have to spend the summer in bed to recover, they told me. No baseball or sunshine or friends or any of the sweet freedoms of summer. I was under house arrest, in a sweaty attic bedroom with no distractions other than my wandering mind. So obviously I thought, "Now might be a good time to dig that guitar out of the closet and see if I can figure it out."

This was the same guitar my mother had bought me when I was six and I had made it through a few lessons before deciding it was a waste of time because I wasn't immediately Segovia. I put it away and tried not to think about it, but, of course, insisted to everyone at school that I was probably the best guitar player they knew. I never actually played for anybody—because I was living a lie and couldn't make an E minor chord if my life depended on it—but I would argue shamelessly with anybody who questioned me. The guitar was my version of the hot Canadian girlfriend who conveniently never visits.

With my bum leg immobilizing me and boredom setting in quick, I decided it was time to learn how to play the thing I'd told the world I'd been proficient at for six years. There wasn't any doubt in my mind that I could do it. It was just a matter of finding the discipline to make any effort whatsoever. I looked at the chord book and fumbled my way through learning a few basic chords. Picking it up all these years later, my hands had grown enough not to be cut to shreds. I still couldn't get anything to sound like a song, but it impressed my family to hear sounds echoing from the attic that sounded even remotely like music.

I made steady progress and showed enough sustained interest, so for that Christmas my parents bought me a white Peavey T-60 electric guitar, which weighed about seven hundred pounds. I'm hardly exaggerating. It's seriously the heaviest guitar. If I'd stuck with that guitar and never played another one, it would have crippled me. Nobody wants them now, except maybe my friend Brian Henneman from the Bottle Rockets. He was into playing Peavey T-60s for a while, and there was a period when anybody who wanted to get rid of any Peavey would bring it to a Bottle Rockets show and just leave it backstage. It was like Henneman had started a wildlife refuge for these inexplicably heavy guitars.

Besides their gross tonnage, Peavey T-60s just weren't cool. On top of that, they were hard to play. The excitement of finally having an electric instrument was literally being outweighed by this bummer of a guitar. Walking by the guitar store, shopping with my mom again in downtown Belleville, I saw a guitar hanging in the window that looked way cooler than the one I had. It was a red Kustom hollow body guitar that looked kind of like a Rickenbacker. I traded in the Peavey, along with a little money I'd saved up, and got it. I think it hurt my parents' feelings, because they felt like I thought the guitar they'd given me wasn't cool, which is true. I felt bad about it, but not bad enough to not get a cooler guitar.

The cooler guitar turned out to be awful, too. In fact, it was even worse than the Peavey. The strings would pop off the bridge with the slightest strum. It was unplayable. So far, the moral of this book might be "Don't get discouraged, get a good guitar." Anyway, my progress had halted and things were looking pretty grim. Then my brother Greg got injured on the railroad, and my guitar problems were solved.

Greg worked for the same railroad as my father, Alton and Southern Railway. He did maintenance, which I guess meant making sure the tracks weren't covered in trash and cows. I honestly don't know. I loved my brother, but what he did at the railroad every day remains a mystery to me. I read in his obituary that his job before he got injured was "filling in holes with gravel to keep the ties stable," which sounds important. He got pretty badly injured—I was never sure exactly what happened, but I think it involved him being accidentally buried in gravel, possibly while filling holes—and because my dad was a company man and my brother was a union guy, my dad talked him into taking a settlement without reporting it. He probably could have sued the railroad for a lot, but he ended up getting a couple hundred thousand dollars. Which for most people in Belleville at that time was huge. This isn't money that someone who fills in train track holes with gravel is accustomed to earning. It was set-for-life money. And one of the things he did with his new fortune was buy me a guitar.

It was a brand-new black-and-white Fender Telecaster, right off the wall. I wanted a black-and-white Fender Telecaster 'cause that's the guitar Joe Strummer played, and it's obviously the best-looking guitar ever made. Surely anything that looked that magical would magically make me better. Both Joe and I were able to afford our guitars because of weirdly fortuitous circumstances. Joe Strummer paid for his Tele after marrying a South African woman looking to become a British citizen, and I paid for my Tele because my older brother almost died doing a job on the railroad that I didn't fully understand.

Now that I was playing a real instrument, a guitar good enough for Joe Strummer, I stopped feeling like I needed to care about learning chords or scales. That has never been the way my brain works, anyway. I just don't learn that way. I struggled and barely graduated from high school because I could never make myself learn on command. I had to find something specific that sparked my interest. Maybe I have a cognitive disability or something; I don't know. I think I ended up well-rounded education-wise only because I'm a naturally curious person and I get restless not knowing things. I've spent entire summers reading about Stalingrad or Persian poetry for no real reason other than someone didn't tell me to. It was the same with guitar. Playing scales always seemed pointless to me. It seems crazy to say, but I could never understand how they would help me write songs, and writing was the goal almost immediately. I wanted to swim in that end of the pool, the deep end. I couldn't listen to the Beatles or Bob Dylan, sit back and think, "Well, maybe if I play an A-major scale enough times, I'll get there someday." It was more like "I want to write a song *right the fuck now.*"

By the end of my one-legged summer indoors, when I started being able to get my guitar to make sounds resembling what I was hearing on records, it wasn't just a sense of accomplishment; it was bigger than that, a naive feeling that I was the first person in the world to do this. Maybe that's a character flaw, but it was a huge part of it for me, elemental to why I wanted to do this at all. It would've been so much harder to keep at it without that feeling. It was the *Born to Run* cassette moment all over again, but now I had something more tangible and satisfying than pressing play on a tape recorder giving me that feeling. I remember when I figured out how to do the standard *da-da-dada* Chuck Berry riff, it was like I'd split the atom. It was that monumental. It was never just "Oh, a lot of people know how to do this, and now I do, too." It was "Holy shit, I just *invented* rock and roll!"

I didn't invent anything, of course, I just discovered it for myself, which is an incredibly empowering way to learn. Years later my wife and I spent a small fortune sending our kids to a Montessori grade school where they were taught *how* to learn, not *what* to learn, and I found myself envious. I would console myself with the notion that if I had been encouraged to embrace that style of learning when I was young, I might not have been driven into the arms of antisocial behavior and rockish redemption. Instead of teaching myself guitar, I might have learned a foreign language or become a scientist or a doctor and been able to really help people. Honestly, I feel guilty about it, like it was my fault. I guess I did somehow save myself, though, and that ain't nothing.

Learning how to play guitar is the one thing I always look back on with wonderment. I'm reminded of "What ifs?" every time I pick up a guitar. Where would I be? I have sort of a survivor's guilt about it that makes me want it for everyone. Not the "guitar" exactly, but something like it for everybody. Something that would love them back the more they love it. Something that would remind them of how far they've come and provide clear evidence that the future is always unfolding toward some small treasure worth waiting for. At the very least, I wish everyone had a way to kill time without hurting anyone, including themselves. That's what I wish. That's what the guitar became for me that summer and is to me still.

3
|||||||||||||||||||||||||

SHRINK-WRAP

BELIEVE IT OR not, the first song I ever wrote was recorded by a band called Joe Camel and the Caucasians. The lead singer in the band was a guy called Joe Camel, although I don't think that was his real name. Or maybe it was, I don't know. He and the rest of the band were Caucasians, so that much was true.

Joe Camel and the Caucasians were from Belleville, and one of the best local bar bands in town. Which admittedly isn't saying that much—it'd be like calling them the best Alpine skiing team in Belleville. We didn't have much to measure it against, but they sounded good. They played mostly R&B covers, and Joe, the lead singer, had a soul patch and played saxophone and had a lot of charisma. I met them not long after forming a band with Jay Farrar. Jay was on guitar, I had gravitated to bass, his brother Wade handled most of the vocals, and Jay's other brother's girlfriend's little brother, Mike Heidorn, who happened to be our age and in the same school but was otherwise unknown to us, was on drums.

At the time, Jay and I were both fourteen, and the idea that a guy my age was playing guitar in an actual band was hard to fathom. How did a guy in my algebra class who didn't have a girlfriend and would sleep on my bedroom floor on the weekends own an amp and a guitar and know how to play it well enough to get asked to do it in *public*?

Jay invited me to see them play a gig at our old grade school, and by "see" he meant "carry our gear and help us set up." I was grateful for the chance. Watching Jay and his older brothers, Dade and Wade, rip through songs like "(I Found That) Essence Rare" and "Brand New Cadillac" was jaw-dropping.

Soon after that, they asked me to join the Plebes, not because I was so clearly a guitar virtuoso but because they needed one more high-school-age member to qualify for a high school Battle of the Bands competition. My guitar aptitude was improving, but only when I was focused on it, sitting on my bed and staring at my fingers. Onstage, when I was flailing around madly, I missed more chords than I hit. Dade, who played bass, was so annoyed he kept turning my amp down when he thought I wasn't looking and, after I had turned it back up a few times, finally and authoritatively turned it off.

Dade eventually quit the band and left town—which possibly had something to do with me, but I may be flattering myself—and I took over bass duties. My mom called up a cousin who owned a Fender Jazz bass guitar and had played in a band before he went to Vietnam. When he got back just a few years later, music had changed so much he got discouraged trying to fit in and his bass sat and collected dust for a few decades until he sold it to me. Thanks, Vietnam.

I figured out how to play it well enough to keep up in about a weekend. I don't remember laboring over it, so it must've come to me pretty easily. We renamed ourselves the Primatives (well, we named ourselves the Primitives, but when our band's business cards came back from the printer misspelled with an *a*, we went with the misspelling, which was a way simpler and more cost-effective solution than confronting an adult business owner about the typo and getting new cards made) and switched gears to more psychedelic garage music, 'cause that's what Jay and I were into. We had a pretty good run for a while, landing gigs everywhere from the basement of a bowling alley (the crashing pins overhead were like extra percussion) to opening for Johnny Thunders at Mississippi Nights in St. Louis. There's a YouTube video of us playing on Halloween 1985, performing *The Munsters* theme while I'm wearing a dress—if you're into seeing something like that.

This version of the band fell apart in 1986, when our lead singer—Wade, the second Farrar to quit our lineup (but not the last)—left to study engineering at college or possibly join the army (I was never clear which) and our drummer, Mike Heidorn, broke his collarbone. The Primatives went on hiatus, but Jay and I kept getting together, having informal (and sometimes impromptu) rehearsals in each other's bedrooms to work on songs we were writing. Despite having no drummer and no lead singer with the same manic energy and onstage charisma as Wade, and no invitations to perform anywhere, it was surprisingly easy to feel confident we were finally on the right path.

Joe Camel and the Caucasians, who were a step beyond us on the Battle of the Bands circuit, would book gigs at the Liederkranz Hall, an old German community center a few miles outside of Belleville, which were basically underage dances with beer, in a town with only one cop, whose main job was parking his patrol car in the lot of the one convenience store in town at the one intersection with a traffic light and making sure no one blew through it. We'd gone to many of these "dances," so when Joe asked us to open for them it was a big deal.

I don't know where Joe Camel got the idea that I knew how to write songs. Actually, I'm pretty sure I told him. I was fifteen or sixteen, and Joe had invited me over to his house because I'd shown an interest in his record collection, which was a meticulously curated assemblage of early rock and roll, R&B, jazz, and country that he mined for his band's repertoire. As we were talking that day he mentioned in passing that he didn't really write songs, but he was trying to because he needed an original to put on a 7-inch they could sell at shows. So I showed him the song I'd just written and told him he could have it if he wanted it. "Your Little World," and yes, I wrote it about a girl.

Your little world
Is much too small
You've got no room
For me at all

Ouch, hurts, doesn't it? I don't remember who it was about—somebody who'd broken my heart, or had rejected me in a profound enough way that I needed to memorialize my hurt feelings in song. They recorded it and released it as a local single. I still have a box of them somewhere. It's not very good, and I think somewhere in the back of my mind I knew that even at the time, but it sure did boost my confidence to have Joe embrace the idea of me as a songwriter.

I had messed around with writing songs for the Primatives, but we were a cover band. In the same bar band mold as Joe Camel and the Caucasians, but focused more on the sixties—the decade after their bailiwick. We thought of ourselves as a garage band in a stylistic sense—not in the traditional sense in that we practiced in a garage—although the basement is usually accepted as a legitimate substitute. We played songs like "Twist and Shout," "Louie, Louie," "Gloria," and "Hang on Sloopy." We also threw in obscure songs that we didn't bother to tell people weren't originals, like the Chocolate Watchband's "Are You Gonna Be There (At the Love-In)," the Sonics' "Psycho," and the Electric Prunes' "I Had Too Much to Dream (Last Night)." We loved anything with a snotty irreverence, even if it made no sense to sing about love-ins and acid trips in the mid-eighties. Eventually we reached a point where we felt like we were cheating.

It felt too easy. We started to draw bigger crowds than the bands we were opening for, because we were in high school and we only had to put a few flyers up at school and everyone would show up. The mass appeal had a lot to do with it being an easy place to get away with underage drinking. My mom would book the hall for us, and collect the money at the door, and look the other way when the kegs were being sold. We started making substantial money, thousands of dollars. Not tens of thousands, but thousands of dollars, even on an average weekend.

My parents were always supportive of my career in music. I think it was, in part, because they were entertainers themselves, even though they didn't have the support to take their interests any further. My mother lived vicariously through me quite a bit. She would always tell me about having wanted to be a singer when she was little, but I don't remember her singing that much.

Later, after I left home, she still treated me like the center of her universe. My old bedroom was transformed into a Jeff Tweedy museum. She would subscribe to any magazine that ever mentioned me, Uncle Tupelo, or Wilco. We ended up with boxes and boxes of magazines and newspaper clippings, dozens of albums and cassettes and 45s, posters and press releases, and every Wilco and Uncle Tupelo T-shirt ever made, including bootlegs. She curated a very, very specific Rock & Roll Hall of Fame.

My dad would have been a great entertainer. He was captivating and charismatic in any public setting, but it required alcohol. Which is sad to me, because he was genuinely funny. But growing up, I didn't know that. I thought he was just hell-bent on embarrassing my mother and me. He bought a karaoke machine so we could sing at family gatherings. People would come over and he would take out the karaoke machine, which had 8-track tapes of backing tracks for not necessarily hits of the day, but hits of *some* day. Hits of *a* day. They were mostly post–World War II popular songs. Songs that my mom and dad grew up with that were basically the pre-rock-and-roll cavalcade of hits. My dad would never be able to resist changing the lyrics to get a laugh. "They asked me how I knew / That your bottom was bluuuue!" It was funny the first, third, or fourth time, not the fiftieth time.

So **THEY WERE** extremely invested in my success, and when I broke the news to my parents that we were going to start writing our own material and even change the name of the band (to Uncle Tupelo), they were very, very confused and disappointed. "Why would you do that when you have such a good thing going?" my mom would ask. "Why can't you do both?" It was hard to explain, but to us it was a cop-out to not commit to doing your own material and making your own statement. Relying on covers felt like leaving training wheels on a BMX bike. We were getting good, but playing other people's songs would never prove it.

Listening to bands like the Minutemen and the Replacements hammered home that conviction. They weren't moonlighting as a party band in between club dates. "Why *couldn't* we just be a real band?" The Minutemen, in particular, could've been guys in our neighborhood, but they were legit because they stuck their necks out and said what they wanted to say with their own songs. To us that was the only calculable difference. They were smaller-town provincial guys, too, but they were fiercely independent and okay with themselves and weren't embarrassed to try. D. Boon was a heavy dude with just a so-so singing voice, and he was making music that was undeniably liberated. We were also listening to guys like John Prine and Paul Westerberg, who were writing songs that weren't that far removed from our own experiences. I wished I had written them, but not in the same way I used to wish I had written Clash songs. Pretending you could be Joe Strummer was like daydreaming about being John Glenn. A perfectly respectable role model, but there's no way I was ever fucking walking on the moon. But being an average-looking dude who wrote super-short indie rock screeds with a proletarian ethos before dying in a van accident at twenty-seven? That seemed doable.

Really the thing that pushed me to start writing songs is the same thing that compels me to keep writing songs today. I listen to music—new records, old favorites, the radio, anything—until I feel like I can't take it anymore, I have to make something or I'll lose my mind. It's as simple as that. Even when I believe I'll never be able to make something even remotely as perfect or beautiful as what I'm hearing, I can't just sit there and let that challenge go unanswered.

I think that may be the highest purpose of any work of art, to inspire someone else to save themselves through art. Creating creates creators. When I was in the hospital going through treatment for addiction and depression, they would have everyone in my group do art therapy. One of the most beautiful things I've ever seen was watching a catatonic sixty-three-year-old woman who had been hooked on heroin for close to thirty years become human again by holding a pencil and being asked to draw. I'm an agnostic by nature, but seeing that made me believe in staying close to the notion of a creator. The one we identify with most easily by finding it in ourselves.

Back to "Your Little World." It wasn't really the first song I ever wrote. It's just the first one that got recorded and preserved for posterity. But looking through some of my old high school notebooks, there's ample evidence that I'd been throwing lyrical darts at the wall for some time. Dig this . . .

I don't trust anybody
I keep my back to the wall
Never raise my hopes so that they don't fall
People just tell lies they never tell the truth

You may be different, but you have no proof
So I can't let you in
(Crossed out "to my world, yeah")

So much poignant heartache. This is on the same page, coincidentally, where I jotted down some half-ass notes on the Middle Paleolithic period, fascism, and Mussolini, and my friend drew a pretty kick-ass illustration of a tongue-wagging ghoul with an elastic body and rotted-out teeth playing guitar.

Here's my favorite would-be chorus:

I used to think that love should be true
But everything is simple when we act like
You need me, and I need you
Ha!

It's the staccato "Ha!" that really sells that one.

Reading these lyrics has made me wonder if I had a deeper appraisal of my parents' relationship in my subconscious than my conscious mind would have ever been able to express. I'm sure it's just your garden-variety teen angst, but if I was trying to intuit the mindset of my parents' marriage when I wrote this stuff, I think I nailed it. On the other hand, it's also pretty "me" to trace the contours of a broken heart with a heart that's yet to be broken.

This same high school notebook also includes a list of potential band names, with some really promising prospects like the Bagworms, the Boogers, Free Beer, the Bleeders, and Spam Hippies.

There's a part of me that's sincerely sad I never convinced Jay to call Uncle Tupelo the Boogers. I'm not sure it would've turned out any better. We would've likely made the same music, and had the same dysfunctional relationship, and it would've fallen apart in the same way. Headlines would have been better: "Boogers Wipe Out," "What Blew It for the Boogers?"

This may explain why I stopped writing down lyrics and musical ideas in general. You see them on the page, and they lose some of their power, especially when they're stupid. With songs, I started to feel like if I'd just sing it enough times, I'd remember it. The chords and the lyrics would go together. I'm sure it was mostly laziness, and I rationalized it by telling myself that if I couldn't remember it, how could I expect anybody else to? There was some logic to that way of thinking. There were so many songs I loved that I didn't necessarily know all of the words to till I looked at them on a page, and at that point, the emotional impact of the song had already been made by the melody and the recording textures. What did the words matter? They were almost beside the point.

We'd written a few things as a band while we were still called the Primitives. I vaguely recall a song called "Christina" or "Christina Come Home," which we played at a few shows, although I think all recordings of it have been burned and buried. It wasn't really until we became Uncle Tupelo that we started writing in earnest. Not long before that, I remember overhearing one of the nicest things that Jay Farrar has ever said about me. He told somebody, "Well, Jeff knows how to write songs." He never said as much to me directly, but the fact that he said it to somebody else, and then that person told another person who told it to me, it still felt like the greatest compliment he ever gave me twice removed. For Jay, that was as close as you were ever going to get to "I love you." "Hey, I heard from a guy who heard from a guy that you allegedly think I don't entirely suck." That's the kind of validation I would have rationed to last years.

If you listen to the early Uncle Tupelo records, you can hear how much more time and energy we were devoting to hammering out the arrangements for these songs. We always made things more complicated than they needed to be. It was never enough just to have a simple melody with some chords that we would sing over. We spent so much time going, "Let's do *duh duh duh*, three of these, and then *duh duh duh DUH*, two of those. Then we'll slow down, and bring it into a new, different tempo for the last part." We wanted to be the Minutemen, but we weren't writing Minutemen songs. We weren't writing minimalist, deconstructed punk rock songs.

It wasn't long after our encounter in freshman English that Jay Farrar and I became constant companions. We might have even thought of ourselves as best friends, but it was an odd bond we shared with an air of duty or obligation. Jay Farrar never even explicitly asked me to join his band. Everything was built on necessity. Who else were we going to play music with? Jay's brothers had moved on with their lives and had relegated music to a semi-hobby status and I had no one else in my life with even a fraction of the same interests. Whereas, Jay's and my obsessions overlapped almost completely. So there was no need to openly acknowledge any interest in being friends. We never said, "Hey, man, I really like you, let's hang out." It was more along the lines of "Hey, um . . . want to . . . Maybe I could come over . . . I'll play my guitar or whatever?"

When he visited, his dad would drop him off with his guitar. We'd stand in my bedroom, and I'd play him Ramones songs I thought I had learned. He'd watch patiently and then shyly correct what I was getting wrong. His skill level was years ahead of mine, so the tutelage was always welcome. When we ran out of songs I wanted help with, we'd talk about bands, compare notes on what we'd read in music magazines, and listen to records. Sometimes he'd spend the whole weekend at our house without ever calling his parents. I couldn't imagine being gone for any length of time without my parents knowing exactly where I was. The weekends never started with him asking, "Is it all right if I spend the night here?" He just showed up and was there all day and stayed for dinner, and then it started getting dark outside and my mom would whisper to me, "Is he spending the night?" And I'd whisper back, "I don't know, I think so." It just happened. Two days later I'd finally ask him, "Jay, don't you need to go home?"

For some reason we rarely spent as much time at Jay's house. It was just outside of Belleville, built on a hill next to a ravine that felt like the edge of a jungle, with birds and frogs and god knows what else chirping from the thicket. It had the cozy vibe of a doomsday prepper's compound. His dad, Pops Farrar, was a retired merchant marine who looked like he'd been drawn by Woody Guthrie. I found him sweet yet intimidating. He made chain-saw sculptures of Civil War generals, and he could play Jim Reeves's "A Railroad Bum" on accordion. My dad listened to one song a year and owned a karaoke machine.

HERE'S A THING about a band name. After a while, you stop thinking about its meaning. It disappears into itself and becomes automatic.

You never think, "Why am I calling this a toaster? That's a weird thing to call an electrical device that lightly burns sliced bread." Do you ever stop and think about the name the Rolling Stones? Face it, that's a stupid name. All band names are stupid. The Beatles is the worst pun. But the Beatles doesn't mean the Beatles anymore. You don't listen to their music and think, "Oh yeah, I get it, they're like beetles but spelled with an *a* because they're rhythmic insects." The Beatles means the Beatles. Sonic Youth? Come on! That's the worst.

Uncle Tupelo never bothered me that much. I didn't think it was the worst band name, so we had that going for us. Our desire at the time was to have a name that didn't come with a lot of baggage, where you know what you're getting before you hear the first note. You don't hear the name Whiskeytown and wonder if it's K-pop. The Sex Pistols, in spite of the vulgar implications, couldn't sound like anything but the Sex Pistols. Nobody in the history of human listening heard a Sex Pistols song and thought, "Well, this is surprising. I was expecting more cello." I like names that are so random and nonsensical that even the explanation adds to the confusion. Hüsker Dü, one of my favorites, was inspired by the Danish board game, but they also added completely unnecessary umlauts. Nothing throws off an audience's preconceived notions like obscure board games and umlauts.

We got the name by creating two lists of unrelated words and then combining them until we stumbled on something we could imagine on an album cover. Uncle Tupelo was on the "maybe" list—Tupelo being a nod to Elvis's hometown in Mississippi—but I don't think any of us were particularly enthused by it until our friend Chuck Wagner made an illustration for us, a sort of band mascot inspired by Uncle Tupelo. It was an old, fat Elvis Presley, but a version of him that never became the King. He's drinking beer, wearing bunny slippers, and sitting in a La-Z-Boy recliner. He's the Elvis who squandered his gifts, never left Tupelo, and just drinks cheap beer in his mobile home every night.

Something about that image appealed to us. Yes, it was a stupid joke, and it had nothing to do with the songs we were writing. But it also kind of did. What if Elvis had taken a few wrong turns on a back road in Memphis and never walked into Sam Phillips's studio? Sam Phillips has a stronger connection to the genesis of rock and roll, in my opinion, way more than Elvis did. So would the history of rock have been recognizably different without Elvis in it? What if he missed his moment, and then life got in the way, his girlfriend got pregnant, and he kept driving a truck to stay afloat? Singing became just something he did in the privacy of his mobile home after downing a case of beer. Every town in America must have some guys like that. Talented guys who just couldn't get their shit together, or maybe never had what it takes, but were just attractive enough to convince themselves they were meant for something better.

The Elvis mascot didn't last—we used that illustration on one flyer before retiring him—but I still think the name hit, in a roundabout way, on the aching heart of what we were trying to express.

THE FIRST SONG I wrote for Uncle Tupelo, with the idea that it might be something I could sing, was "Screen Door." I wrote it while skipping class at Southern Illinois University in Edwardsville. It was my first attempt at higher education over a three-year span that ultimately ended at Belleville Area College. Three years of college in which I managed to not accumulate a single credit. An accomplishment I'm oddly proud of. You try it.

SIU was close to my parents' home, so I could drive there, and then just hang out in the library and listen to music—they had amazing listening rooms with music I'd never been able to find anywhere else, like Morton Subotnick and John Cage albums—and big pod-like chairs that were like cocoons where I could lose myself and let my mind wander and imagine worlds that had nothing to do with a midwestern kid writing lyrics like "Down here, where we're at / Everybody is equally poor" while wasting his parents' money on a college education he did not desire.

Jay and I had vastly different approaches to lyric writing. He was always zoomed out by a power of ten to a height that outlined the edges of a big picture I could never quite make out from where I stood. I don't remember feeling as negative about where we lived until I met Jay and we started writing songs, and he wrote about factory towns and unemployment and alcoholism and things like that. I mean, he wasn't *wrong*, Belleville was a depressed community economically and psychologically. Almost everything was bizarre and depressing, like the time I spent working at this giant liquor store. I was promoted to part-time night manager before I was even of legal drinking age. But that's not the crazy part. The fact that I was night manager meant that I was required to make night deposits at the bank. And according to the head honcho of this booze depot, this required that I carry a gun, which they kindly provided but never taught me how to use or even how to remove from its holster. One of the managers I worked for did a lot of cocaine. When he was eventually fired for embezzling and for, like, being an unreliable guy on coke all the time, he returned to the store after a few days, not to retrieve his belongings but to rob the place. With a gun. During store hours. In broad daylight. Without a mask! Guess what, they caught him.

The bottom line is that it was not a healthy or happy place. And I do believe whole towns can be collectively depressed psychologically like it's a local dialect. If you have a fairly isolated community, and people maladapt to their internal psychological stress by drinking or willfully numbing themselves in other ways, porn or gambling or whatever, and there's a dwindling supply of hope, people get swept along, and they wake up and they're old and the world has passed them by. And most of the time their kids never see anyone get better, so they grow up with no idea how it happens or what it looks like. So, I get where Jay was getting this. It's just that, as a teenager trying to write music, that wasn't how I saw things. I had plenty of internal torment and self-doubt, but very little of it was directed outward, looking for someone else to blame. I wasn't looking at the community around me and thinking, "This town is a cancer that's eating us all alive." Even early on I was more likely to believe that if something feels bad, it must be my fault.

You could sum up the creative worldviews in that first demo cassette we put out in '87, shortly after we changed our name to Uncle Tupelo: *Colorblind & Rhymeless*. Jay has a song on there called "Before I Break," which is about a guy drinking himself to death and losing any hope to even see beyond tomorrow and he ends up "half drunk in a ditch by the side of the road." Me, on the other hand, I contributed "Screen Door," which is about wearing loose clothes because it's too hot, skipping school, and playing songs with your friends on the front porch.

Jay was pretty much fully formed right out of the gate. He had a gift for lyricism, and an authentically great voice that made everything he sang sound like the Old Testament. My voice, on the other hand, sounded like the kind of pubescent warble one might hear squeaking through an Appalachian fast-food drive-through speaker. When I hear those early recordings I'm just mortified. I used to chew tobacco, and crazy as it sounds, in an effort to quit, I started smoking, which is a stupid way to quit chewing tobacco, but I thought it would at least add some grit to my voice. No such luck. Now I was a pubescent hillbilly with a chest cold. My voice was the worst. Early on I would try to get Jay to sing my songs so I wouldn't have to. Now I'm glad he made me do it.

In the end I took a lot of inspiration from Bo Diddley to come to terms with my limitations. Not how he sang and not necessarily the way he played guitar, but how he got there. Bo Diddley had big hands. I never actually met the man or his hands, but that's what I've heard anyway. The man himself once described his hands as "meat hooks, a size 12 glove." His hands and fingers were so thick, he couldn't pluck at the strings like they do in most country and blues songs. So he developed his own style, one that used his limitations rather than tried to compensate for them. He played the violin as a kid, so he tried that same technique on a guitar. He tuned it to an open E and then moved his hands superfast across the fretboard like it was a violin bow. He permitted himself—he *liberated* himself—to play guitar like that. I wanted to do the same thing, to allow myself to play music to my strengths rather than my weaknesses.

I do not have a voice that I have a lot of comfort with sustaining. So when I started writing songs, I stayed away from melodies with

sustained notes. It's one of the reasons I like using capos on my guitars, because they tend to eliminate some sustain. I might as well be
writing and recording music on a ukulele, 'cause that's about as much
sustain as I can tolerate. I've also figured out ways to mute strings
and make sure I don't get too much ringing. I've gotten better at the
guitar over the years, and I can deal with it better now, but what I still
look for in an instrument is something that reflects my less-than-
perfect voice.

Sometimes you're just stuck with the guitar you're stuck with. Especially if you're a teenager in southwestern Illinois and you're lucky
to have any guitar at all. Whatever it is, you need to learn how to
manipulate it so it's working with you rather than against you. For
example, I learned pretty early on that I don't like new strings.
They're so bright and cheery. I hate everything about them. I need
strings that are weighted down by history, inhibited by their own
filthy past. I need a guitar that isn't a soaring instrument, because my
voice can't compete. It's just not going to rise to that occasion. I need
the strings to come down to my level.

I've heard people complain about my guitar when I play solo
shows. "Why does he insist on playing that guitar? It sounds like it's
strung with rubber bands." To which I say, Um . . . Shut the fuck up,
get your own guitar and ring like a silver bell for all I care. I need a
guitar with strings that don't sound like a twenty-year-old who
wakes up at five a.m. and has a venti iced Americano and is ready to
seize the day! I need strings that sound like me, a doom-dabbling,
fifty-year-old, borderline misanthrope, nap enthusiast. I should
probably tell you that's all bullshit. I just like the way old strings
sound better because I love old records, and old records don't have as

much high end, which would make even new strings sound less bright. Plus, strings are expensive so they never used to change them in the old days.

Truthfully, what I was most concerned with was coming up with songs that seemed even remotely to belong in the same company as Jay's songs. He was always more comfortable writing from a moral-authority position. I tried to follow his lead, but it didn't come as easily for me. I liked "Screen Door" because it was authentic; to me it had a sort of defiant, punk rock stance, just being proud of who you are and where you're from, even if it looks boring and stupid to everybody else. I wanted to write songs like the Minutemen's "History Lesson—Part II." That knocked me out the first time I heard it. "We were fucking corn dogs." So were we! And one of my favorite lines of all time, "Our band could be your life." What a victory that would be, to make a song that a listener hears and goes, "It's like it knows me." Maybe "Screen Door" wasn't that song, but it was humble and had good intentions.

I tried to get closer to Jay's social consciousness with "Train." It started out as a song about how often you had to wait for trains when you drove around in Belleville. Being so close to St. Louis, we lived near the highest concentration of railroad tracks in the country, so you couldn't go anywhere without crossing tracks, and if you didn't time it right, a two-minute trip to the corner store could take half an hour. We were also close to Scott Air Force Base, so every time you were stopped at a railroad crossing, there was a pretty good chance you'd be watching military hardware being transported. It was like this constant reminder of "Oh yeah, we spend a shit ton of money on tanks in this country." I may have laid it on a little thick. There was a line in there about worrying about being "the first one to die in a war." I wrote this in 1989, a year before the Gulf War. There was no military conflict and no draft. I didn't know anybody my age worried about dying in a war, and that includes the kids who planned on enlisting.

I think for most songwriters, unless they're very singular and gifted, it takes some time for them to find their voice. There's a lot to be said for faking it till you make it. You just do it until it becomes real. You work, and you work, and you work, and hopefully you get it right eventually. "Gun" is the first song that made me feel like I was getting somewhere. It wasn't a moment of divine inspiration, where the clouds of uncertainty magically parted and this perfect little song floated into my head. I was becoming more disciplined about working at songwriting every day. Which meant picking up the guitar even when I didn't feel particularly inspired. In other words, I didn't pick it up for comfort because my heart was breaking, I wrote "Gun" in spite of a broken heart.

I had a girlfriend who was in the class above me and had gone away to college as I started my senior year in high school. She left Belleville to attend SIU–Carbondale, a two-hour drive southeast. She met a guy there during her first semester away and started seeing him while she and I were still technically dating. I was devastated. I'd experienced rejection before, but not the world-shattering feeling of betrayal. It may even mark the beginning of the first identifiable pattern of depression in my life. When you're prone to depression, this is the kind of catalyst that can bring it on and turn something upsetting into something debilitating and seemingly insurmountable. It also happened in the fall, which couldn't have helped. I know now how susceptible I am to SAD, seasonal affective disorder, but back then I just knew it as "Oh shit, it's starting to get dark at five p.m." It was a perfect storm of mood-altering circumstance. I was inconsolable.

I can remember her calling me to tell me she had met somebody. She said she'd kissed him or he'd kissed her, she wasn't sure, but it was at a party, and it didn't mean anything. The way she said it, it made me nervous. It was like she was confessing to a crime while simultaneously taking it back. "I killed a guy . . . But it's okay, he isn't actually dead, and I don't know why you're making such a big deal out of it!" I drove down to Carbondale to see her, and I found her walking hand in hand with a guy toward her dorm room. They went inside, and I waited outside for a few minutes, wondering what I should do, and then I knocked. They were already in bed.

God, it was a mess, a full-on catastrophe. It was almost comically hurtful. And as ridiculously inconsequential in the grand scheme of things as it all was, at that moment I couldn't see it as anything less than the end of my life.

I wrote "Gun" a little while after that, not with that consciously in mind. But later I was grateful all that pain hadn't gone to waste.

Crawling back to you now
I sold my guitar to the girl next door
She asked me if I knew how
I told her, "I don't think so anymore."

That was probably the most honest and direct I'd ever been in a song up to that point. Telling the world that I'd sold my guitar wasn't saying I'm going to kill myself, but it was close. To me, it was almost the equivalent of killing myself at that point. I was in so much pain;

I was willing to give up the one thing in the world that was sustaining to me, the *only* thing that mattered. That might seem like a martyrdom fantasy—"If I can't have what I want, I don't want anything!" It is grandiose, but I also think I was serious. The feeling that "anything is better than this," even giving up the only thing you love if it would just make it go away, is real. I can still identify with that. When I play this song, that's what hooks me in. It's not about remembering this act of betrayal, but the memory of being gripped by so much despair and helplessness that I didn't even care if I ever touched a guitar again. I felt that exact way years later when I went into rehab. "I don't care if I ever write another song again, I just want to feel better. I don't like feeling like this." That's why I can still sing "Gun" and not feel silly. It's not about that moment in history, it's about that feeling of despair and being willing to do anything to make it go away.

Not that I think suffering is necessary to create worthwhile art. I hate that idea, and I think it's bullshit. It makes me think of my brothers, who are a great source of regret and sadness for me. Greg was a local guy, happy to be working on the railroad, and had gone through his drinking and drugging phase. If he were alive today, he'd be the type of guy you'd maybe see profiled in articles about Trump voters. Steve was a grandiose intellectual. I'm pretty sure he never finished any of his degrees—he went to Washington University, he went to Oregon—but he instilled in me a passion for literature, his passion for learning. My mother always said he was the smartest person she ever knew. I always contend that that's why he's been unable to get the help he needs to stop drinking—because he's convinced that he's smarter than everyone. And you need to be able to accept that you're not. Something I heard a lot when I was in rehab was this totally awesome way counselors would shut someone down when they started arguing that they didn't have to listen, they were going to do it their own way. The counselors would point out that "Your best thinking is what put you here." Most of the time everyone would laugh at the undeniable truth of it. Seriously, if you were smart enough to fix yourself, wouldn't you have done it by now? That's what I always want to say to Steve.

He really makes me sad. He was a good older brother, and he was a mentor. He gave me inspiration and insights to follow. And at the same time, assessing his situation, looking back on his life, it's a series of uncompleted tasks. He aspired to be an author but he never finished writing the books he would start. The cruel assessment is that he chickened out, and sadly, I think that's the accurate assessment. Alcohol was a pretty safe refuge from his fear of finding out that he's not as special as he thinks he is. No one is. I could write a whole book about him, but generally, I've worked on me, and the parts of him that make me sad—I've come to terms with the fact that it's not my fault. I spent a majority of my life feeling responsible somehow, but I didn't do it to him.

Preparing my parents' house to be sold last summer, I came across this quote that Steve had scrawled on the wall: "No writer ever becomes great until they've been greatly hurt." I don't know if that's an actual Hemingway quote, but my brother thought it was. Even at the time, that seemed pretty maudlin. I'm antithetical to that. I think everybody hurts deeply. And certainly there is a therapeutic element that might lead some people's suffering through certain types of issues to creating art and making things. But I just don't buy the argument that we suffer deeper, or harder, than anyone else. Anyone who makes stuff lucked out that they found an outlet for what most of the world has as a condition.

That quote, and that type of hero emulation of Hemingway and other writers, really damaged my brother.

Even when I was a kid, a quote like that seemed painful—he looked at it in a totally different way than I did. He looked at it as if you're supposed to inflict or invite pain upon yourself to make art. Even then, my reaction was "I hope nothing bad happens to me so I become a good artist. I hope that's not true."

Because I think that artists create *in spite* of suffering, not because of suffering. I just don't buy it. Everyone suffers by degrees and I believe everyone has the capacity to create, but I think you're one of the lucky ones if you've found an outlet for your discomfort or a way to cope through art. At the very least, one's suffering must be fairly manageable to even contemplate art. To exalt an artist's suffering as being somehow unique or noble makes me cringe. When someone's heart aches because a girl said she still loved him but really she was sleeping with somebody else and that made him sad, at best they're plugged into something universal—if we all learn anything from being alive on this planet, it's that people will lie to you, especially about how much or little they care about you. And I would guess there's a lot more similarity in how we suffer than the way we experience joy. Rejection stays with you, but I don't think people register it when they're happy. They don't say, "I need to remember what this feels like." It just goes by, and it's perfect and awesome, and you feel grateful that you get to experience even a fleeting moment of pure, unbridled, unsarcastic bliss. But when we experience pain or trauma, we're acutely aware that something is wrong. You want answers. "What is this? How do I get rid of this? Why is this happening to me? I don't want this." That's why so much art, and music, in particular, becomes a great commiserating balm for pain. Joy doesn't need to be audited. We're just grateful to have had it at all. But pain, goddammit, we demand to know *Who's responsible for this?*

However, there is an emotional hierarchy I do find hard to shake. I definitely love sad songs the most. The ones that expose the rawest vein, that I'm most reluctant to sing out loud, always feel the most authentic. I used to try out new songs on my mom. She was a tough audience. Not because she was critical—if anything, she loved everything I wrote *too* much—but because the more real the song felt to me, the more the words got frozen in my throat. You don't need a crowd to find out if a song has worth. An audience doesn't have a consciousness, one person does. If it's one person who's sitting so close you can see their eyes and hear their breathing, that's when it becomes as intimate as a conversation. You're confronted with what a song is capable of. It really has to work on one person at a time. If you feel exposed when you're singing to someone and each word gives you a distinct terrifying thrill resembling embarrassment, that means you're doing something right.

That's what made me feel like I could be a songwriter. It's not about being able to write the perfect lyrics or a melody that will crawl up inside a listener's head and never leave. It was realizing that I'm okay being vulnerable. I don't care. My comfort level with being vulnerable is probably my superpower. I wasn't the cool kid. I wasn't the strongest. I wasn't the one you could depend on if things went wrong. I wasn't the smartest person. I wasn't the one you turned to if you had a question. I wasn't ruggedly handsome or boyishly charming. I wasn't the captain of the football team, or the kid everybody in school voted was the most likely to succeed. I *was* the guy who could burst into tears in front of his peers and not care what they thought. I had a bone-crushing earnestness, a weaponized sincerity, and I was learning how to put all of those feelings into songs. That may not sound like a superpower, but when I discovered it, it was not any less remarkable than Peter Parker realizing he could walk on walls. That was the moment of reckoning. I was different. I had something to offer. I was impervious to my peers' shame. They couldn't make me recoil with their snickering or judgmental sneers. I'd sung these same songs to my mother, in the quiet of our kitchen, and if I could open up to her and not be destroyed by a disapproving arch of an eyebrow, what could a crowd of strangers possibly do?

I became a songwriter not when I composed that perfect couplet, or experienced the right amount of pain. It's when I realized that whatever I wrote, even if it meant gutting myself in front of strangers, letting all those raw emotions come flooding out, making a fool of myself with my own words, was exactly what I always wanted to do with my life.

EVEN BEFORE WE started booking gigs, we made that demo with all of our original songs on it: "I Got Drunk," "Screen Door," "Before I Break," and a couple of instrumentals. It was an odd collection of lo-fi 4-track recordings and rehearsals we'd recorded on a boom box.

I'd made copies to hand out to clubs on my dad's primitive home karaoke machine that were barely audible. It wasn't enough to make the record companies come calling, but having any kind of demo tape did help us land regular slots at Cicero's, a basement bar below a pizza joint in University City on the west side of St. Louis, a short walk from the Washington University campus. It was our favorite venue in town and it was pretty awful. The acoustics were exactly what you'd expect from a dank concrete basement with super-low ceilings prone to leaking. We'd often have to put our amps up on cinder bricks, because sometimes the water would get high enough to flood the slightly raised part of the floor they generously referred to as a stage. It made me a little nervous plugging in a guitar amp while standing ankle-deep in water. Cicero's was almost all bar, with a stage at the far end that had an inconveniently located pole, which was holding the ceiling up. Cicero's had electrical outlets that were always sparking and hissing angrily. Combined with all the cigarettes being lit and dropped—this was during the eighties and nineties when even preteens chain-smoked—it was a huge firetrap. Unless it was raining, then you just had to worry about getting electrocuted. (It was also a lot of fun.)

Things happened to the band slowly, until they started happening fast. For a few years, we played a bunch of shows, but mostly stayed close to home, rarely venturing east of Chicago. We recorded a few more demos, including one called *Not Forever, Just for Now* that contained most of the songs that would become *No Depression*. I also talked Tony Margherita, the manager at Euclid Records—who was also now my boss, since I'd started working at Euclid as a part-time clerk—into managing the band. I brought a cardboard box full of Uncle Tupelo cassettes to the store and casually gave one to Tony. I may have gone a little over the top with trying to seem indifferent.

"It's nothin'," I told him. "Just some stuff my band's been messing around with. Check it out if you want to . . . ? No biggie. I mean, you can tape over it if you want . . . It's cool . . . I'll just leave it here on your jacket."

He took one of the cassettes home, and the next day we made plans to get together so I could ask his advice on where to send the tape and book more gigs. Not that Tony necessarily had any idea—his experience as a music industry insider involved making sure the record store was stocked with cool records—but there was something about him that made him seem perfect for the job. Maybe it was the glasses. He was also really tall and imposing, and he looked like he'd be convincing with a baseball bat in his hands. Whatever it was, it inspired confidence.

I asked Tony to be our manager without clearing it with Jay first. I didn't think he'd care, and I was right. When I mentioned it to Jay a few days later, he barely managed a nod. Jay didn't often concern himself with the business side of the band. That was my responsibility, I guess because I worked at a record store and I had more exposure to "the industry" than he did at his mom's used bookstore. I also had a different skill set for communicating with people. Namely, I could kind of do it. As time went on, Jay would become suspicious that Tony and I were aligning against him, which was patently absurd. I'm not even sure how we could've done that if we wanted to. How could we promote the band while simultaneously sabotaging him? We'd have to somehow get audiences to say, "I sure do love Uncle Tupelo, except for that guy with the great voice."

Tony had been a positive influence on me almost from the beginning. It started like so many—all—of my friendships over the years, with conversations about music. It wasn't just something we did to pass the time, we talked about music because it was our job. All record store employees have an inordinate number of brain cells devoted to records, even records they don't personally care about. To acquire even a semi-encyclopedic mental inventory of records demands an intense amount of focus and a lot of public shaming by your record store elders. Get caught putting Jethro Tull in the *T*'s once and you'll know what I'm talking about. It's stressful.

Record store employees are not always honorable and selfless contributors to the greater good. I'm not sure what it's like now because it's been a few decades since I manned a register, but back in my day we were dicks. Hey, spend your day being "brought up to speed" on bebop by a grad student in a beret and ridiculed for not knowing which Genesis record is the one before Peter Gabriel left and you, yourself, might snap at a customer pathetically asking for help finding the Beatles' White Album. *"It's the white one!"*

Another perk of working at a record store, besides the free-ish records and not getting fired for shrink-wrapping the boss's office, is that you can drink on the job. One evening about an hour before closing time, Tony said he was running out to get some beer to keep us entertained while we restocked the shelves. He returned with a six-pack of beer.

"Is that it?" I asked him.

"Yeah," he said. "What, did I get the wrong kind?"

"No, it's just . . . I thought you were getting beer for both of us."

He looked at the six-pack and tried to make sense of my complaint. "I did," he said, opening a bottle and offering it to me.

Up to that point in my life I had honestly never seen anyone buy just a six-pack of beer.

I was flummoxed. I didn't know anybody who could drink just a six-pack, much less split one with somebody. My dad drank a twelve-pack of beer every night. That was his minimum workday evening intake. By the time I got married he was still going strong. In fact, he brought his own cooler of beer to the ceremony when Susie and I said our vows onstage *at her bar*. One of the last times he came to see me play, our tour manager offered him a bottle of water, to which he replied with disgust, "Now, you know I don't drink water on game day. Get me a goddamn beer." So again, the idea of anybody splitting a six-pack was surreal.

Good things began to happen when Tony officially came on board as our manager. We got a record deal with Giant (soon to be renamed Rockville), we were touring *outside* the Midwest—we even played a sold-out show at CBGB in New York, on the same stage where a lot of our heroes had performed—and we'd been invited to Boston to record our next album. Everything felt like it had been cranked up a notch. Even our songwriting was starting to feel more confident, like we were taking real steps toward having our own voices and a collective style. And to top it all off, we had a new van! A van we could drive on a highway and not think, "This is how I'm going to die, in this van."

A van was one of the best things about being in a touring band with a limited income. It was empowering, that feeling of rolling into town for a gig, like the Minutemen, always on the way to somewhere else, just one tank of gas away from being homeless. We'd owned a few ill-advised vans over the years. The first was Old Green, a Dodge van with a paint job reminiscent of dried snot. The floorboard fell out, just collapsed under our feet, and rather than continue to drive it like a *Flintstones* car, we traded it in for a 1970 red Ford Econoline van that we named . . . wait for it . . . Old Red. This was a spectacularly dangerous van. The steering had about a foot of play before it made any turn, and the brakes needed to be pumped a minimum of thirty seconds before you wanted to come to a stop. It had broken tie-rods and leaked oil—we had to stop and put oil in it every fifty miles or so—and only occasionally did it have any brake fluid in it whatsoever. We loved it, mostly because the Minutemen had also toured in an Econoline van, and if it was good enough for D. Boon, it sure as hell was good enough for us.

Tony came along on some early road trips with us, and he was not impressed with Old Red. I believe his exact words were "Let me out." I've never seen such a large man look so legitimately afraid. We were unmoved by his arguments until he reminded us that D. Boon's beloved Econoline van was the same one that killed him when it flipped in the Arizona desert and snapped his neck. We conceded that he had a point, and when we returned to Belleville, he drove the van directly to a used car lot. Their mechanic looked under the hood and recoiled at what he saw.

"You *drove* this here?" he asked. "How are you alive?"

Old Red had apparently been within days, maybe minutes, of bursting into flames. They gave us $50 for a trade-in, and along with a couple thousand dollars loaned from Tony—I think he had to mortgage his house to come up with the money—we purchased a blue Chevy Beauville van. We called it . . . I shouldn't have to tell you . . . Old Blue.

THE LABEL WE'D signed with wasn't exactly Warner Bros. We were with a little independent label, which gave us $3,500 as an advance, just barely enough to make a record. As it turned out, making records was expensive. We ended up at Fort Apache South, a recording studio in Roxbury, a Boston neighborhood we were advised not to walk around in by ourselves. Sometimes, recording late at night, we'd hear gunshots, and we'd look at one another and one of us would say, "Hey, why don't we just sleep in the studio tonight?" Which we had to do anyway, because, as I mentioned, a few grand doesn't go a long way when you're making a record, so we didn't have any money left over in the budget to pay for a hotel.

When we didn't sleep at the studio we stayed with Three Merry Widows, a St. Louis band that had moved to Boston because it was a more vibrant scene. They had one couch we somehow split three ways, which is mathematically impossible. I'm not saying any of this out of sour grapes. We were grateful. We were ecstatic, even. We were making a record! A record that was going to "come out" and be in record stores! The guys producing us, Sean Slade and Paul Kolderie, had helped make records for bands like Dinosaur Jr. and the Pixies at Fort Apache, which was why we were in Boston in the first place. They even let Jay play on the same 1961 Les Paul that J Mascis had used on *Bug*. It's hard to overstate how huge it was to us. Weeks earlier, just knowing that they had heard our demos would have felt validating and now their names were going to be on our album jacket alongside our own. We only had ten days to record everything—even with the gunfire outside, studio time is expensive—but as young and irreverent as we were, nothing was taken for granted. We didn't want to blow it. Every one of us worked hard to make it great. Sean and Paul took good care of us. They were fun, like cool older brothers, but they still knew when to crack the whip. They knew what we lacked more than anything was confidence. It's crazy the wonders some simple sincere validation can provide. Thanks to Sean and Paul, in just ten days we became a real band. We left believing we were good. They told us we were, and it became so.

4

‖‖‖‖‖‖‖‖‖‖‖‖‖‖‖

HOW IT ENDS

THIS IS HOW it ends.

I'm waiting in our apartment for Jay to come home. A few days earlier, he'd called Tony and told him he was quitting the band. It wasn't fun anymore, he said, and he didn't like me. To me, his timing couldn't have been more bizarre. We were coming off an incredible year, better than I could have ever dreamed. We had just released our fourth album, our switch to a major label hadn't been nearly as compromising as we had feared, we made our first TV appearance, and our record was well received. We were touring the country and splitting hotel rooms, a huge step up from sleeping on the couches or hardwood floors of strangers who took pity on us after the shows. The night Jay called Tony and complained about the unacceptable amount of fun he was having, we had just played a sold-out show at Tramps in New York City, and *The New York Times* had published a review of our latest record, *Anodyne*, comparing us to Hank Williams, the Flying Burrito Brothers, and *Exile*-era Stones.

There had been some changes along the way. Mike had made the disappointing but understandable decision of opting out of the touring lifestyle in favor of a well-paying job at the local daily newspaper and living closer to his girlfriend. After that we tried out a drummer for a few months whom Jay struggled to connect with before moving on to Ken Coomer from Nashville, Tennessee. Ken was big and confident and hit his drums twice as hard as anyone we'd ever played with. Lord, he was loud. Mike was self-taught and had learned how to play right alongside us, so all of his inconsistencies and idiosyncrasies were baked into the band and belonged to us all. Ken, on the other hand, felt like a real professional rock drummer, which was exciting and a little overwhelming at first.

For *Anodyne*, our first record on a major label, we had decided that the way to guarantee maximum control of how the record sounded would be to record it live in the studio without any overdubs. I'm not sure what we were afraid they would want to change about our sound or why we even thought they would care enough to try and mold us into a more commercial act. Our minds just worked that way back then, I guess. To make it easier to get a full band sound without resorting to overdubs, we rounded out the lineup with a couple of friends we'd made traveling around the country, including John Stirratt, who we'd met and become fast friends with in Oxford, Mississippi, after Uncle Tupelo played a show with his band the Hilltops. John was the first person we'd ever met outside the St. Louis area who had a copy of our demo tape. He'd taken it from his college radio station and had invited us to share a bill shortly thereafter. And then there was Max Johnston, who we met . . . Well, it's a long story I'll get to later.

Tony called me with the bad news about Jay leaving when we returned from New York. I was hurt, but mostly furious. This wasn't one of Jay's bands with his brothers I'd talked my way into. This was Uncle Tupelo, which I had helped create. I felt at least some ownership of it. To just say, "Nah, I'm over it," and close it down, after all those years of touring and building something together, felt unfair, and to do it without even letting me know something was wrong, I took as betrayal.

I really wanted to talk to Jay about it—maybe even yell at him—but he'd disappeared. Several days went by, and there was no sign of him. He could've been at his parents' house, or possibly working at his mom's used bookstore. I could have called, but instead I sat and waited in our second-floor apartment on Eleventh Street, right off Main Street in Belleville, that we were still sharing with Mike Heidorn. The place had seemed like a sanctuary when we found it: a sprawling flat above a dance studio that used to be a train depot now run by an inattentive landlord. Oh, and the rent was $80 a month! When we moved in, there were four of us living there. That meant we each paid $20 per month. I could pay my portion of the rent by looking for change in the couch a few times a month. My parents lived less than a mile away, so regular meals and laundry were still free. It was adulthood with training wheels.

That still didn't make it easy enough, though, and after several years of neglect and treating the place with roughly the same love as a highway rest stop, it no longer seemed like home sweet home. The furniture, which was already second- (or third-) hand by the time we'd dragged it in, looked and smelled like we kept raccoons as pets. There were pizza boxes stacked to the ceiling and garbage bags filled with dirty dishes that deserved a decent burial. There were more blankets hanging over doorways than actual doors and a fridge that contained little more than beer and ketchup.

I sat there for days and stewed. When you've committed yourself to stewing and watching the front door, you have a lot of extra time for taking an inventory of your life. I started to put the pieces together, thinking back over the last year, and with hindsight, it all seemed so obvious. Some of the clues were right there in the songs. I thought "Chickamauga" was about a Civil War battlefield, and maybe it mostly was, but there was another layer that was clearly foreshadowing. "Solitude is where I'm bound." Ugh. How did I miss that? If the record was a conversation between us, I was all "We'll get there eventually," and he was "The time is right for getting out while we still can."

I was also starting to take stock of our shared space. Both Jay and I were twenty-six, deep enough into what could fairly be described as adulthood. We had a major label record deal; shouldn't our living conditions not be best described as camping? Things that I'd never noticed before suddenly came front and center. "Why is there a garbage bag filled with dirty dishes?" I thought. "Whose idea was that? That is the worst idea in the history of bad ideas. Seriously, a plastic dish rack costs maybe a buck."

Too much reality can be depressing and I was up to my eyes in it. Especially since, up to this point, I'd convinced myself that we lived in an indie rock version of the Monkees' house.

The Monkees' living arrangement was such a formative memory

for me that I've chased the fantasy my whole life. I truly believed that a band was supposed to live together and have antics and adventures. To be fair, though, it was the Beatles who technically came up with the utopian ideal of a cohabitating band in *Help!* Ever since the moment I watched all four Beatles walk through separate doors and all end up in the same sprawling shared living space, I've pictured all bands in communal homes. I loved every detail: Ringo's vending machines, John's revolving bookcase and relaxation pit, Paul's giant church organ rising out of the floor. *That*, I thought, is the only way it makes sense to call a band a band.

The Monkees just upped the ante. Their house was a little more practical, but it still had a spiral staircase and bunk beds. During the first season, Davy and Peter slept in the downstairs bunk beds, and Mike and Micky slept upstairs, but they had all moved into the same bedroom by season 2. Which, again, made complete sense to me. Of *course* you all sleep in the same room. What if somebody gets a musical idea in the middle of the night? You need your bandmates nearby for emergency jamming. The Monkees had no parental authority figures or real governing body other than a mannequin named Mr. Schneider, who gave advice when you pulled a cord. In my prepubescent brain, this wasn't just a fantasy in a sitcom universe. It was aspirational. For me, *The Monkees* might as well have been a documentary.

I grew out of those childish ideas, and then grew right back into them when I got older. The Loft, my recording studio in Chicago, is pretty much built on that template. It's got bunk beds, enough for every member of Wilco and the Wilco crew that lives outside of Chicago. We've had a few sleepovers over the years, while in the midst of making records, preparing for tours, et cetera. The Loft has a kitchen, a desk for each band member where their personal mail piles up when we're out of town, a pinball machine, and enough nooks and crannies to get lost in.

But as I sat in our ramshackle excuse for an apartment in Belleville and waited for Jay to come back, it was so glaringly *not* a Monkees house. Not just because there was no spiral staircase or advice-dispensing mannequins. It wasn't a true Monkees house because it was empty. There was never an episode of *The Monkees* where Micky Dolenz said, "This isn't fucking fun anymore, I quit," and then disappeared. That wasn't even a remote possibility. As bad as things could get, they were in this thing for life. Maybe Micky wouldn't sleep in the communal bunk bedroom for a few nights, just to let his temper cool off, but he'd always come back. Then one of the guys would find a magical monkey's paw, and they'd be distracted by the next madcap adventure.

A LOT OF WHAT has been covered in the press over the years regarding my relationship with Jay Farrar has made it sound like we were always at odds, but we weren't. We had good times. Lots of them.

Like the time we were recording our second album, *Still Feel Gone*, at Long View Farm in western Massachusetts, a few hours outside of Boston. That album title, by the way, is about being on the road too long, which we'd only recently started to experience. When you've been traveling for so many weeks and months that it all starts to blur together, and you close your eyes and get the sensation that you're in the rear seat of a van speeding down the interstate even when you're back home in your own bed, that's when you still feel gone.

Long View Farm was an actual farm, with horses and rolling fields and a big barn that was built in the nineteenth century and had a state-of-the-art recording facility. The Rolling Stones used it in the eighties when they were rehearsing for their *Tattoo You* tour. They converted the hayloft into a stage so Jagger could practice his . . . Jaggering? I don't remember why we ended up there. We had a slightly bigger budget this time, and Sean and Paul, who had produced our first record, were pushing for us to go there.

Long View is famously haunted, but I never saw any ghosts. Mike swears he did, though. We were staying at a little cabin on the property, and one night Mike was doing the dishes, and he turned around and noticed a woman standing behind him, dressed in nineteenth-century garb and just staring at him. His first reaction was "Oh, that's cool," and he waved at her and then turned back and continued washing dishes. When he turned around again, a few seconds later, she was gone. Which is . . . weird, I guess? I don't know. I thought it was probably a cleaning woman.

Either way, the talk of paranormal activity had put us all on edge. While Mike and I argued about the maid ghost, debating whether she existed or whether he was high enough to hallucinate, Jay stayed quiet, which we read as on edge. Stoicism can act as a sort of emotional Rorschach test, and it's easy to project your mood onto the silent one in the room. Later that night, Jay snuck into the barn when the rest of us were out and found an old pipe organ. He cranked that thing up, and when Mike and I showed up for a late-night rehearsal, we were still fumbling for the lights when he burst into a deafening rendition of Bach's *Toccata and Fugue in D Minor*, the piece always used as a cartoonish shorthand for spookiness.

It was a beautifully executed and effective fright. My heart raced and the hair stood up on the back of my neck. Then we saw Jay bent over the organ. He was nonchalant, but there was no mistaking the intent. He was pranking us. His underselling of his conscious ploy was almost funnier than the prank itself. Jay Farrar scared us out of our wits by playing scary organ music in a dark barn without ever even acknowledging us. I mean, come on, that's the kind of hijinks never associated with Jay and Uncle Tupelo.

There were plenty of other moments like that, when Jay would surprise us by being spontaneously silly, but the hard feelings that went with our demise somehow made it easier to relate the ones filled with dread. It makes sense you would reinforce the narrative that things needed to end than the equally valid point of view that we were buddies and it all ended with an unfulfilled promise. It really was a struggle at times, though. Like when we realized good news had to be gingerly broken to Jay. "Oh crap, we were offered the opening slot for the Yo La Tengo show in St. Louis. How are we going to tell Jay?" "Oh no, *Rolling Stone* wants to interview us. Who gets to tell Jay?" Nobody wanted that thorny task. It was always difficult to present good news to him because I think he was suspicious of good news. He'd find the negative side of anything. "Oh great, *Rolling Stone*, is Madonna going to be on the cover?"

Another great/bad piece of news we had to break to Jay was the opportunity to make an album with Peter Buck, the R.E.M. cofounder and lead guitarist. We first met when he came to see Uncle

Tupelo in 1990, before we'd even put out our first record, at the 40 Watt in Athens, Georgia. I think he only went on the recommendation of Debbie Southwood-Smith, the Rockville A&R woman who signed Uncle Tupelo. There were maybe twenty people in the audience for our first show at the 40 Watt, and four of them were R.E.M., which was a pretty crazy ratio for a band without a record out, but I assume it happened quite often in those days when R.E.M. was pioneering a new kind of rock star persona. A homespun, accessible, weird, and overall friendlier sort.

Peter asked us to meet him after the show at a place called the Grit, a nearby vegetarian restaurant. When we walked in, there was no sign of him, but I saw Michael Stipe sitting alone at the bar, so I tapped him on the shoulder. "Excuse me, Mr. Stipe, do you know if Peter is here?" He turned to me and replied, with no facial expression or emotion, "I'm not Peter's keeper." Ah, okay, noted. We eventually found Peter, and we hung out deep into the night, bonding over records and books and southern diner food. At some point he offered to help us make a record. We'd only made one record, so we weren't quite aware how generous and sweet an offer that was.

EVENTUALLY WE FIGURED it out and spent five days in March of 1992 making... well, *March 16–20, 1992* with Peter Buck producing us at John Keane Studios in Athens, Georgia, and John Keane, himself, engineering and lending a hand with some banjo and pedal steel overdubs. We stayed at Peter's house, a big old Victorian mansion, which saved us enough money to stay under budget. I remember wandering around the house, looking for a bathroom, and opening a door to what turned out to be a closet filled with gold and platinum records. Every day he'd get his mail, there would be more. He'd say, "Oh, wow. Gold in Israel," and then he'd go put it in the closet with all the others. He was a bona fide rock star at a time when that meant something, but he didn't really act like one. Having known him now for a couple of decades, I can safely say any idiosyncratic behavior he's ever exhibited would've pronounced itself at some point even if he never was in one of the world's biggest bands.

When we lived with him, he wore his pajamas most of the time. Even when he left the house—we'd stay behind to work on songs, and he'd say, "I'll be back in a few hours to see how it's going"—he'd walk out in pajamas. I'm not sure if he even bothered to put on shoes. While we were staying with him, he brought in cases of beer—I guess our reputation preceded us—and when I told him I didn't drink anymore, he brought in cases of pop, too. Peter was a very hands-off producer, not in an aloof way, but in a laid-back "It'll all work out somehow" way. There were times when I noticed him reading a newspaper while we were in the middle of recording a song. But it never felt like we were being ignored. He had a calming presence; it simultaneously lifted our anxiety and made us want to try harder.

There's a great story that Roger Hawkins tells. He's the drummer on some of Aretha Franklin's most iconic songs, like "Respect" and "Chain of Fools." As part of a group of studio musicians in Muscle Shoals, Alabama, he was drumming on hugely important R&B songs when he was just a teenager, far too young to have any sense of, or ego about, his talent. So one day Hawkins was playing on a session that Jerry Wexler from Atlantic Records was producing. Out of the blue, Hawkins claims, Wexler walked down from the control room and into the studio and told him, "Roger, *you* are a great drummer." Wexler wasn't involved in some larger conversation with Hawkins. He just wanted to tell him. Hawkins's reaction to it, in his own words: "So I became one."

That story always made sense to me. I've had that same moment of feeling like everything's changed because of one compliment, one tiny bit of encouragement. That, in a nutshell, is what Peter Buck did for me. Not that he ever walked into the studio just to tell me how great I was. No, but he made me feel like an equal.

Just a few years ago, I was on tour with Tweedy, the band my son Spencer and I formed to take the songs we'd been recording in the studio on the road, and Peter was playing with the Minus 5, who opened for us on a few dates on the West Coast. We asked them to join us for a song, and I introduced Peter as the guy who believed in me way before I believed in myself. He walked out and gave me a hug, and then whispered to me, away from the microphone, "You've always made it easy to believe in you, Jeff." It brought a tear to my eye, for real.

Still, my best memories of Jay are playing music with him—the only time I feel like we were truly present with each other—and the odd moments offstage when something distracted him from being the grim protector of music's sanctity. Like when he broke both of his ankles in a car accident in 1987, rolling his Toyota Celica into a ditch, and I had to carry him upstairs for band rehearsals. The awkwardness of our friendship and our discomfort with even necessary physical contact inhibited my attempts at being his Sherpa and always worked to turn my efforts into a comic spectacle.

Or when we went on our first European tour in '92 and spent a few days in Copenhagen enjoying the pleasures of legal hash. It was the first time in my life I'd gotten high and not experienced any paranoia whatsoever. Jay was into hacky sack at the time, believe it or not, so we spent a lot of that trip just hacky sackin' in the sun. Those are the days with Jay that I have the warmest memories of, when there was no tension or anxiety or neurotic thoughts: "What is he thinking? Does he hate me? He probably hates me." Jay and I were just two stoned twentysomethings kicking around the sack with our band on the road.

Not forever, just for now.

JAY FINALLY CAME home to our Belleville apartment, acting as if nothing had happened. I confronted him, demanding explanations, but he offered none. He agreed to finish the tour if only to help pay back Tony a little of the money he'd invested in the band. After that, he was done. The reasons why weren't worth discussing anymore, he said, because I already knew why.

"I really don't," I insisted. "Would you mind giving me a hint?"

He ignored me, and we sat in opposite corners of the room, avoiding eye contact.

"Why do you hate me so much?" I asked.

I sincerely had no idea what I had done to fill him with so much disdain. The image I had of myself was that of a person 100 percent devoted to Jay, his songs, and our band.

Almost twenty years later, I was shocked to learn from a magazine interview with Jay that there was an "incident" that he saw as the last straw. Something that I'd completely forgotten about. An "incident" that, because it had happened well before we had released any records, I had forgotten before the band even ended. Apparently still an "incident" he'd never forgiven me for.

We had just finished a show in St. Louis, and this was back when I was still drinking—I quit drinking cold turkey at twenty-three in an effort to sidestep my genetic destiny—so it was before our first record deal. I never made another record with alcohol in my bloodstream after *No Depression*. I've ingested plenty of other things while making records, but never booze. But on the evening in question I was quite drunk, as I often tended to be in the band's early days. Jay's girlfriend, Monica, had also gotten tipsy during the show, and she fell asleep in the back of our van, waiting for us to load out. Jay was our designated driver for the night, so he was (mostly) sober.

After we loaded out, I stumbled into the van and sat next to Monica. She woke up, and we started talking, not in the way two sober, rational humans have a conversation, but the incoherent babbling of two individuals who'd been overserved. We were leaning in to each other, and I was earnestly slurring, "I love you, Monica. I've always loved you." Monica was sweetly slurring right back, not without pity, "Aw, I love you, too, Jeff." Innocent stuff. Obnoxious, yes, but not anything with sinister motives. I was just a drunk having a bad case of loving everyone. Over the past hour, I'd told numerous people—some of whom I knew, some of whom I didn't—that I loved them. I may've also professed my love to our van, Old Blue. If there's one thing that's 100 percent true about every intoxicated person in world history, it's that you shouldn't believe them when they say they love you. The only difference between you and that slice of cold pizza back at their apartment is that they haven't met the pizza yet.

Jay heard it all and watched our inebriated snuggling unfold from the van's rearview mirror. He was upset, which he had every right to be. If some drunk started weepingly confessing his love for my girlfriend, I'd be pissed, too. Jay confronted me about it when we got back home, and it was apparent he had a very different version of events. He thought I was hitting on her, or trying to seduce her. Even in my drunken stupor, that hadn't been my intention. I was trying to tell a friend how much she meant to me, and because of the alcohol, I was doing it stupidly. There wasn't any pawing at her, no attempts at kissing, nothing even remotely sexual. It was just two drunks telling each other, "I love you, man." As drunks do.

That was still too much for Jay to bear. When we got back to Belleville, we unloaded our equipment and then Jay laid into me. I apologized, he quit the band, and I'm pretty sure I cried. It was a big deal. I took him seriously. I knew I'd fucked up, and it inspired me to quit drinking, which I somehow managed to do. I was losing control more and more often and waking up in strange places with people mad at me and I was starting to get scared.

Jay came back to the band—I thought he had forgiven me, but it was really just that he wasn't ready to give up on Uncle Tupelo yet—and we survived for another four years and three more records before he quit again, this time for good. He never mentioned Monica among his reasons at that time. Years later, when he was interviewed, he talked about that night in the van like it was the ultimate betrayal, the moment that killed Uncle Tupelo. His telling added details that were villainous, like that I'd been stroking Monica's hair (doesn't sound like me), and when he confronted me, I called him a pussy (really not in my repertoire, being one myself). He claimed that I was crying to garner sympathy. Um . . . Okay, that's probably partly true. I did cry a lot, and quite often it would result in being tended to in maternal ways by our female friends and our male friends most in touch with their feminine energy, but it was never a calculation I was conscious of. I know that because I can remember how desperately I wanted to not be crying. Even without alcohol I still have an impulse from time to time to mope and feel sorry for myself and want to be taken care of. The cure? My badass wife. She simply won't have that shit. Not even a tiny bit.

"Why do you hate me?" I asked Jay again in our Belleville apartment. I was going to keep asking until I got an answer out of him.

He didn't deny it. If anything, he looked surprised that I didn't already know the answer. "You have no idea what it's like to stand onstage with somebody every night who loves himself as much as you do," he said.

"You're right," I said. "I don't have any idea."

That wasn't my attempt at a zinger. I meant it honestly. I had. No. Idea.

Every time I played with Uncle Tupelo, I would feel stupid after a show. Early on, it was because I got drunk and acted like a buffoon onstage. Later, when I stopped drinking, I would still get wrapped up in the music, but for every brief moment I spent uninhibited, losing myself in the moment, I could stop somewhere just shy of feeling truly liberated and retreat back into my overthinking mind, inside my stupid head where I would remain, awkward and painfully self-aware. I was certain my self-consciousness was visible from outer space. Immediately afterward, when the show was over and we were off to the next town, I would be remorseful. I'd feel real shame. I'd replay the show in my memory and be tormented by mental images of me taking myself way too seriously. The self-loathing was constant. In my head, it was a nonstop ticker tape of "Why did I . . . ? Uggghhh!" "Who do I think I am?" Jay didn't appear to be burdened in this way at all. In fact, what I was learning was that he was just as suspicious of me as I was.

What Jay could have said, if he was paying attention at all, was "You have no idea what it's like to stand onstage with somebody every night who struggles with and sometimes overcompensates for debilitating self-doubt, a guy sadly aware he's disappointing a bandmate he's spent his entire adult life trying to please."

He quit the band and walked out of our filthy apartment. I sat on a stained couch watching him go and wondering what the fuck I was going to do now.

"WE'VE BEEN PRACTICING in Belleville all week. So this is our first show ever."

That's how I introduced Wilco to the world, on November 17, 1994, at Cicero's in St. Louis. Actually, we were performing under the name Black Shampoo, which might seem a curious choice. Was it really necessary for a band that had yet to release an album to use a fake name for their live debut? Wilco was about as recognizable to the world as, well, Black Shampoo. I don't recall the exact logic for why we did it, other than that we were performing at Cicero's, where

Uncle Tupelo had played so often over the years that we practically had a key. There were fans in town interested in what I was going to do next, but that was maybe three hundred people at most, not enough to necessitate a fake name to throw off their scent. We didn't have a good reason, other than that Ken Coomer was an avid collector of cult films, and he'd introduced us to *Black Shampoo*, a terrible blaxploitation movie from 1976 about an L.A. hairdresser who makes love to a staggering number of women before killing some white mafia guys with a chain saw. It's a truly horrible yet hypnotically entertaining movie, and calling ourselves Black Shampoo seemed like a funny, self-effacing way to begin our musical second chapter.

Wilco was new, but not *new*. It was me, John Stirratt on bass, Max Johnston on banjo and fiddle, and Ken Coomer on drums. The only new guy onstage with us was Jay Bennett, on guitar. It was basically Uncle Tupelo minus Jay Farrar.

Only ten months ago, Uncle Tupelo, with Jay Farrar, had headed out on the final three-month tour that we'd agreed to do to pay back some of the money we owed Tony. The mood was pretty grim. The only thing we were looking forward to was that it was going to be our first tour in an actual tour bus. Someone—Tony or Warner Bros.?—had decided that the grueling schedule and the added tension in the band might be alleviated somewhat by the relative comfort of bus touring versus Old Blue.

It was a nice idea. It might have even been a gambit to see if the camaraderie of sharing a luxurious living situation might heal the band's broken bonds. So we loaded all of our gear into the parking lot behind our apartment and waited for our new accommodations to arrive. Everyone, I think even Jay, was excited about the prospect of spending at least some small part of our lives seeing what it was like to tour in style. That was until he laid eyes on the Ghost Rider. What we were picturing was sleek and non-ostentatious like the buses we had seen parked in front of theaters at sold-out shows by the likes of R.E.M. or the Replacements. Instead, what we got was one of Kiss's old touring coaches—a seventies-era Silver Eagle decked out with an airbrushed mural in a style I can only describe as "black-light poster–esque," depicting a pirate ship buffeted by a stormy sea with a screaming skeleton standing in the crow's nest holding a Gibson Les Paul aloft and being struck by lightning.

The look on Jay's face was tragic. I felt bad for him. This was not a serious vehicle. I'm not sure how we talked him into climbing aboard, and once we did, I have no idea how we got him to stay, because the interior was even worse. White leather, mirrored ceilings, and a purple neon sign in the back lounge informing everyone, in cursive, that they were aboard the "Ghost Rider" lest they forget. So we embarked upon Uncle Tupelo's last tour learning how to sleep while being shot at eighty miles per hour down the highway inside a metal box that looked like the VIP room at a strip club and made us all feel like we were living inside a cocaine straw. Ghost Rider indeed.

The tour did not go well. In February, at Cat's Cradle in North Carolina, I almost punched Jay in the face. Not onstage, of course. The near fisticuffs happened after the show, in the club's parking lot. I'm the one who lost my temper first. I was pissed off because Jay wouldn't sing harmonies on my songs. It was the thing that finally pushed me over the edge. I knew he was leaving, I knew this tour was primarily to tie up loose financial ends, but what the fuck, at least pretend you want to be there. You don't have to like me or enjoy my company, but for the hour and change we're onstage, could you at least do your job?

No fists were thrown. Just a lot of voices raised to aggressive registers. We went back to the hotel room and had a band meeting, and Jay made sure everybody knew that the problem was me. So fine, there it was. I didn't have the energy to disagree. Maybe I *was* the problem. I didn't think of myself as just the "bass player" anymore. I was starting to write songs I really believed in, and I was feeling more and more confident that my songs were worthy enough to sit alongside Jay's.

This might have been the biggest problem. The year previous, before Jay announced he wanted to leave, we found out we'd been booked on Conan O'Brien in a few weeks. It had already been decided that we'd play "The Long Cut." Not by me. The record company and the show's producers had requested it. Jay didn't say anything, but it was painfully obvious he thought the fix was in. It confounded me. I would have rather played one of Jay's songs for a lot of reasons, but coming at this head-on and asking Jay if he wanted to talk through the problem would have been a disaster. That just wasn't a viable tactic, given our poor communication. Plus, the pressure was already suffocating and we were going on national TV for the first time. Wasn't that the good news? People are going to hear about our band? Who cares if it was "my" song or "his" song? Weren't they all Uncle Tupelo songs? When did we stop being a band and start a competition? Every success for Uncle Tupelo was a success *for Uncle Tupelo.* To think otherwise was nuts. Warner Bros. wasn't paying us per notes sung on TV. "Well, Tweedy got slightly more singing time on national platforms, so it's clearly his band. Let's give him a larger chunk of the residuals." That's not how it works.

Our very last show with Jay—the one where we played our songs together in a public setting for the last time—was in May at Mississippi Nights in St. Louis. But that was more like a raucous wake. I was ready for it to be over. There were some nice reunions—it was heartwarming to get to play with Mike again—and we managed to pull off a cathartic and truly monolithic "Gimme Three Steps" with the Bottle Rockets. That was fun. Overall though, it felt like something that needed to end.

AT THE CICERO'S show that next November, Wilco's first song of the night was "I Must Be High," which was also the first song on *A.M.*, our first album as Wilco, which wouldn't be out for months. It was also the first song we recorded in the studio as a new band, and we liked the first take well enough that we put it on the album. The song is about regretting the sad ending of a relationship and thinking you must've been nuts (or chemically altered) to walk away from it. It wasn't a song about Jay or the end of Uncle Tupelo. I'd already written one of those—a raw, caustic ballad about what happens when a musical partnership falls apart. We never recorded it, because even back then I realized it was a colossal mistake. I didn't want to sing about Jay Farrar.

We recorded *A.M.* in Memphis, Tennessee, at a place John Stirratt recommended called Easley Studios. He'd recorded there with his band the Hilltops, and I'd been curious about it since learning that Jon Spencer recorded *Extra Width* there. It was another one of those glorious indie studios in a bad part of town. We recorded some demos in June, and Reprise liked them enough to commit, so we finished the record in August. I ended up with the same Reprise/Warner Bros. deal that I'd had before. They basically reset Uncle Tupelo's contract with each of us individually.

Everything was happening at breakneck speed, which wasn't by design. There was no reason to be in a hurry. Outside of St. Louis, the world wasn't exactly clamoring for more of our music. The urgency was all in our heads; it felt like we had to figure this out before our momentum died down or common sense caught up with us.

In Uncle Tupelo, I wrote songs to go alongside Jay's songs. That was always at the forefront of my mind. But now there was nothing in my songs to counterbalance. They existed on their own.

Nothing I had written for *A.M.* felt like it broke any new ground, but I felt like I had a solid batch of quality songs to work with. I'm not sure I was even trying to break any ground. Just refining the types of songs that I could say with confidence I knew how to write felt like enough of an achievement. In my semi-deluded mind I might have even thought that the more accessible nature of my songs in the context of Uncle Tupelo would make a whole album of my little gems feel like a greatest hits collection.

"Passenger Side," in particular, felt like a song that I had tried to write a few times already. It might not be obvious to anyone listening, but I relate the narrator of that lyric with the same sort of hyper-me character that I picture singing "New Madrid" or "Screen Door." A fictionalized version of me as someone who gets in more trouble and has more friends. To me, at the time, "Passenger Side" along with "Casino Queen," "Box Full of Letters," and "I Must Be High" felt like progress—not so much in terms of content, but in my ability to craft sturdy, memorable country-tinged pop songs.

It was an exciting feeling to finally play the songs we'd recorded together. Wilco could be whatever we wanted. That was freeing, and also terrifying. What the fuck was Wilco going to be? At least for *A.M.*, we settled on the answer "Just like Uncle Tupelo, but with a different name and without one of the voices that had given us our musical identity."

"I really would like to thank you for, up to this point, not hearing anyone yell, 'Whiskey Bottle,'" I told the crowd at Cicero's. "I appreciate that. Nothing against the song, mind you."

I was making a joke, but not entirely. The ghost of Uncle Tupelo was very much haunting the basement that night. Nobody shouted for Farrar songs, but there were more than a few people wearing Uncle Tupelo T-shirts and baseball caps. We played some Tupelo songs—six, if anybody was counting—but tried to focus on the new stuff. We wanted people to hear *A.M.*, to like these songs as much as the old ones. We had something to prove. I was still stinging from a conversation with our A&R guy, Joe McEwen, who was Jay's A&R guy, as well. After he listened to *A.M.*, his first comment to me was "This is going to be a great way to set up Jay's record." Way to read the room, Joe! How could he think I'd be into the idea of making a record just to set the stage for Son Volt? It was profoundly confusing to me that he thought Jay and I were still operating as a team. I didn't mean Jay any ill will, but I sure as hell didn't make *A.M.* as a marketing tool for *Trace*.

We weren't just trying out new songs at Cicero's. We were

breaking in a new guitarist, Jay Bennett. For all my fears about that night, that we'd lost our momentum and the audience wouldn't care anymore and everything we'd built would crash and burn, Jay Bennett's presence put me at ease. He had none of the emotional baggage from Uncle Tupelo. He didn't give a shit if people were hoping to hear more *Still Feel Gone* songs. Everything we played was new to him—he'd learned it all just a week or so earlier—and he was happy just to be there.

Jay Bennett was from Champaign-Urbana, about three hours northeast of St. Louis. I didn't really know him, but I'd known about him for years. I saw his band Titanic Love Affair open for Soul Asylum at Mississippi Nights in 1988, and I remember being impressed.

Years later, he was the guitar player for Steve Pride and His Blood Kin, and they opened for Uncle Tupelo a few times, at Lounge Ax in Chicago and, I think, in Champaign. That band couldn't have been more different from Titanic Love Affair. He was playing pedal steel guitar licks on guitar and nailing it. I remember saying to Farrar, "That guy's really good, huh?" Farrar just shrugged in a noncommittal way and said, "Kind of notey." I guess because he played a lot of notes, which was . . . bad? I wasn't aware that there was a correct number of notes, and if you exceeded that limit you were just a show-off. I laughed at Jay's put-down so he thought I agreed with him, but in my head I couldn't stop thinking about it. Jay Bennett could do two things really well that were foundational pillars for me: punk rock and country. At that time those styles of playing weren't often seen in the same package.

Brian Henneman had played lead guitar when we recorded *A.M.*, and he had done such an incredible job that we asked him to join the band, which he declined, rightfully so. He was getting the Bottle Rockets off the ground; he needed an outlet for his classic pop-perfect country tunes. So I knew we needed to find a real guitar player. I was never going to get close to playing Brian's precisely crafted parts, much less while trying to sing. Brian Paulson, who had produced *Anodyne* and *A.M.*, recommended Jay Bennett, so I gave him a call, we talked for a bit, and I sent him an advance tape of our record. He called back days later with an excitement that caught me off guard. "You got such an incredible vocal sound on the record," he told me. I remember that line specifically. I'd made five records already, and nobody had ever said to me, "Your vocals sound incredible." I don't know if I was more disoriented by the compliment or that his unguarded enthusiasm was so unfamiliar that it threw me for a loop.

Looking around that night at Cicero's, I was proud of what we'd built. I don't know where the strength or the grit and determination to rebuild came from at all. But when Jay Farrar quit the band, I went really quickly from being despondent to some place of excitement and curiosity. It really was the cliché of one door closing and another one opening. It transitioned, almost instantaneously appeared. It went from commiserating with Tony about Jay to Jay quitting to realizing, "This is going to be great. This is going to be amazing. Because I work really, really hard at this, and if I have the reins, and I can work really hard at my own pace and toward my own ends and goals, that would be fun. I wonder what will happen?"

And it was happening, right around me and right in front of me.

5

||||||||||||||||||||||

PAPER PRODUCTS

T HIS IS THE story my wife, Susie, and I always tell when someone expresses any interest in the dynamics of our relationship.
Like most couples, we've gone through some rough patches in
our marriage, and during one such stretch we sought help through
some counseling. At our first session, the therapist asked to meet
with us separately first, and then brought us together to talk at the
end. "I don't usually share what individuals tell me in their initial
interviews," she said. "But I think I need to make an exception here."

During her one-on-one with Susie, the therapist had asked her,
"What was your first impression of Jeff?"

Susie replied, "I didn't understand how anybody could survive
with so few paper products."

In the handful of times she visited me in Belleville, back when I
was living in the Uncle Tupelo apartment, I never thought twice
about bringing her there. It seemed perfectly inhabitable to me. In

hindsight, okay, the lack of paper products might have been a problem for somebody accustomed to, say, toilet paper. It's true we rarely had toilet paper in our apartment. How, you might ask, could four humans sharing a living space tolerate such a state of affairs? Well, it's complicated. I think a combination of incompetence, poor financial planning, and resentment had resulted in a standoff among us over who would blink first and grudgingly supply the others with the luxury of toilet paper. It was an insane game of chicken where you became weak in the others' eyes if you weren't resourceful enough to maniacally crumble up pages from a phone book to the texture of a chamois. Maybe we were early pioneers of repurposing and recycling. We certainly lived like pioneers. Anyway, I failed to mention this household quirk to Susie before she excused herself to use our bathroom during her first trip to our place and she returned shaken, and pale. Disturbed, really.

When I met with our therapist, she had asked me the same question. "What was your first impression of Susie?"

I answered immediately, "I thought, wow, I've never seen so many paper products."

It's true. The first time I walked into Susie's apartment—where she lived alone, I might add—I was stunned by massive stockpiles of paper towels and tissues and toilet paper; not just a roll next to the toilet, I swear she had pallets of the stuff. "This is the smartest woman I've ever met in my life," I remember thinking. To this day, after close to twenty-seven years together, I don't think we've ever come within a hundred rolls of running out. In fact, I'd be willing to bet we're still using Kleenex from the cache I first laid eyes on that day.

I MET SUSIE IN person for the first time at her thirtieth-birthday party, at a bar across the street from Wrigley Field in Chicago, while she was pretending to be pregnant.

I was nineteen, not legally old enough to be a patron at the Cubby Bear, much less a performer. Susie was the club's booker, and she'd begrudgingly given Uncle Tupelo the opening slot for the New Duncan Imperials, a Chicago band known for kazoo solos and their affinity for Jägermeister. It was her last night—she was leaving to launch her own music venue, Lounge Ax, with co-owner Julia Adams—and the owner of the Cubby Bear had hired a security guard to shadow her, just in case . . . I don't know, she tried to steal a bunch of shot glasses? It was weird.

Susie claims she doesn't remember much from that night, but I remember more than I usually do about shows that happened so long ago. Actually, I couldn't tell you much about our set that night, but I remember Susie. I remember she had one of the basketballs from the arcade hoops game stashed under her dress, which was a habit of hers—part gag, part sincere desire to be a mom. I remember not liking the New Duncan Imperials; not so much because of their music, but because I didn't like that the drummer—who called himself "Goodtime," which didn't do him any favors in my book—was dating Susie. I remember what Susie was wearing. She had on paisley leggings that for some reason she called "choppers," and a big, oversize dress. The type of dress I later learned she referred to as an

"Episode." To her, any flowing gigantic dress, designed for comfort, not to flatter or accentuate, was an "Episode." The nickname was inspired by my father-in-law, Peter, who had been troubled to find his daughter wearing such an unflattering dress at work. He called her brother Danny and asked him, "Is Susie having a psychotic episode?"

I don't think I exchanged more than a few words with her that night. She was the star of the evening and the star of the room, and it was apparent to me that she was just a Star, period. The first real star I'd ever met. Getting there, meeting her in person, and playing on one of her bills, had taken a lot of work. I had a composition book—which we rediscovered years later when we moved in together—that was filled with notes to myself, page after page after page, that just said: *Call Sue Miller. Call Sue Miller. Don't forget to call Sue Miller.* It was in service of the band. I only knew that Sue Miller was the club booker in Chicago who put together the best shows, and whichever club she was working at was where you wanted to play. It still came across a little stalkery when you flipped through my notes.

Up to that point in my life I'd only had a few girlfriends, and I'd been pretty content taking things slow since my first sexual encounter at the age of fourteen. Now, if you're a fan of mine, then you've presumably been enticed to read this book by the hypersexual nature of Wilco's oeuvre, and you've probably been wondering when I'm going to get around to the scintillating details of my sex life and, in particular, how I lost my virginity.

The unfortunate truth of it is, the specific type of sexual initiation I experienced is still romanticized and sold as a "You hit the jackpot" kind of fantasy. The older woman taking a male virgin and teaching him carnality is a scenario still shockingly accepted as not just okay but ideal. Any naysaying to the contrary is casually shamed into silence by the pervasive and dominant masculinity of our collective mind-set. Well, the truth is, it was as wrong and damaging as would be easily accepted were the gender roles reversed.

At fourteen, I wasn't anywhere near being emotionally prepared to dive into that end of the pool. As usual, the story centers around the record store near my house. I hung out there so much I got to know all of the employees, and in particular I enjoyed hanging out with Leslie. She was twenty-five and loved great music. She was funny, and I thought of her as my friend. Toward the end of the summer before my sophomore year in high school, she informed me she was planning to leave Belleville and move back to her hometown. As she told me this, she inconspicuously slipped me a note saying she had something to give me before she left. When her shift ended, we went over to her house. We listened to music for a little while, and then she said we should leave because her roommate was coming home soon. She grabbed a bottle of champagne from her fridge, a blanket, and took me to a nearby park. It was dark and empty, and we laid on the blanket and passed the champagne back and forth, and then she climbed on top of me.

I didn't fight it, but it felt very wrong. I don't know what I was expecting to happen, but I swear a part of me was still waiting for her to give me an album or a card or some token to remember her by. So that's how it happened. Technically, I was consenting, but only so far as a fourteen-year-old can consent to anything. I told a few friends, trying to find a way to express the pain and confusion of the whole ordeal. Instead, rumors started to spread and, of course, because I was a guy, among my guy friends and acquaintances alike, my statutory victimhood was celebrated. Even to the point of jealousy at my good fortune. Jay started mockingly calling me "Mr. Laid." As in "Oh, you think you're Mr. Laid now," "Whatever you say, Mr. Laid." I got quiet about it fast. I was embarrassed and disoriented, and then I was ashamed of being embarrassed and disoriented. Should I be high-fiving my friends? Why am I sitting here by myself in the dark?

The worst part was lying to my mom. Even at that age, I talked to her about everything. I was a fundamentally honest kid. She knew something was wrong, but I was sickened by the thought of sharing any of it with her. "So, Mom, you know that lady at the record store I always talk about? Yeah? Well, we had the sex, sooo . . . What's for dinner?" One of the things that comes up a lot in recovery from addiction is the notion that you're only as sick as your secrets. This is a pretty good example of that. I had a secret and it made me sick.

So I guess that's the bulk of the baggage I was carrying around when Susie and I got together. Susie had her shit together. She was way more mature than anyone I'd ever been with, not just in terms of age—she likes to point out that, our birthdays being a week apart, we've never shared a decade; in other words, when I turned thirty, she had just turned forty—but also in attitude. By the time we had met, Susie had followed through on her biggest dream. She quit her job to become a business owner, running a music venue in which she wasn't just responsible for booking the talent but paying a staff and dealing with city ordinances and making sure the toilets weren't overflowing. That was unfathomably adult to me. She also owned her own home. During her twenties, she kept a note on her refrigerator to remind herself that she would buy a house before she turned thirty. By twenty-nine, she bought a three-flat on Chicago's North Side. Her mother lived with her in one of the downstairs apartments.

The amazing thing is, no one would walk into her house and think, "Well, obviously a serious businesswoman lives here." Susie is a lifelong accumulator of pop culture ephemera. So every shelf, counter, and square inch of space in her home—and that includes living rooms, bedrooms, and even bathrooms—was occupied by some toy or nostalgic curiosity. On top of being an exquisite curator of countless trash culture items she's collected as an adult, she literally has every single item from her childhood. I mean every single note that was ever passed to her in class. Everything. Nothing has been thrown away. She still has everything. In our house we have the usual items people have, like books and plants and framed photos of loved ones, but they might share space with a Fisher-Price play family set or a Flip Wilson/Geraldine doll or an Evel Knievel lunch box or a Mr. Potato Head (from when they still used real potatoes) or a Donny and Marie thermos set or maybe a rusty metal Band-Aid box from the seventies. She has unopened boxes of cereal. Anyone care for some Urkel-Os? She has a giant jar full of plastic food, like miniature turkeys and waffles and eggs. We still have a melted radio from when our apartment caught fire. She has Mercurochrome in a scary bottle, an old dentist chair, and her hip-hugger elephant bells from high school, which were so wide at the bottom that she could (and would) go to school barefoot without anybody noticing.

She calls herself an archivist, but she is also kind of a crazy person. To me, it just made her more fascinating. Besides, what's not to like about Easy-Bake ovens and Rodney Dangerfield and *Bewitched* board games?

Uncle Tupelo slept at her three-flat many times before we started dating. A lot of touring bands that played Lounge Ax did. Susie kept a closet filled with dozens of sleeping bags from the sixties and seventies—Cracker Jack, Spider-Man, Hawaiian Punch, Campbell's Soup, the Flintstones. If it was pop culture on a sleeping bag, she had it. On any given night, her house would become an ad hoc adult orphanage, with musicians lying shoulder to shoulder in sleeping bags on Susie's floor, surrounded on all sides by monuments to her undiscarded childhood and a shared schlocky past. Have you ever fallen asleep looking at a Fonzie lunch box being cradled by a Pee-wee Herman doll? Your dreams can't compare.

Uncle Tupelo did sixteen shows at Lounge Ax over the next four years. That was sixteen sleepovers at Susie's. We started to know where all of the light switches were, and where the bathroom was without asking. Usually after a show, we'd hang around her apartment to keep the party going for a while until she kicked everybody out, sending us downstairs to her mom's apartment (who often slept at her boyfriend's place when Susie needed more room for guests). One night I got brave and asked if I could stay.

We made out until it started getting light outside and then dozed off in her bed. I still don't get how anyone found out about us making out, but the next day, when we returned to the club, Susie's staff had already given her the nickname "Cradle Robber," which she did not appreciate.

We started kinda dating. Not *really* dating, because we lived in different cities, and she was very clear with me that she doesn't "go steady" with people who don't live in Chicago. She actually said "go steady," by the way. Whatever we were calling it, I kept looking for excuses to drive up to Chicago. I just wanted to be around her, as often as possible. I'd take the train when my car wasn't working. I'd tag along with other bands passing through St. Louis on their way north. I took every opportunity that came my way to get to Chicago. It was the only hope I had of her ever calling me her boyfriend.

I can pinpoint the exact moment we officially realized we were destined to be together. I know this because it's a story Susie and I have often repeated, telling and retelling it so often I sometimes wonder if the details have gotten conflated in our brains. Maybe. Brains are unreliable narrators. But turn the page and you'll see how I'm pretty sure it happened.

I MOVED TO CHICAGO a few years later, in 1994, the same year that Uncle Tupelo dissolved, which made the decision easy. It was difficult enough being so far away from Susie, but sticking around St. Louis would have been masochistic. Susie hadn't given me an ultimatum, but she refused to call me her boyfriend unless I lived in Chicago. So I packed my personal belongings—the entirety of which fit inside a thirty-one-inch footlocker trunk from Target—and drove to Chicago in a 1980 Chevy Malibu Classic. That car didn't last one winter in its new home. It got stuck in the ice in an alley, so I took off the plates and left it there. It might still be there, for all I know.

I wouldn't have picked Chicago if Susie wasn't there. Or maybe I would have, I don't know. I never gave much thought to geography.

ADMIT TWO
SAT, OCTOBER 10, 1991 9:00pm 21/over
THE MOMENT IT HAPPENED
JEFF TWEEDY + SUSIE MILLER
2438 N. LINCOLN AVE

LOUNGE AX
HOME OF BALLHARVESTER

IT WAS 1991, AND *UNCLE TUPELO* WAS PLAYING OUR FIRST BIG HEADLINING GIG AT *LOUNGE AX.*

Art © George Eckart

I HUNG OUT *AFTER THE SHOW,* HOPING TO SPEND SOME TIME WITH *SUSIE.*

SO, WHATCHA UP TO?

UM, I'M *WORKING?*

IT WAS LIKE A **BOLT OF ELECTRICITY** HAD HIT US BOTH AND SENT AN ELECTRICAL CHARGE THROUGH US. IT **WASN'T** STATIC ELECTRICITY. IT WAS A **FULL JOLT** THAT WENT THROUGH **OUR WHOLE BODIES.**

THERE WERE ONLY THREE POSSIBLE EXPLANATIONS:

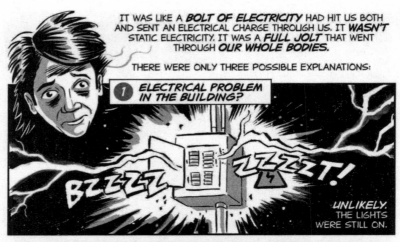

1 **ELECTRICAL PROBLEM IN THE BUILDING?**

BZZZZ ZZZZZT!

UNLIKELY. THE LIGHTS WERE STILL ON.

2 **ATMOSPHERIC CONDITIONS IN CHICAGO?**

KAB-O-OOM

UNLIKELY. WE WERE IN THE BASEMENT.

3 **WE FELL IN LOVE?**

HMMM... **POSSIBLE!**

I had no loyalty to Belleville or St. Louis, but also no huge desire to get out. It was just the place where my parents lived, so I lived there, too, because that's where their house was. Chicago was where Susie's house was, so that's where I headed next. Like Bob Dylan once wrote of New York, it was "as good a place to be as any." It didn't matter to me.

I don't remember if Susie explicitly invited me to move in with her. I think it was just assumed. She knew me well enough to realize I wasn't quite capable of taking care of myself. I didn't have the wherewithal to find my own apartment and sign a lease and fill it with furniture and set up utilities. That was just not happening. It'd be like asking a six-year-old to fill out a tax return. I'm not saying this with false modesty, or admitting I cooked up some half-baked ruse to put our relationship on the fast track; I honestly couldn't do it. I had no checking account. I'm fifty years old as of this writing, and I've still written maybe four checks in my entire life.

Moving in with Susie meant living in the same house as her mother, which was a big learning curve for me. I was not accustomed to having any relationship with a girlfriend's mother, much less living one floor above her. Luckily, for whatever reason, Susie's mom took a liking to me. She was boisterous and brash, with a big personality, bright red hair, and a deep raspy voice like Harvey Fierstein. She would say things like, "All of Susie's boyfriends have been losers, except for Jeff, who's *darling*," and then she'd blow me a big air kiss. "M'wah!"

Because Susie spent most of her time at Lounge Ax, that became my second home, too. It was located in a Chicago neighborhood that was just starting to gentrify, on a block where taquerias and bodegas sat alongside sports bars and college bars and college sports bars. On the corner, there was a great bookstore, Guild Books. I bought *Guitar Army* directly from its author, the MC5's former manager John Sinclair, when he worked there for a while before it got priced out of the neighborhood. Directly across the street from Lounge Ax was the Biograph Theater, where John Dillinger was gunned down by FBI agents in the 1930s. You could stand in the alley where Dillinger bled to death, which is apparently a thing that tourists like to do. Lounge Ax was the best place ever. I can close my eyes and recall every detail of it; I can smell the stale odor of beer and cigarettes (which for some reason smelled more comforting and welcoming at Lounge Ax than it did anyplace else). A scene from the John Cusack movie *High Fidelity* was shot at Lounge Ax, when Cusack's character goes to see Lisa Bonet's band. I wasn't there when they filmed it, but I heard that the director warned the actors to avoid the bathrooms or to only use them "in an emergency."

I can recall the details more vividly than almost any other place I've ever been. It was one long wooden bar with a tiny stage under a low ceiling of what looked like painted-over cobwebs and dust. There was a couch with no legs, an egregious lack of ventilation or air-conditioning, and bathrooms down a steep and narrow wooden staircase.

Like any Island of Misfit Toys, it had its characters. There was Dan Orman, the doorman. Who I always assumed had filled out an aptitude test in high school and when it came back, it said *D. Orman* at the top, and he read no further. Seriously, though, he was born for the job. An unyielding bulldog, he was. There were no exceptions given, even for people he obviously recognized. He carded me the first time I walked into Lounge Ax, and he carded me the last time, more than a decade later. He'd sometimes babysit my son Spencer while I was onstage performing. Didn't matter when he was working the door. It was always "Welcome to Lounge Ax. May I see your ID? It's a five-dollar cover tonight."

"Dan, it's me, Jeff. Susie's husband. I'm performing tonight."

"Congratulations, Jeff. I'm going to need to see your ID, and it's a five-dollar cover tonight."

Fred Armisen was a regular at Lounge Ax, as a performer and a part-time assistant to Susie. He'd stamp hands at the door and answer phones, and occasionally his band Trenchmouth would play. Fred claims Susie gave him his big break when she asked him to host karaoke night once a month. Each month he'd come as a different character: Jesus, a guy with a head injury, a priest, and one time he hosted as Hitler, but not the evil Hitler, Fred's Hitler was trying to soften his image and had taken up writing poems for a vegan fanzine.

Before our kids were born I was there every night Susie was. I never asked who was playing. It didn't matter. Get close enough to the stage to watch any band good enough to catch Susie's attention and life was suddenly worthwhile again: Silkworm, Trumans Water, Neutral Milk Hotel, the Mekons, the Jesus Lizard, Thinking Fellers Union Local 282, Guided by Voices, the Coctails . . . just so many great bands.

I got to be friends with a lot of them—or if not friends, at least friendly. I'd pick up bands at the airport and bring them to our apartment. Just because I'd moved in with Susie didn't mean she stopped hosting. At night, the sleeping bags would be laid out, and there'd be the arguments over who gets the top bunk of the red bunk beds. Whenever the Young Fresh Fellows stayed over, we all wore matching pajamas. It was like living in a summer camp that never closed.

Lounge Ax was also the first place I ever played solo acoustic in front of an audience. The casualness and intimacy of Lounge Ax made it feel like a safe space to try out a song for the first time. Most of *Summerteeth*, especially the songs I wasn't sure I should be singing in front of other people, were played for the first time at Lounge Ax. "Via Chicago" and "She's a Jar" made their debut on that stage before the rest of Wilco even knew I'd written them.

Susie and I also got married on that stage at Lounge Ax, in August 1995. She wore a pretty lace dress, and I wore a vintage suit I'd recently acquired for $10 at the AMVETS Thrift Store. An hour before the ceremony, our friend the famous horn player Max Crawford decided that the thing our wedding was missing was a marching band, so he made some calls, scared up some drums and horns, found enough musicians among our guests and Lounge Ax regulars to play them, and after a crash rehearsal of the wedding march, we were on our way down the aisle (or the Lounge Ax equivalent of an aisle) behind a raucous marching band. Lana Levins, a waitress at Lounge Ax who was also a fully ordained minister thanks to a Universal Life Church certificate, led the ceremony. I married Susie with my mom's wedding ring, which my dad had bought for her at the army commissary for $10.

Anyone paying attention might have gotten a kick out of the Junior Walker song "Shotgun" being the first song the band played that night, or that the movie advertised on the marquee at the Biograph

Theater across the street was *Nine Months*. Or they might have even noticed that Susie was, in fact, a touch pregnant.

I'm willing to bet some of them put it together when Spencer was born four months later.

And then we lived happily ever after. The end.

A Conversation between My Wife and Me about How Much of Our Private Life She Thinks Is Fair Game to Be Included in This Book:

SUSIE: Can you just leave me out of it?

JEFF: Completely? I don't think so.

S: I don't see how it's anybody's business. Just write about your songs or whatever. Don't bring me up at all.

J: I think it'd be nice to include a few things.

S: Like what? You're going to make me sound awful.

J: Are you kidding? No, no, not at all. It's all going to be positive and funny.

S: Funny how?

J: You want to see my imitation of you?

S: Oh god.

J: Trust me, it's good. Here, I'll show you. [*Scrunching up face.*] "Is that how it's going to sound?"

S: That's supposed to be me listening to your music?

J: Yeah. [*Laughs.*] Nailed it.

S: How about when I got cancer nine months after we started dating?

J: Um . . . Maybe. Is that a positive story?

S: It has a happy ending. I had this pain in my chest, and I told every-body at Lounge Ax, "I have a tumor!" And they were like, "No, no, relax; it's nothing. You just need to stretch more." But then I went and got X-rays, and the doctor told me, "You have a tumor all right. Big tumor right there in your chest. But it's benign, so it's not going to kill you. We'll just cut it out."

J: They sawed you in half.

S: They cracked my fucking chest open to take out the tumor, and the doctor was like, "Whoops, looks like it was cancer. But we got it, so you're fine now."

J: Was I helpful during any of that?

S: Yes, and you were, what, twenty-three at the time? Not an emo-tionally mature age for most guys. I think that's what turned my parents around. That's when they decided they liked you.

J: They hated me before?

S: No, not at all. But, you know, you were a musician. It's not every parent's dream that their daughter ends up dating a guitarist who doesn't know how to use a checkbook.

J: Your mom thought I was darling.

S: Yeah, I saw you included that. That's seriously the only thing you're going to write about her?

J: Not good?

S: She did that *one* time, and it's become the story we've drilled into the ground. Are you going to tell the fudge story about my dad?

J: Remind me.

S: It was the first time we had dinner with my parents as a couple, and we were at that barbecue place with the fishing poles on the wall. My dad leaned over to you and said, apropos of nothing, in his big booming voice, "Do you *like* fudge, Jeff?"

J: I couldn't have been less prepared for that question.

S: I think the restaurant sells a fudge cake, so it was probably on his mind. It was just a weird thing to say out of nowhere.

J: That's why we and the kids say it all the time to each other. It's how we recalibrate a discussion that's gone off the rails. "Do you *like* fudge, Jeff?"

S: So you are or aren't including that story?

J: I haven't decided yet. I don't know if we need to fill the whole book with stories about our parents.

S: Your mom is in there, right?

J: Oh sure.

S: Did you include the story of her throwing a baby shower for us at that bowling alley? And she invited all of those people I haven't seen before or since?

J: Um . . .

S: Those women apparently thought I was deaf, 'cause they kept whispering really loudly, "She's much older than him, you know." And then one of them said, "I worked for Jews once. They do everything differently."

J: Oh boy.

S: There was a giant ham, and I don't like ham, not because I'm Jewish, I just don't like it. But I ate some and immediately got violent diarrhea. You had to go through the poolrooms to get to the bathroom, and all these men were drunk and playing pool, and I'm going back there every five seconds.

J: I'm trying to stay away from diarrhea stories.

S: And the presents that they gave us! A powder-blue leather Precious Moments Bible: New Testament.

J: Didn't we return it to the Bible shop?

S: We did, yeah. They asked why we were returning it and we lied and said, "We already have one." But they only gave us store credit.

J: I was thinking we focus on stories about us, not necessarily our families.

S: Something romantic and mushy?

J: Sure. Do we have those?

S: You used to write me letters when you went on tour, and you could get pretty mushy. You wrote about wanting me to be your one and only.

J: I used the phrase "be my one and only"?

S: You did. That's an exact quote.

J: Wow. It's a wonder I didn't end up writing for Precious Moments.

SUSIE'S FAVORITE SONG has nothing to do with me. I didn't write it, and I've never sung it. It's A9. That's its number on her jukebox, a gift from the boys and me for her fiftieth birthday. The jukebox came loaded with a ton of great records, which she's added to with favorite records from her childhood. A9 is the Staple Singers song "I'll Take You There." In our house, when we hear that familiar riff blasting from our living room, we know it's Susie's way of saying it's time to dance. It makes her happy in ways I'll never be able to make her happy with my music. I'm fine with that.

The way I feel about Susie, the way she's loved me and changed me, it can't be in my songs. It's too big for songs. Maybe, occasionally, I can get a part of it to fit. Sometimes it gets deep in the track where I can feel it but it's never put into words. If you've ever been in a relationship that you took for granted, even when it was the one thing holding you together, and you somehow didn't lose it despite acting like an idiot, then you know how difficult it is to convey that amount of gratitude, much less set it to music. I wouldn't know where to begin.

6

MORE KETCHUP THAN YOU CAN IMAGINE

JAY BENNETT ATE a lot of ketchup. Like way more ketchup than you could imagine. Arguably more ketchup than food. This is not comic hyperbole. You have not witnessed the dozens and dozens of empty ketchup packets lying on his bed in a hotel room, a room in which you're also sleeping, and you have to tell him, "This is too many empty ketchup packets. It's making me uncomfortable." Jay Bennett would laugh at my protests like he thought I was joking, but I was sincerely concerned. Who uses that much ketchup? Jay Bennett would put almost an entire packet on each bite of fries. That is a crazy disproportionate condiment-to-food ratio.

I loved Jay Bennett, he was smart and funny and earnest and weird and a great collaborator. He was my friend. I loved him, but he was also a pain in the ass sometimes. I think most people who were friends with Jay will tell you that. That never stopped anyone from loving the guy, though, including me. Only at the very end of his time in the band did his difficulties start to outweigh his virtues. Jay was burdened with the kind of issues that show no regard for intelligence or kindness or social status. Maladies that destroy without taking into account what one has to offer the world, like all diseases. I wish I could have done more to help him in the same way I wished I could have saved my brothers from suffering and my dad from living a life less than to its fullest.

When Jay Bennett joined the band, I only knew he was a great guitar player. That's all I thought we were getting when I asked him to join Wilco, and that would've been enough. But it turned out he had a lot more to offer.

During a trip to West Virginia during the *A.M.* tour, we did a radio show called *Mountain Stage*. We were going to play a few acoustic songs, just Jay Bennett and me and Max Johnston, our fiddle player (and Michelle Shocked's younger brother). I met Max when Uncle Tupelo was one of the opening acts, along with the Band and Taj Mahal, on his sister's *Arkansas Traveler* tour in 1992. We left the tour early—the scene got a little nutso for us—and we took him with us. I don't think Shocked was too happy about that. Sorry. That day, the four of us arrived at the theater for soundcheck and tried to figure out how to arrange our songs for the environment. *Mountain Stage*, then and now, is a weekly live radio show that gears itself toward the country/folk and acoustic end of the musical spectrum. The idea was to play acoustic, but we didn't want it to just mean "Today we're playing our loud songs soft. You're welcome."

Jay Bennett noticed that the studio had a baby grand piano, and he sat down and plunked out the chords to "Passenger Side."

"You play piano?" I asked him.

"Not really," he said. "I can fake it pretty good."

It sounded great to me.

This might sound ridiculous, but I don't like too much confidence from a musician. Sometimes, I think overconfidence allows simple musical choices to be replaced with technical choices that require thinking, and when you're thinking, it's hard to be listening, too. Jay was a very confident guitar player and I appreciated it most of the time, but on the piano he didn't have that certainty anymore. For some reason I felt it more when he was struggling a little bit. I didn't watch him and feel like everything was going to be okay.

"You should play piano instead of guitar," I told him.

"No. Really? Are you sure? All right, what the hell." He laughed and shook his head.

That was always a great thing about Jay Bennett. He was game for just about anything. I'd love to say I had a master plan from the very beginning, but it wouldn't be true. Plus, I didn't even know he played piano. The guitar was still the main appeal of bringing him on board and really upped the overall musicianship of the band, but having an inspired amateur (maybe even drunk) piano player sure made a lot of my songs make more sense. The sad songs sounded sadder, the wobbly rock songs sounded wobblier, and the pretty songs got roughed up a bit. It sounded right to me. It made me like my voice more, which we've established is flawed and sounds jarring when surrounded by too much virtuosity, clarity, or precision.

It also introduced sonic textures I'd never had any access to. I appreciated the usefulness of Jay's knowledge of classic pop architecture and his studio literacy, but I loved his willingness to try anything, to fuck things up with me. A lot of the bands I grew up listening to and admiring were weirder than what Uncle Tupelo was. Jay Farrar and I listened to plenty of off-the-beaten-path records, but we were focused on concocting some reduction of our musical influences into a disciplined and cohesive sound. We were narrowing it down for ourselves the way people try to narrow down the world into more manageable points of view and simpler sets of rules. Almost like refining a religion into some splinter sect. Wilco's philosophy was forming as a reaction to those constraining impulses. Now it seemed more exciting to contemplate how much one band could embrace.

Jay Bennett was a great match for me and the rest of the guys. Like everyone else in Wilco, Jay had absorbed a lot of music and could slip in and out of styles pretty effortlessly. He was also happy and willing to dig in with me to find ways to subvert classic song structures. We complemented each other well in this regard; he approached songs like an architect and I approached them like a wrecking ball.

It's easy to write songs in shapes you've heard before, and there really isn't anything wrong with using prefab song shapes to pour your ideas into. If it works, it works, but it didn't always satisfy me, especially when I was trying to communicate something more damaged about myself. For a lot of the lyrics I was writing, it made more sense to me to undermine their stability and familiarity. Not to be weird just to be weird, but because I felt the lyrics more when they sat atop shifting sands. Luckily, I enjoyed moving my fingers around the fretboard however long it would take to find the chords that would skew a song just enough to excite my ear, and Jay seemed to relish the math problem that the wrong chords I had come up with would represent. Sometimes he would put pen to paper to show me why a chord change shouldn't work, but only in service of showing me how cool it was to be so wrong. Other times, when I'd get frustrated by my lack of theoretical training, I'd ask him to present me with chord substitutions until one would shake something loose melodically.

There was something about his personality; he needed to know how all the pieces fit together. Not just with music, with pretty much anything. When I reached out to him about joining Wilco, he was working for an electronics repair shop in Champaign, which was the perfect job for him. He could take apart anything and put it back together again. He would go to garage sales and estate sales and pick through people's garbage, pulling out the bits and pieces that looked interesting to him, and he'd bring them home and see how they fit together, and if they didn't fit, he'd find something else to do with them.

Working with Jay created possibility. He wasn't just a kindred spirit and talented guitarist. He had a wildly different skill set, a mathematical approach to music completely foreign to me. It was a symbiotic and rewarding collaboration. I couldn't stop making up songs and presenting them as problems, and Jay never got tired of solving them.

It was similar, I suppose, to some of the dynamics Jay Farrar and I had going on. They both had enviable attributes (both unlike mine and each other's) that anyone would benefit from being around, but there were key differences in the way we interacted. Jay Bennett and I had way more of an ability to be open with each other about our musical aspirations. I was still young and insecure . . . but not *as* young and insecure. Neither of us were ashamed of wanting to make something great. Plus, Jay Bennett actually made an effort to be in Wilco. Let me tell you, in 1994 that was just slightly more lucrative than working at a VCR repair place and way less certain. So if he wasn't into it, I told my self-esteem, why would he even bother?

BEFORE JAY BENNETT joined the band, when we recorded *A.M.*, Uncle Tupelo had only been defunct for a little over a month. I can hear something missing when I listen to that record now, and it's understandable to me in a way that it never would have been then. Since we were in high school together, every song I had written was meant to sit next to Jay Farrar's songs. Now Jay's songs were missing, but I could still hear them. They were still in my head, to be honest. I was still in the mode of writing songs as if they were one side of a conversation. Which explains why *A.M.* can be as annoying to me as the guy loudly sharing his end of a phone call in a quiet restaurant. One of the things that happens when you're in a band with two songwriters, or two singers, is that it's inevitable that, after the show, at the bar, somewhere, someone comes up to you and says, "I like your songs more than the other guy's." And still to this day, people argue about Son Volt versus Wilco.

But back then, there were enough people in my ear saying things like that that it was hard not for me to think, "If I made a record of stuff that was just like the music I made for Uncle Tupelo records, it's going to be amazing." It's really curious—I really did look at myself as being a part of Jay's musical world as opposed to being a part of my own. It was certainly rewarding, and I channeled my energy and creativity through that perspective and that lens, but it wasn't fully formed in terms of me having a voice that was independent.

The songs on *A.M.* were generally perceived to be lighter than Jay's songs. There was less of a contrast and less shading. That's what people kind of expected, and that's the way it was received critically.

"This is the lightweight version of Uncle Tupelo—that's what I thought it would be." But half of that record are songs that we still get asked to play all the time. I don't have any embarrassment about anything. That was the reality of what it was at the time. And I think the songs are quality songs, for the most part.

Being There, which we recorded next and the first album we recorded with Jay Bennett, is the light going off in my head of "I don't have to limit myself to the musical interests that Jay Farrar and I had in common." It was a real epiphany. "I don't have to worry about being thought of as pretentious or inauthentic by acknowledging that I like Devo." Not that there's any Devo influence evident on *Being There*, but the palette, from that point on, could draw from just about anything I'd ever listened to, and every recording could move toward incorporating some further reach of my musical interests. Growing toward a point where I felt free to incorporate noise, or found sound, or even things that I'd only read about.

Two out of the four Uncle Tupelo records had been recorded virtually live, and overall the approach we had taken toward the studio had been to use it as a means to document rather than embellish. So allowing performances to be layered with overdubs and songs to be set against atmospheric backdrops felt like yet another magical discovery of something others had long accepted as common practice. Maybe being deprived for so long added to the excitement. What had started out as tentative and traditional—piano, organs, doubled-backing vocals—quickly escalated to experiments with tape manipulation and atonality.

The song "The Lonely 1 (White Hen Version)" is an example of the loosening reins. We had taken the finished mix and set it against a heavily chopped-up, rearranged, and purposefully mangled recording of Jay Bennett and I walking to the store to buy cigarettes in an attempt to create a deeper sense of isolation by placing the vocals inside a city landscape. The idea was that nothing can quite make you feel alone like being around a lot of people. I thought it really worked. But on the album we opted for an ad hoc string arrangement, which in itself was uncharted waters for us.

Some of our excursions into the unknown did make it onto the record, though. "Misunderstood" is a collage of whole band performances layered on top of one another with the added dimension that for each take we had been passing our instruments to the bandmate on our right. I'm not sure what the idea was with that particular exercise but it ended up adding some unpredictability to a fairly repetitive, barely two-chord song. It also helped keep the whole proceeding from coming off as overly dramatic. It's hard to take yourself too seriously when you have no idea what you're doing.

Being There was also the first record I made as a dad. On "Dreamer in My Dreams," at the end when you hear me say, "I'm leaving," that's me really walking out the door to go pick up Spencer at Lounge Ax.

UNCLE TUPELO HAD opened for Billy Bragg in St. Louis in 1991. It was at a chapel on the Washington University campus, and he invited us to play soccer with him in the parking lot before the show. Other than that, I don't remember much about the evening. I ran into him again years later, in London, when Jay Bennett and I were on a mini–European promo tour for *Being There*. He came to our show—or said he did, but he actually slipped in at the end—and told us about a project he was working on, writing music for unpublished Woody Guthrie lyrics. He was looking for a backing band, he said; "a band who could play country and folk with a rock sensibility." "We know a band sort of like that," I joked. I later found out that Billy had approached Jay Farrar first and he'd said no.

I wasn't originally into the idea, either. We were already planning to head off to Willie Nelson's studio in Texas to start our third album, which would become *Summerteeth*, when we got back to the States. Also, I couldn't imagine any circumstance where I would want Wilco to be a backing band for anyone not named Neil Young or Bob Dylan. Not that I didn't admire Billy, but our musical styles were starkly different to me; it just seemed like an odd match. I later learned Bragg claimed he picked us because we were "the ultimate Midwest Americana red-dirt band." I'm glad I didn't hear that at the time because that would have convinced me to stay away. I really didn't want people to think of us with a label attached—roots music or Americana or whatever brand they were peddling that week.

It just didn't feel right when we were working so hard to fight those preconceptions. But Jay Bennett was pushing hard for the collaboration to happen. He was a huge Bragg fan; he'd even named his last band, Titanic Love Affair, after a Bragg lyric. ("Our titanic love affair sails on the morning tide.") We kept in touch with Billy, and when we found out that Woody's daughter Nora had agreed that we'd also be allowed to write music for Woody's unpublished lyrics and visit the archives in New York to search for them ourselves, how could I say no.

Nora and the Guthrie family and Woody's old manager had collected and archived thousands of pages of Woody's writing, written longhand, covering just about every possible genre. There were love songs, political songs, children's songs, holiday songs (both Christmas and Hanukkah), unbelievably filthy songs about fucking, songs about Roosevelt (pro) and Hitler (anti). A lot of it was brilliant, and a lot of it was the kind of stuff writers fear people will find when they die and undo their legacies. It was like reading the unedited transcripts of an artist's creative process, and it was wildly liberating. It didn't seem like Guthrie agonized over every word; he just wrote down whatever came into his head, unfiltered and uncensored, and maybe never looked at it again.

There were also lists mixed in with the lyrics, lists of things he intended to do or wanted to do or worried he might forget. One list was of personal goals for the year, with suggestions like "drink less," "smoke less," and "womanize less." There in the midst of all the vices he wanted to overcome, he included this: "Write a song every day." That's the best advice I've ever gotten as a songwriter, and it wasn't directed at me. It was written by a man who died two months after I was born, as a reminder to himself.

Nora made authenticated copies of the lyrics we'd chosen and we made a plan with Billy and arranged to meet in Chicago in December to start demoing our songs. On tour that fall, while I was carrying around Woody's words and getting excited about how they were starting to speak to me, I became convinced I needed a guitar that I didn't have. A guitar that felt like those lyrics to me. My main acoustic was a 1957 Gibson J-45 at that point. It's the one I'm holding on the back cover of *A.M.*

It was the first decent acoustic guitar I ever owned, but for some reason I just didn't think it was going to work for the Woody Guthrie record. At a shop in San Francisco, I found a 1930s Martin 0–18 that

I couldn't put down. Seriously, I wouldn't even let them put it in the case for me. It's been mine since the moment I touched it. I'd never really played an old Martin before that day, but I have a lot since, and I've yet to find one that makes me feel like that guitar does. I don't remember the exact dollar amount, but as a musician with a mortgage, a new baby, and zero hit albums, it was more than I could reasonably justify paying for a guitar at the time. I bought it anyway.

By the time we got back to Chicago for the initial *Mermaid Avenue* demo sessions, I'd written music for almost every set of lyrics I'd taken from the archives. It was supposed to be an informal get-together to start working out arrangements and to record our rehearsals and run-throughs as we taught each other the tunes we had each come up with for Woody's words. We'd play a song for Billy, and he'd play one for us. When the session was over, it turned out that we had recorded the final-album versions of most of what we had written for the album. In Dublin, where the album was finished, we spent most of our studio time working on full band arrangements of Billy's contributions. So if you hear me singing on *Mermaid Avenue*, it's most likely a recording that was intended to be a demo.

I THINK THERE WAS a real suspicion of roots music and nostalgia in the band at the time we made *Mermaid Avenue* that helped us to be a bit more irreverent and unburdened by Woody's legacy and the weight of the historical context than we had any right to be. The way some bands at the time were working so hard to come across as authentic by adapting their image to some backwoods chic was really making us skeptical about taking inspiration from looking back musically. Our heads were pointed much more in the direction of pushing ourselves into some sort of new sonic pop territory, anything that felt unexplored by us. We had already made some studio breakthroughs, so when we took a break to work on *Mermaid Avenue*, it felt like we were vacationing from the future. Or at least our future.

There was a sense of—not being above the *Mermaid Avenue* material—but feeling like where we were was beyond that style of recording at the moment. But at the same time, we were very much invested in it and happy to be a part of it.

Summerteeth was partly a reaction to how defined the band had become by the alt-country tag, or roots rock, or No Depression—whatever they were calling it that month. People assumed we had this sort of identifiable, philistine range of influences, and we, in our heads, knew that wasn't the case. That there were things we'd been recording that no one had heard yet that weren't that at all.

"Via Chicago" and other songs on *Summerteeth* were treated almost like collage. They were fragmented, or mosaic, almost. We were trying our best to find ways to undermine songs that are really, at their core, simple two- or three-chord folk songs. This was the time that I began to write songs in the way that became my standard practice for many years, definitely up until *Sky Blue Sky*. When I write in this mode, I write for myself first, pretending that the audience isn't even there, and will never be there. I can get things off of my chest, I can invent versions of myself that are better than I believe I am . . . or worse, are even downright awful and murderous. I can expose shadow selves that I believe I should keep my eye on. I can admit things about myself without really having to take ownership of anything. Having it all feel private and insular creates a sense of authenticity I'm not sure I'm able to explain in an understandable way. It's a trick I play to coax myself into being okay with exposing things that feel powerful and intimate because they're the types of things people often hide about themselves, or even from themselves. This style of writing felt new and exciting, and even more so when it came to perfecting the songs and recording them.

Jay Bennett and I were probably at our most compatible in terms of our creative relationship during the making of *Summerteeth*. In hindsight, it was a pretty unhealthy environment. I was probably as unhappy as I'd ever been. I was insecure, homesick, and drug-addled. The insecurity fueled some paranoia, but as they say, just because you're paranoid doesn't mean they aren't out to get you. And in reality, there was a side of Jay that was kind of maneuvering to be my right-hand man, my main collaborator, yet at the same time fomenting some resentment toward me with the other guys when I wasn't around.

When it would just be Jay and me, Jay would say, "You and I could play everything." Jay really did like playing the drums, and he played the drums on some songs on that record. I play bass, so he'd say, "We can make this whole record ourselves." And when I wasn't in the room, and the other guys were there, he'd say, "Elvis thinks he's going to make this whole record by himself." So, clearly immature, typical band stuff. But there was still a lot of creative progress being made. It wasn't dysfunctional to the point of grinding everything to a halt. Music was still by and large a conflict-free zone.

On one hand, I felt insecure, paranoid, and unhappy, and on the other hand, I was still fully capable and engaged. I've had a lot of different periods like that. The part of me that could cope and had developed some healthy adaptations to all of those problems was ultimately in charge. The contrast and confusion comes from the idea that you can't be two things at once. And I definitely disagree with that. I think you can be completely confident and comfortable with your talents, and in an undiluted way, pushing forward with your best abilities, and also debilitated by and maladapted to issues that never really go away. But that you only notice when you aren't being distracted by something you're good at.

I think it's bad for people to believe they're only supposed to have one emotion at one time. Are you ever really only happy? Or sad? Or angry? I'm ambivalent more than anything, and a lot of the time I'm totally unsure how I feel. It's ambiguous. That's the part I think people really can't tolerate. We humans hate ambiguity more than almost anything else in the world. So we pick an emotion and stick with it.

That's what *Summerteeth* was like for me. And all of that is just a roundabout way to say, it was a difficult time—that's the record that's hardest for my wife to listen to. I still hadn't grown up in any significant way emotionally, and like a lot of men, I relied upon my spouse for an unconditional motherly type of love that isn't particularly healthy. When a child was introduced into that dynamic, I became a fucking jealous baby. I made really stupid choices because I wasn't getting enough attention. How pathetic is that? One of the reasons that painkillers were such an attractive drug to me was because they feel maternal, there's a warm sense of well-being that comes with opioid use. It's nauseating to me in hindsight, but I had no idea what was going on at the time. I had more love in my life than I'd ever had, and I was still lonely.

7

THE FLOWERS OF ROMANCE

WHEN I WAS fourteen years old, I made a list for my parents of the records I wanted for Christmas. The first record on that list was *The Flowers of Romance* by PiL. Reviews I'd read included words like "confrontational" and "heretical" and phrases like "not music." Plus, I was a fan of Johnny Rotten, who on this record was calling himself John Lydon, so I was intrigued. I never expected my parents to actually *buy* it. It was like asking for a pony, or claiming the only gift you want is world peace. Somehow, implausibly, they had found it at the mall and it was wrapped and waiting for me under the tree on Christmas morning.

I sat on the floor and studied the album cover—which featured an angry-looking woman with a rose in her mouth, holding a heavy kitchen masher like she intended to hit somebody with it.

"Hey, Jeff," my dad yelled from across the room. "We need to liven this place up. Why don't you throw on that new record we got you and play it for everybody?"

Our house was full of family for the holidays. Aunts, uncles, cousins, grandmothers. Even a few neighbors had stopped by to say hello. They had been eating plates of potato salad and glazed ham and drinking and smoking and loud-talking at one another, and I'd been carefully avoiding interaction. Now all eyes were on me, waiting for something to happen. I nodded and slowly carried my record over to the family turntable. I slowly lowered the tone arm onto side one and braced myself. I had no idea what was going to come out of the speakers, but I knew John Lydon was Johnny Rotten and Johnny Rotten had been in the Sex Pistols, and I knew there wasn't a single note of the Sex Pistols that I would want to be dropping the needle on at that moment.

Electronic insects? Loud snare cracks . . . "*Aaaalllaaah!*" John Lydon began ululating. "*Aaaaallaah!*" "*Doooom sits in glooom . . .*" Lopsided drumming. "*Deeeeestroy the iiiin-faaaah-dellll!*"

Wow, did that kill the mood, instantly, with extreme prejudice.

"What in *God's name* is that?" my father screamed. "Boy, are you trying to kill me?"

He hopped over presents and piles of wrapping paper strewn about our living room floor and yanked the needle across the record—*rwiiiiiiieeeeeppppp*—which oddly sounded like a part of the song.

It's one of my favorite records. I still have that *exact* copy, with the scratch across it from my dad's Christmas rampage. It's a document of a perfect musical experience. In a way, that was all I ever needed from *The Flowers of Romance*, just enough to get a sense of its power before it was ripped away. The potential of the rest of the album might have been even more powerful, left to my imagination after that.

It's similar to how I sometimes prefer demos to a finished version of a song, especially when it's a song of my own. I love that moment in the life of a song that is all possibility and potential. When I can imagine all of the different directions it could go. I find that just as enjoyable, maybe more enjoyable, than when it's fully realized. A finished record is just . . . finished.

When a song is finished, and it has its final coat of paint, it makes me sad. I mourn all the choices I didn't make. I can still hear the overdubs I didn't add, the notes that were left out, the guitar parts that are just all wrong. That's when I realize I've ruined it. That's not false modesty. Any song that ever originated in a person's imagination and was translated into notes and words is inherently inferior to its potential. When a song is rattling around my subconscious, it's still limitless, which means I haven't found a way to fuck it up yet.

Once a song goes out into the world, that's when it really gets ruined. Other people get to listen to it and make it worse, by misreading intentions and judging and weighing in with opinions. I'm right there with them. Not just my songs, but *all* songs. People ruin everything. My songs are never as good as they were in my head when they had limitless forms and belonged only to me. It's a leap of faith every time to share them. I do it willingly, because if I held on to my songs I'd eventually be the one to break the spell and I'd be the one ruining them. And that's the only thing I can think of that could be worse than other people's opinions.

MELODY IS KING. Songs are ruled by melody. I believe that melody, more than lyrics, is what does all the heavy lifting emotionally. When I write lyrics, or when I adapt a poem to a song, my goal is to interfere as little as possible with whatever spell is being cast by the melody. At the same time, I hope—at best—that the words enhance the song somehow, add meaning, or clarify and underline what the melody is making me feel.

I think that's why I often don't bother with lyrics for a long time, because I don't want them to get in the way of the emotion coming from the instrumental track. In fact, one of the primary ways I write lyrics is to sing and record vocal sounds without words—vowels and consonants that sound like what I hope the lyrics will sound like. I call them "mumble tracks." I've gotten pretty good at making it sound like I'm singing actual words. So much so that a lot of times when I play people a track at this stage, they'll think they're listening to finished lyrics. I keep them mixed really low, so they're almost a struggle to hear, but just loud enough to make out the rhythmic phrasing and melody. I almost always prefer to have a finished track before I commit to a lyric. So having a mumble track in place is an easier way to keep working without losing sight of the bigger picture.

To translate a mumble track, typically, I might take a rough mix out to our cabin in Michigan and sit around for hours listening without trying to think too much, just writing down the first words that pop into my head that fit the meter. Once I've transcribed everything line by line, I'll take a look at what I've got. The lyrics at that stage are often pretty meaningless and nonsensical—though sometimes they're not, which fascinates me.

The next steps after translating are to add however many more rounds of revisions and reshaping it takes until something coherent begins to come across. Usually, there has to be an image in my mind that guides me through the song—some narrative, even when it's impressionistic or fractured. For me, that visual connection is important—I have to be able to see something to remember it. I think this process works because it makes use of how our brains are wired to make sense of things. When you listen to a mumbling voice, your brain wants to hear words, the same way it wants to see animals or faces when we stare at clouds, because our brains are sense-making machines and we have a low tolerance for ambiguity. Sometimes I have to listen over and over again just to make out a single word. Other times whole sentences appear at once; they come like slips of the tongue.

If I sing something like "Shay clom fum-ah dif tansh," by the eighth time I play that phrase I might hear it as "Blum blum *from a distance.*" *Oh, hey, that sounds right.* So I keep listening till I stumble onto the first part of that line. I'll eventually get to the feeling of "Well, that's obviously what I always meant to sing there"—which is strange and wonderful, because no words were intended at all. But I do think it means something. You're not just playing Mad Libs with a melody. It's a process where you trust your subconscious, and you allow it to come up with ideas and phrases that don't need to make sense to your rational mind right away.

I think I'm drawn to this approach to writing lyrics because it keeps me attached to a song in its early state, the way it was before I'd thought it through and figured out what it was. I don't feel like I'm always trusted to make the best choices consciously. I trust myself enough to commit to a process, see what gets made, and respond with feeling and intuition, but when my ego gets involved I know I'm just going to cater to it, in other words, avoid embarrassment, be clever, show off. There's nothing that makes me crazy like a song that just wants to be clever.

It's a type of writing I've tried hard to avoid, where you can almost picture the songwriter sitting in a café and pulling out a notebook. "What rhymes with *vestibule*?" they wonder aloud, tapping a pencil against their lips. And then, inspiration! "Aha, *cesspool*! Perfect!" That mental image breaks the spell for me. Music is most magical when everyone can lose the burden of self and be put back together as a part of something bigger, or other. I think of it as egos blending, singer into musician into listener. Something like that feels right to me. Anyway, it's something worth aiming for.

THE PAINTER AND photographer Chuck Close once said that younger artists too often sit around and wait for inspiration to strike while "the rest of us just show up and get to work." I assume by "the rest of us" he means anyone making art when they're old enough to have realized inspiration is way more likely to come around when you already have your tools out. A pen on paper, a brush on canvas, a guitar in your hands. I'm that old now, but I've believed in that kind of work ethic for longer than I've been old.

I try to make something new, something that wasn't there when I woke up, by the end of every day. It doesn't have to be long or perfect or good. It just has to be *something*. I used to fill up notebooks with poems and lyrics, now I do it with my phone. Sometimes I'll give myself a time limit of no more than twenty minutes to write and re-cord a song into my phone.

I used to assume that the people who were great at writing songs were just more talented than everybody else, and that they always had a very clear understanding of what they were trying to accom-plish and the intent behind it. As I've gotten older I've concluded that this is rarely the case. The people who seem the most like geniuses are not geniuses. They're just more comfortable with failing. They try more and they try harder than other people, and so they stumble onto more songs. It's pretty simple. People who don't pick up a pencil never write a poem. People who don't pick up a guitar and try every day don't write a whole lot of great songs. If you don't ask, the answer is always no.

Too much ambition gets a bad rap in my line of work. If you grew up in the late twentieth century loving or wanting to be a part of the punk or indie rock scene, you were expected to at least give the ap-pearance of not caring and giving the least possible amount of effort. Of course, it's a lie. Does anyone think Devo just happened with minimum effort?! The Ramones?! Pavement?! I'd be willing to bet every band you've ever heard of worked hard and had crazy ambi-tion. Maybe it went away at some point or they got content to coast, but trust me, at some point they worked their asses off and dreamed grand and triumphant dreams. Listen, it's a cop-out to hide ambition and pretend aspirations are shameful. It's a way to protect yourself. Preemptive sour grapes.

Here's an aspirational thought I've had about what I do that kind of turns Chuck Close's quote inside out. Sometimes I think it's my job to be inspired. I work at it. That's what I do that most resembles work. It seems to me that the only wrong thing I could do with whatever gifts I've been given as a musician or an artist would be to let curiosity die. So I try to keep up with other people's creative output. I read and I listen. I'm lucky that's what I get to do with my time—keeping myself excited about the world and not being discouraged when it loses its spark. By now I've been doing it long enough to say with some confidence that if you can remain open to it and you're not afraid to call it work sometimes, inspiration is limitless.

Back in the late nineties, I came across *The Conet Project*. I saw it in the record store and thought, "Huh, a CD with nothing but Cold War–era spy transmissions sent over old-school shortwave radios. This looks cool," and I grabbed it. I listened to it in the car on the way home, and I was hooked. The voices were so eerie, like long-dead ghosts trying one more time to make contact but not really sure anymore how to use language or even who they'd been trying to reach in the first place.

I kept expecting the novelty to wear off, but I kept coming back to it. My mind kept wandering back to *Conet*. These recordings of cryptic and indecipherable shortwave radio messages, which may or may not have been encrypted orders to undercover spy operatives, were as fascinating to me as anything being made by actual musicians using actual instruments. I found it satisfying much in the same way as my dad's album of steam engine recordings was satisfying.

I wanted to know why it was so hypnotic to me. Why could I listen to hours of this stuff, even though I had no clue what any of them were saying? That question became the foundation for *Yankee Hotel*

Foxtrot. The way people communicated or ultimately failed to communicate in *The Conet Project*, it's not all that different to me than my own efforts to communicate. Most of the conversations I've been involved in during my adult life are just slightly less awkward versions of *The Conet Project.* I've been to dinner parties and other social situations where I can't even pretend to get with the small talk. I want to be nice, and I want to be there, but I'm not on that wavelength. I can't get there. I can't just abruptly turn to the person next to me and say, "Where do you think we go when we die?" Even though that's what I'm thinking. That's what's going through my head. And it feels like an attempt at real communication to me. Everything else, well, there's such a fine line between saying to somebody, "The Cubs are doing pretty well this season, huh?" and making uninterrupted eye contact while informing them in a blank-faced monotone, "I AM A NORMAL MALE HUMAN, I AM A NORMAL MALE HUMAN."

Every time somebody asks me, "How 'bout the Cubs?" I want to respond with "Yeah, the Cubs, they're going to die someday. Do you ever think about that? All of them. *All of them.* Rizzo. Bryant. The one with the goatee. The other ones. The entire team. Some of them probably soon, you don't know. They could be dying right now while we're sitting here making conversation about baseball. Death is lurking."

Susie always wants me to come with her to these type of gatherings and she almost always regrets it.

I'VE CARRIED AROUND a lot of books over the years that I've never bothered to read.

I'm not that way with *all* books. Just the books that I'm waiting for, anticipating some turning point when I'll be ready for what's inside. Other books I don't feel are necessarily to be read. Sometimes, I think it can be just as inspiring to imagine what a book is about. I might crack it open and read a sentence or two to get a feel for the language, but I don't always need a larger context. I don't need to read them from start to finish. My relationship with them is mostly my imagination of their potential. I'm guilt-free when it comes to books. I make an honest effort to read what I know is important, but I don't grade myself. Life is too short to pretend you finished a book or understood it. Who cares?

I suspect that almost anyone claiming to have read *Finnegans Wake* is a liar, but it sure is a fun book to carry around, just feeling its weight in your hands. That's a powerful thing, to have access to the mind of James Joyce right at your fingertips. I didn't need all of it. It's exciting enough to open to any page, find some crazy long sentence and see what kind of sense you can make of it.

Books are my companions. I love books and I'm always in the middle of several at a time. I don't think of them as mountains to climb, or chores to accomplish for some notch in my belt or a badge to buff. Sometimes I'll read a book about a book without even once feeling like a fraud for not having read the book the book is about. You understand. Sometimes I'll read them with a highlighter, marking phrases that excite my lyric-loving mind. Otherwise I lose the plot. William H. Gass, who has written more than a few of my favorite sentences, has turned up in some of my songs. There would be no "Something in my veins / Bloodier than blood" without his genius.

Bits and pieces from Henry Miller have found their way into my lyrics, especially while I was working on *Yankee Hotel Foxtrot*. "Quiver like a toothache . . . When we were still innocent enough to listen to poets . . ." It's amazing how many things I've been singing for years that I'll find highlighted when I revisit the warped City Lights paperbacks I traveled with circa *Summerteeth*. I'm a little embarrassed to admit how much of the imagery from "Ashes of American Flags" is sprinkled throughout the first 150 pages of *Tropic of Cancer*. None of it is in the same order or context as the song, but the language is almost all there.

"I assassin down the avenue" from "I Am Trying to Break Your Heart" doesn't really mean anything. It comes from a writing exercise. A lot of my lyrics originate this way. You could take, say, all the verbs from an Emily Dickinson poem and set them side by side with all the nouns from "The Battle Hymn of the Republic" and see what happens. It might start as gibberish, but it's amazing how hard it is to put words next to each other without some meaning being generated. It would have been so much harder to memorize some of my more abstract lyrics if they had remained just gibberish.

Originally the line was "I assassinate down the avenue," it started as an exercise where you make a list of ten or twelve verbs that you may associate with a vocation, in this case "a spy," and a list of random nouns. For the next step you take a pencil and draw lines randomly between the two, until something surprising happens in the way they interact. Can I assassinate an avenue? Can the avenue assassinate? When we're left to our own devices, verbs and nouns tend to pair up in clichéd ways, but when a verb is acting on an unfamiliar noun it can really be exciting. It stimulates the language. In the end the noun "assassin" sang better within the meter of the song and, for me, having it used as a verb made it somehow even more disorienting and evocative. I love it when words wake up and sound new again.

I have an easier time explaining the process of writing lyrics than I do explaining what they mean. Do people really need to know? Does it make the songs more enjoyable? Does it really matter if what they think a song is about is vastly different than what I think it's about? I assume part of the reason I feel that way is because when I listen to other people's songs, I'm never particularly interested in knowing what lyrics are "supposed" to be "about," especially after I have already found them to mean something to me.

Knowing this about myself might have given me the confidence not to sweat being too clearly understood lyrically. Most songs are open to interpretation anyway, so why not leave a few more gaps for the listener to fill in with their imagination? The trick I was trying to teach myself at the time was how to find a balance between leaving enough room for someone to pour themselves into a song and giving them something concrete and engaging enough to want to be intimately collaborating with you on meaning. "You Are My Sunshine" is the perfect balance to me. I've never come close, but that's the ideal I'm always aspiring to. Most people think of that song as being simple and easily understood, but I don't know anyone who agrees on exactly what it means.

After a song is created I'm really kind of done with it. I can enjoy the process of writing and recording it, but after that, it's not something that helps me disappear anymore. It stops being useful to me as anything other than another song to write on a set list. It's other people who give it a long or short life. Songs become vessels for other people to pour themselves into. And that's great. That's amazing, but that's as far as I can go.

Unless it's "Heavy Metal Drummer," in which case I can tell you exactly what it's about. It's a reminder to myself to lighten up occasionally. That's all. I guess a lot of my songs function this way, now that I think about it. If I have some epiphany that I'm sure I'll eventually forget, I make a mental note to stash the basic premise in a song somewhere so I can have the lesson refreshed from time to time. In this case, I was reflecting on the sudden realization I had once while watching a heavy metal cover band at a club in St. Louis after an Uncle Tupelo show. I'm not proud to admit this, but we were snobs. Just miserable. Hanging out on the sidelines stock-still in thrift-store flannel and work boots watching the spandexed gyrations of our peers—these pimply kids with massive hair actually having a fun time and yet still convinced of our superiority. Based on what? Our inability to enjoy ourselves? That is the kind of bullshit I need to remind myself not to indulge in, with song if need be.

THANKFULLY, AT SOME point I stopped giving a shit. In a good way. I don't mean I stopped caring about music. I stopped caring about things that don't matter, or at least things I can't control. For instance, I don't have control over how someone judges a song I write. If I can entertain myself putting a song together, and several months later still care for it enough to share it with the world, and then it turns out someone takes a strong dislike to it, those are pretty low stakes. No one gets hurt. I didn't leave a surgical sponge in someone's abdomen. It's okay.

I just like writing songs. It's a natural state to me. I like to believe most people's natural state is to be creative. It definitely was when we were kids, when being spontaneously and joyfully creative was just our default setting. As we grow we learn to evaluate and judge, to navigate the world with some discretion, and then we turn on ourselves. Creating can't just be for the sake of creating anymore. It has to be good, or it has to mean something. We get scared out of our wits by the possibility of someone rejecting our creation.

It bugs me that we get this way. It bugs me a lot. I think just making stuff is important. It doesn't have to be art. Making something out of your imagination that wasn't there before you thought it up and plopped it out in your notebook or your tape recorder puts you squarely on the side of creation. You are closer to "god," or at the very least the concept of a creator. I understand destruction can be creative, too, but I think it becomes a lot more thoughtful and intentional when you've allowed yourself to be a creator. I'm pretty naive, I admit, but I'll always believe that destruction would be an impulse a lot more difficult to indulge if more people were encouraged to participate in their own tiny acts of creation.

I also kind of believe that even the greatest works of art ever created mean almost nothing individually. If a work of art inspires another work of art, I think it has fulfilled its highest duty. People look for inspiration and hope, and if you have it you share it. Not for your own glory, but because it's the best thing you can do. It doesn't belong to just you.

The Chicago historian Studs Terkel asked Bob Dylan in the

sixties about how he went about writing a song and trying to outdo himself, or at least being as good as the last song he wrote, and his response was pretty damn perfect. "I'm content with the same old piece of wood," he said. "I just want to find another place to pound a nail . . . Music, my writing, is something special, not sacred." If the songs Bob Dylan wrote aren't sacred, then nobody's songs are sacred. Nobody's. No one has ever laid on their deathbed thinking, "Thank god I didn't make that song. Thank god I didn't make that piece of art. Thank god I avoided the embarrassment of putting a bad poem into the world." Nobody reaches the end of their life and regrets even a single moment of creating something, no matter how shitty or unappreciated that something might have been. I'm writing this just weeks after returning from Belleville, where I sat next to my dad's bed in my childhood house and watched him die. I can guarantee you that in the final moments of his life, he wasn't kicking himself for all those times when he dared to make a fool of himself by singing too loud.

I said this recently to my son Sammy, when we were talking about creative choices and how much weight to give other people's opinions. I told him: "You can't pants me anymore. I've had my pants taken down enough times in my life." I meant that both figuratively and literally. I'm hard to shame by an outside opinion. Obviously, there are still things that could happen during a show that might rattle me and knock me down a peg. Somebody in the crowd could shout out, "You suck," and it would make me feel less than enthused about myself. I'm still a person. Mostly, I'd be curious why they would bother to spend their hard-earned cash to inform me of my lameness.

Here's what I still think about when I'm writing songs. I think about when I moved to Chicago twenty-five years ago and I was using this crappy RadioShack cassette recorder that didn't work all that well. It was just something to get ideas down on tape so they wouldn't disappear, but it was an awful machine. So Susie let me use her old-school Dictaphone, about the size of a dictionary. I was in love with it. It sounded so much better than you'd ever imagine, considering it was an arcane piece of clunky seventies technology. It had a plastic handle so you could carry it around like a lunch box. Susie would get cassettes from bands who wanted to play Lounge Ax, and the ones that didn't pass muster I would confiscate and record over with my own songs. (I'm sure most of them were perfectly fine bands, and they made songs that they cared about a lot. It wasn't personal. I promise it won't happen again!) I'd fill up an entire tape with new material, coming up with a new tune every night as my set goal.

I'd sit in our apartment with my guitar and Susie's gigantic Dictaphone and I'd listen to everything on the tape, whatever I'd recorded the previous nights, everything up to the blank space on the tape. Then I would imagine, "What comes next? What does the next song sound like on this album I'm making up as I go? If I was a teenager again, listening to an album in my bedroom, what would I want to hear next?" There's so much power in that silence, just imagining what could happen but hasn't happened yet.

8

GR-OOD

IN THE YEARS before *Yankee Hotel Foxtrot*, I felt good about how my songwriting had grown. For years I'd been gauging the quality of my songs based on how easy it was to picture someone else singing them. Now it meant more to me to write songs that only made sense if I sang them. Almost everything I'd written up to that point, even the stuff I was proud of, had an emotional core that I maintained some distance from. Keeping other people's voices in mind when writing had been a self-imposed guideline because I had aspired to write songs that were universal. I think working that way had helped me grow as a songwriter, but these were *my* songs. Finding my voice and feeling more confident about who we were as a band made it that much more disheartening when the people charged with helping us find an audience didn't have any clue what we were working toward.

It especially hurt coming from Joe McEwen. He'd been my guy for years. Back when Uncle Tupelo was starting to get some notice from the major labels, and there was a brigade of dark-haired A&R women with bright red lipstick following us around, McEwen stood out for being so socially awkward, which to us was an asset. He didn't seem capable of being too much of a bullshitter because he was even more uncomfortable than we were having conversations with strangers. We were being inundated after shows with peppy and insincere label reps, practically shouting at us, "You guys were great!" But with McEwen, he was more like, "Yeah, so yeah . . . What I think, a major label . . . You know what I'm saying? . . . I think it could be good for you guys. It's just, you know . . . Putting that out there."

McEwen was the master (and maybe the inventor) of the A&R guy dance. When he was watching a band, he'd close his eyes and slowly shake his head no. It was impossible to tell what that meant. Was he loving it, or saying, "No, this isn't good at all"? I never had any idea. I've seen him do this same move to countless bands, and I've learned to love it over the years. It's so perfectly ambiguous. It's also much easier to find it hilarious now that I'm free of worrying too much about what Joe McEwen thinks.

One time, he came backstage after a Wilco show and said, "That was really gr-ood." He changed his mind *mid-word* and decided he couldn't commit to "great." Which made me like him, because he was so awkward and trying to be real. He didn't want to lie and say he thought something was great if it wasn't actually great. So he made a mid-word reassessment. McEwen was also Dinosaur Jr.'s A&R guy, and J Mascis and I have shared some notes about him. He once came into the Dinosaur Jr. dressing room before a show, five minutes before they were supposed to be onstage, and said, "Hey, J, what's happening? Wow, you put on a lot of weight."

As much as I had a love-hate relationship with record labels and the business side of things, I also wasn't completely against playing by the rules. I was never the self-sabotaging contrarian brat our public interactions with the music business have led some to believe. I thought it was an industry set up to work for you in some ways, but against you in other ways. I was unwilling, and maybe even incapable, of compromising the music we were making, but I could certainly see good reasons to take their advice on other decisions. Like whether to attend an awards show. Getting a Grammy nomination wasn't something I had ever dreamed of or even thought about. I'm not saying that because I think it's cool not to care about awards. It just hadn't occurred to me. Sure, it's an honor just to be nominated, but some of my favorite musicians have had decades-long careers and are yet to be acknowledged. And yes, it's true countless artists I love have indeed won Grammys, but the prestige has also kind of been ruined by giving Grammys to some of the worst crap anyone has ever sold as music. It's like if you were an athlete and you made it to the Olympics and found out they award medals to the best athletes in the world but also to people who have really awesome fake Chinese symbol tattoos. Why in the world would I covet something like that, other than that winning a Grammy would make my parents happy? My dad was especially proud when we got Grammy nominations, and used it as a form of currency. Several people in Belleville have told me that my dad offered them Grammy tickets over the years. I've heard stories like "I'll never forget when your dad found out that the bartender at Fletcher's was a huge Wilco fan and he promised VIP Grammy tickets for her and all her friends." First of all, you only get two, and you have to pay for them, and they're non-transferable. I don't think I've ever invited my dad to the Grammys, much less given him tickets that he could dole out however he wanted. But he loved being a beneficent big shot, even if his generosity was all smoke and mirrors.

But I went to the ceremony anyway, at least the first time, when we were nominated for *Mermaid Avenue* in 1998. The record company wanted us there. Maybe they had marketing algorithms that indicated how many more units ship when a scruffy musician appears for a few seconds on a TV screen before a Grammy they're up for goes to Lucinda Williams's amazing record instead. It seemed silly to me, but I wasn't going to argue with Warner Bros. They'd been gracious enough to put out our album, and they thought this was important, and them thinking this was important was okay by me. So I flew out to L.A. with Susie and the Wilco guys and their significant others, put on an ill-fitting suit that made me itch and squirm like a little kid at a funeral, and sat through a production that at times resembled a fever dream. Except for Ricky Martin. His performance was the good kind of fever dream. He had women on stilts with streamers, and drummers who looked like they were hitting the peak of an ecstasy trip marching through the audience, and Ricky was gyrating within an inch of his life in these ridiculously tight leather pants. It was like a Hieronymus Bosch painting come to life.

Later, we all went to the bathroom together, like a gaggle of teenage girls, and Susie and the rest of Wilco went to pee while I waited outside and held everybody's programs. That's when Sean "Puffy" Combs—or P. Diddy, or Colonel Combs, or whatever he was calling himself at the time—and his entourage wandered over. They didn't make eye contact with me, but somebody in the group reached out with a bejeweled cane and tapped the thick stack of programs I was holding. It was jarring. I wasn't sure what was happening. But then I realized, "Oh, I get it, they think I'm handing these out. Of course they do!" Why would Sean Combs or anybody who works for Sean Combs have any clue who I was? All they saw was a pale white dude standing in the middle of foot traffic and holding a bunch of programs. Obviously, I'm an usher. It didn't offend me; it would've been way more surprising if one of them had said, "Hey, it's Jeff Tweedy! Thank you for 'Passenger Side,' man!"

Here's a fun fact that you absolutely don't need to know but I'm going to tell you anyway. The guy who runs Sean Combs's clothing brand, the president and CEO, is named Jeff Tweedy. He got the job in 1998, ironically the *very same year* that Combs and his posse mistook the *other* Jeff Tweedy, me, for an usher.

A BAND IN THE nineties wanting to get any attention at all also had to make videos. I wasn't interested in being a visual artist or selling music that way, but I also wasn't a puritan who was adamant about *not* selling music that way. The way I looked at it, Bob Dylan and other songwriters far more talented than me had done promotional videos. So who did I think I was, a fucking artist? My line in the sand over what I will and won't do has always been really instinctual, and I've tried to keep it separate from ideology. My goal was to not put any unnecessary impediments in the way of being heard. By refusing to do a video, you're basically telling the people trying to help your band be heard that they don't know what they're doing. From early on, we erred on the side of letting them do their job. As long as their job wasn't interfering with the music, we tried to trust them. We signed a contract to make records and deliver them, that was our job. And their end of the bargain was to sell them, that was theirs. If they were staying out of our way, why would we stand in theirs?

Even when they wanted to change the music, there were times where, to me, it didn't feel worth it to push back. Like when they asked if they could have a mix of "Monday" with no horns so they could release it as a single, that didn't bother me. If they thought a horn arrangement was what was going to keep Top 40 pop radio from being interested in Wilco, they weren't evil, they were stupid.

Still, we weren't looking for anyone's input when we delivered *Summerteeth*. It wasn't a work in progress. It was done, as far as we were concerned. But *they* were concerned. David Kahne, the head of A&R at Reprise, told us they needed one more song, something more obviously pop that they could release as a single. That made no sense to me. I was sure *Summerteeth* was full of pop music. That was the point of it. We made a record that was wall-to-wall our idea of bubblegum pop music. But they were convinced they needed one more song, and what that really meant was that their egos weren't invested enough in our "project" for them to wholeheartedly "work the record" without being able to point to something they had done to make it huge on the off chance it did get huge. Kind of like "Hey, nice little record you got here, it'd be a shame if something didn't happen to it." Even then we felt they'd been mostly good to us up to that point, so we said, sure, we'll make another song. We love being in the studio and I love writing songs, so it wasn't the worst thing that could happen to us.

We told them, "You want one more song? Fine, but you pay for it. We don't want to pay for it. It shouldn't come out of our budget, because we delivered on our contract. We delivered the record that we wanted to make. If we hate it when it's finished we're not putting it on the record. That's the deal." Surprisingly, they agreed and coughed up some money and I wrote "Can't Stand It" on the flight out to the session they'd booked in California. They said they liked it when it was done, but they wanted to "tweak" it. Fine, we said, do whatever you want to it. David Kahne volunteered to remix it. He'd mixed a lot of hit records, like "Walk Like an Egyptian" for the Bangles, and worked with people and bands like Paul McCartney, Sublime, and Sugar Ray. You don't get more pop than David Kahne. I flew back to L.A. and sat with him at his studio and listened to a mix he'd already started on. He had cut it up digitally and put it on a metronomic grid and added some samples and backward effects. I smiled and said, "Sounds great." I really did like it. I wasn't sure if I agreed with all of the changes, but he didn't try to cut the line about prayers never being answered again, so I was happy about it being on the record.

As long as they left the rest of the album alone, I was okay. We'd just plop the new song on the front end of the album, like a sonic aperitif. If an overly edited "single" made by too many cooks would get the label more excited about helping people find our record, it'd be worth it. "Can't Stand It" fit in lyrically with the rest of the album. It matched the mood, so it didn't stick out like a loud drunk at a wake. The way we'd sequenced it, the first track was initially going to be "She's a Jar," and in retrospect that may've been too much. That's a rough way to ease somebody into an album. "Hey, here's some domestic violence set to a sad melody. And that's just to get us started!"

The process made me more cynical. Not because it didn't make a difference. Although it didn't. "Can't Stand It" never became a radio song, and *Summerteeth* ended up selling about as many records as it would have without them weighing in. What they told us: "If you jump through this hoop and this hoop and this hoop, it'll translate to *x* number of plays on *x* number of radio stations." Didn't happen. It wasn't because they were just wrong and the formula that worked for one band wasn't going to work for us. What made me cynical was the realization that they weren't really concerned with keeping their promises. On tour in Atlanta right after *Summerteeth* had been released, I was picked up by a Warner Bros. rep tasked with driving me to a radio interview, and when he opened the trunk of his rental car, it was completely filled with boxes and boxes of Alanis Morissette's *Jagged Little Pill*. He had two copies of *Summerteeth*. So obviously the big push wasn't happening. I got it. I could see with my own eyes what it really looked like to be a priority. We were not a priority. Now I knew.

A few years later, we turned in *Yankee Hotel Foxtrot*. David Kahne, the same guy who insisted that *Summerteeth* needed a single, had recently taken over as (interim) president at Reprise after Howie Klein resigned or got pushed out. He listened to *Yankee* and decided he didn't like it. Neither did our new A&R guy, Mio Vukovic, who had taken over for Joe McEwen. They thought it was all wrong. It wasn't radio friendly, there were no hits, we'd have to scrap everything and start over or, if we insisted on going with what we'd recorded, be dropped from the label. That last idea seemed pretty good to me.

If that sounds brave, let me tell you, it wasn't brave. I was fed up.

The music industry depends on artists being insecure and needy, willing to crawl across cut glass to be famous. Historically it's given them incredible leverage when it comes to negotiating contracts. If you're not willing to walk away from a deal, and the other side knows it, you are screwed. For some reason I've always been stupid or arrogant enough to walk away from negotiations when they start to feel gross or insulting. It looks like it'd take a lot of confidence to do that, but I don't feel like an exceedingly confident person. I think I'm just content and stubborn. Content in that I've never really felt like it takes a lot to meet my needs. I hate wanting things and I hate feeling greedy. "No record deal? Okay, welp, it's back to phone book toilet paper for me." And I'm stubborn because there's only so much I'm willing to compromise artistically. Allowing something you've created to be undermined to a point where you can no longer believe in it or stand behind it feels suicidal to me. I don't think I would have survived it. What would be the point if you stopped feeling good about the main thing that makes you feel good?

At the same time, I really don't subscribe to the notion of selling out. Or at least not in the same way I did as a kid. I'm sure there are many out there eager to point out, "Of course you've revised your idea of selling out, you did those commercials!" To which I say, "You're right. That, to me, is not selling out." Licensing my songs to be used in car commercials used to be a big decision. Now it's a check in the bank. The music isn't altered, the lyrics aren't altered, the meaning isn't altered; unless you think the image of people listening to "The Thanks I Get" on a car stereo corrupts the song's integrity in some way, in which case I think you need to calm down. To me there is a huge difference between saying no to a record label that wants to change your song and saying yes to a car company that wants to pay to use your song, as is, in a commercial. Plus, if I had told my dad, "We turned down two hundred and fifty thousand dollars from a car company because we have integrity and would prefer to avoid selling out," he would have said, "You're a fucking idiot! It took me four years to make two hundred and fifty thousand dollars!"

Parting ways with Reprise seemed like a very straightforward decision. There wasn't a lot of second-guessing. At that point we just weren't meant to work together. It's art, it's subjective. What I think makes a great record and what the business people think makes a great record doesn't always line up, and it doesn't have to. To their credit, Reprise made it easy for us. They offered to let us buy back the master tapes for $50,000, and then after some negotiating they changed their minds and let us have them for free. It made sense why they wanted to be rid of us. Their objective was to sell as many records as they could and move away from catalog artists. They weren't interested in the slow-build model anymore. They wanted huge paydays *right away*, and we weren't worth the trouble even if we were technically showing a small profit. To be honest, if it was just about paydays, it was hardly worth the trouble even *for us*. What we were making from record sales wasn't even close to what we could make by tacking a few extra dates onto a tour. Record sales weren't paying our bills. So for us, it was a choice of making a record we didn't like and not making any money, or making a record that we loved and not making any money. That's no contest. There was no bravery involved.

So now with an unreleased record that we owned and no record label to put it out, we were ready to get back on the road, which was really the only way we'd ever been able to make a living—playing music. Touring was what kept us alive. Every year we made a little more money playing live and every year record revenue stayed about the same, no matter what we did. At that point in history, the Internet was just starting to be a realistic place for people to hear music. So we thought: Let's put *Yankee Hotel Foxtrot* online, let people hear it for free. We were proud of the record and wanted it out there. It was never a strategy to "build a buzz" or leverage a bidding war with other labels. We weren't scheming to blow the lid off the record business by re-inventing the economic model of how artists distribute content to their fans. We just wanted to play our songs on tour and not have audiences go, "What the fuck is this? Play something we know, goddammit!"

THE MOST REVEALING scene in the Sam Jones documentary *I Am Trying to Break Your Heart* is one nobody talks about, and maybe nobody but me thought was all that important. The entire thing takes less than a few seconds of screen time.

The band is in the studio, trying to figure out the transition from "Ashes of American Flags" into "Heavy Metal Drummer." Jay Bennett and I argue about it, I get annoyed with him, then he gets annoyed with me, then I go vomit in a bathroom stall, then I come out and try to give him an apologetic hug, but he's still pissed. None of that is the revelatory moment. It happens right in the middle of that scene when Bennett is coming unraveled and he asks me, "Can I explain myself, please?" I shoot a look at the camera, a pained expression you might give a stranger at the next table in a restaurant if you've been fighting with your wife and you realize that they've been listening to everything and you want to tell them, "We probably both look insane to you, don't we?"

If you're an armchair critic who's watched the movie countless times, looking for clues for how it all went wrong between Bennett and me, you've probably been dissecting all the wrong things. It's not something he did or I did or he said or I said. It's never as obvious as you think it should be. The only moment that matters is that tiny blip of acknowledgment, when I remember that we're being watched, and I remember to think about not just what I'm seeing, but what *other* people are seeing, and whether what they're seeing is a better reflection of what's really happening than what I think I'm seeing from my vantage point.

I never understood critics who called it a "fly on the wall" documentary. I don't know how any documentary could ever pull that off, but it sure as hell wasn't the case here. A fly on the wall is unnoticed, but we were acutely aware that there were cameras following us around. I'm self-conscious enough as it is. There was no way to forget. The camera becomes an observing ego in the room. It's always in your periphery, and it makes every conversation feel like an out-of-body experience, where you're floating over yourself and diagramming how you interact with the world. Maybe it is like a fly on the wall. But it's a type of fly that you always know is there, and you can't stop thinking about it, and it makes you more self-conscious and inhibited, and you start seeing your world through the fly's eyes and thinking, "I wonder who the fly thinks is the asshole in this situation. Holy shit, it's me! No, now the fly is shaking his head!"

I'm not actually sure if Jay Bennett's behavior changed when there was a camera around, or if maybe he'd always been that way and I was only aware enough to notice. One night we were working late at the Loft, the camera crew had left for the night, and we were struggling with how to end "Poor Places." I suggested we try something a little ridiculous: Let's see if we can create sounds without any human inter-action. We each set up a station with an instrument playing itself. Like an organ with some keys taped down, or a tape echo feeding back on itself, or an electric fan strumming a guitar. It was just about making some noise in the room that didn't involve us; it was just the objects making their own music. The plan was to come back the next morning, turn all of our self-playing instruments back on, and hit re-cord. But when I got to the Loft, Jay Bennett was already there, walk-ing the camera crew through all of the different stations, and talking about how he'd put it all together. He had all of the instruments go-ing, the whole room was buzzing, and he was fielding questions from Sam Jones about his sonic experiments. I didn't say anything—I knew it was petty and I didn't want to get into another fight in front of the cameras—but I was furious. That was a *group* idea; I'd suggested it, everyone added to it, and we had all worked on it together.

Jay Bennett liked to see himself as a bit of a mad scientist in the studio. And he was adventurous, and he did apply some unortho-doxy to how he approached recording, so it wasn't completely un-founded for him to believe that about himself. It was a myth, but like all myths, it was built on something true. I was starting to worry about him. The cameras seemed to be pushing him toward that idea of himself to the exclusion of all other aspects of his personality, like an actor pouring himself into a role. He was becoming more and more focused on and protective of that particular piece of who he was. It was confusing and sad because we all wanted the cameras to see him the way we all saw him: sweet and funny and talented; one of us; a "Wilco"!

Reality TV wasn't much of a thing then, but now it would be easy to see what was happening as a fairly common type of psyche that emerges on shows like *Survivor.* He started pitting people against one another, whispering rumors and stoking paranoia. If you weren't in the room, there was a good chance he was talking behind your back or diminishing your contributions. I heard about all the nasty things he'd been saying about me when I wasn't around—I guess it never occurred to him that the rest of the guys in Wilco would compare notes—and when it was just Jay Bennett and me alone in the studio, it was the rest of Wilco that wasn't pulling their weight. "Let's just finish the record without them," he'd tell me. "We could be done already if those guys weren't slowing us down."

When Jones was putting together the edit for his movie, I'm sure a lot of less-than-flattering footage ended up on the cutting room floor. He came into the project as a fan of the band, so he wasn't looking to do a hatchet job or intuit what reality TV would become. So the movie is an interesting snapshot of our process, but not really all that complete or accurate. Even the music that's featured in it is mostly takes of songs off of the album that I was never really satisfied with. Those versions are what the record company liked and were encouraged by. Each new round of mixes we would subsequently send Reprise after Sam Jones stopped filming studio footage elicited this direct quote from our A&R guy: "It keeps getting worse!" So I always feel like the movie skips the most important part of making *Yankee,* the exciting surgery we started when Jim O'Rourke came on board and we stripped everything down to its skeletal remains and built new bodies using tape edits—splicing old recycled parts with whole new appendages matched and fitted like bionic limbs.

I had become a Jim O'Rourke fan in 1997 when a CD of his album *Bad Timing* became a constant traveling companion. It's such a beautiful album; four songs, no words, just Jim playing acoustic guitar, and then out of nowhere herds of interloping horns or strings charge through. It made a bigger impact on me than anything I'd heard in years. The songs were so simple and unhurried. I was mesmerized by the patience and discipline it took to arrange long meditative songs into performances with the immediacy of a pop song.

In 2000, the Noise Pop Festival in San Francisco was looking to expand to Chicago, and they asked me to participate. The original idea was to pair me with Jon Langford of the Mekons and the Waco Brothers. Langford is great, but it felt kind of obvious to me. The Mekons had pioneered a lot of what Uncle Tupelo was known for, so maybe I felt self-conscious about that. And in any case, it didn't feel that surprising for us to work together. So I asked them, "Do you think Jim O'Rourke would be interested?" They got in touch with him, and it turned out he was a fan of *Summerteeth*. I didn't know him at all—Susie knew him, but she knew everybody—so our first rehearsal together was the first time I met him in person. I was immediately enamored with him. He was open and exuberant, hilarious and brilliant. He also had bona fide roots in experimental music, which I loved but had never had many opportunities to bond over. Everyone had always been so super serious about it.

But when I met Jim, I found somebody with the same passion and excitement for listening to two violins play the same note for a half hour as he did for Supertramp. He wasn't an academic elitist who appreciated it primarily as an intellectual exercise. That felt like an affirmation to me. I took it to mean that I wasn't crazy, that this kind of music could be visceral and warm and cathartic and inviting. It was okay to enjoy it. It was even okay for people to see you outwardly enjoying it.

Jim and I spent a lot of time together listening to records. Mostly Jim's, because his apartment was more conducive to loud listening and long sessions. It was almost entirely empty except for about ten thousand records, a record player, and some chairs in front of a pair of electrostatic speakers and a pair of McIntosh monoblock power amps. He was the opposite of so many people I'd known in my life with great record collections. He *wanted* to share it. I was more accustomed to the pathological, possessive, and secretive world of record store clerks and their inclination to hoard musical discoveries like stock tips. They don't want you to hear it; they don't even want you to be aware it exists, because on some unhealthy level it becomes their whole identity, not to mention some sick sense of job security. But Jim has a generosity of spirit where he can't *wait* to play you something, and he's pulling out record after record, and you lose track of time until you realize it's 4:00 a.m. and you've smoked a pack of cigarettes and now you're lying on the dirty wooden floor of a tiny apartment listening to Arnold Dreyblatt and the Orchestra of Excited Strings, and you think, "I should probably tell my wife where I am."

For the Noise Pop show, we decided it made more sense to come up with our own material rather than just do covers of each other's songs. So Jim would come over after Spencer went to bed and we'd hang out in our family room and improvise on guitars until we found something that we liked. Jim eventually brought over the drummer he'd been playing with, Glenn Kotche, who joined in seamlessly. Glenn was great, intuitive and patient, and he played at a reasonable volume, which was not something I was accustomed to. He'd show up with a floor tom and a snare and nothing else, and still fill out every corner of a song without ever running out of ideas.

The three of us came up with a bunch of droney, acoustic, vaguely English folk–sounding songs, and gave them stupid names like "Laminated Cat" and "Liquidation Totale." After we played them at Noise Pop it seemed like a drag to never hear those songs again, so we booked some studio time and recorded the first Loose Fur record in four days. That should've been the end of that. But I kept finding reasons to work with them again. Glenn showed up to see me do a solo acoustic show at the Abbey Pub in Chicago, and I convinced him to grab a drum kit and join me. He played half the show without ever having heard the songs before, and it felt more comfortable and rehearsed and natural than with any drummer I'd ever played with. Then I asked Glenn to come to New York with me to help write and record a soundtrack for Ethan Hawke's film *Chelsea Walls*. A few weeks later, he came to the Loft for a friendly visit and I talked him into doing percussion overdubs on a few *Yankee Hotel* tracks. Every time, it was easy. I didn't have to explain things to him. And that's not a criticism of Ken Coomer. Talking about music is hard; the more you can avoid it, the better. Drums in particular are almost impossible to talk about at length without someone losing their mind. "*Nooo!* Four *blap blap kashunks* and *then* a *shrap shrap caflump.*" I'd program drum machines just to try to show Ken what I wanted without talking. But with Glenn, I didn't have to say anything. It's like he would either know what I was thinking or blow my mind with a part I could have never dreamed of. I was in love.

I asked Tony to call Ken and tell him he was being replaced. I wish I had done it differently. I thought I could call him later and explain myself and repair the relationship, but I should have called him first. It was stupid of me. It shut down any opportunity I might've had to talk to him for too many years. I still don't think he likes me very much, and I don't blame him.

After letting Ken down like that, I was determined to do things right with Bennett. He and I sat down in the Loft and I told him it was over. I laid out my case for why it wasn't working and wasn't going to work. I don't think he saw it coming. He wasn't happy about it. He argued with me, told me I was wrong, and explained at length exactly how wrong I was. But the band had unanimously backed the decision and my mind was made up.

There were many reasons I didn't want to make music with Jay Bennett anymore. For one thing, it wasn't a healthy situation for either of us. There were lots of prescription medications being consumed at the Loft. Not by me, at least not in that particular moment. I knew I didn't have the tools I needed to be around them and resist, so I stopped going to the Loft when Jay was there, and he was always there. Like most addicts, I went through periods where I was clean. "Oh, I've figured out a way to do this. I don't need to go to rehab. I'm not taking anything." It works for a while, but like they say, quitting isn't the problem, not starting again is the part that's hard.

But Jay Bennett wasn't there. He wasn't close to even being ready to admit there was a problem. I was scared for him, but I was even more terrified for myself because I was just learning how much danger I was in and how hard it was going to be to stay healthy. So it was a selfish move. It was about self-preservation. I fired Bennett from

Wilco because I knew if I didn't, I would probably die. That sounds like hyperbole, but it's really not. I told him I knew what was going on. That's one of the first things I said to him. "You've been getting FedEx packages full of pills."

"What?" he said, laughing. "No, come on. Who told you that?"

"You're here at six in the morning," I said. "There's no reason to be here at six in the morning unless you're waiting for a FedEx package."

"You sound paranoid. None of that happened."

It had. The guy who was running the Loft for us would see him there in the mornings, counting his pills on a desk in the back. I told Bennett we would help him. If he wanted to find somebody to talk to about addiction and maybe get into a program, we would pay for everything. But he was incredulous. "If I had a problem I would admit it."

Jay Bennett had been out of the band for almost eight years when John and Glenn knocked on my hotel room door in the middle of the night to share the tragic news of Jay's overdose. It was hard to be surprised, but that didn't make it any less heartbreaking. I wish he were alive. I wasn't in touch with him after he left, but I kept waiting to hear through friends that he'd landed on his feet somewhere. I wouldn't have been surprised to see him onstage with Jackson Browne or Elton John or even Paul McCartney. He would have made almost any band better if he'd been able to get help.

I get it when Wilco fans are still angry at me about Jay Bennett. I don't like it, but I understand. They don't think Wilco is as good now as it was when Jay Bennett was still in the band, because he's on all of the Wilco albums that mean the most to them.

I understand wanting to cling to the idea of a band. I grew up believing that a rock band was a merry band of ne'er-do-wells that took care of one another and managed to get their act together to provide the rest of us with some beautiful art. But that's obviously fiction.

I had my feelings hurt when Jay Farrar told me that Uncle Tupelo was over. I couldn't believe it. How could he do this to *our* band? After everything we'd built together? But he was right to end it. I didn't realize this until years later, when I found myself in the awkward position of being that guy in another band. If he wasn't getting the same joy from playing with me anymore, then why would I want him to keep doing it? A band isn't a sacred bond. I can still remember the sting of that moment. It hurts to have the rug pulled out from under you. But there's something valuable to surviving rejection, to realizing your hurt feelings aren't the end of the world.

I might still be in Uncle Tupelo if Jay Farrar hadn't ended it. When I had to start over again with Wilco, I had that same fearful protectiveness. Keep the band together! It doesn't matter if it feels miserable sometimes, or if trying to make music in this environment fills me with self-loathing, or if drugs keep making things chaotic. You stick with it because the band must persevere. The band must survive! The band! The band!

It was an amazing relief to realize, "No, fuck this, it doesn't have to, it's just a band. I don't have to keep these relationships alive at any cost. It doesn't matter." That kind of devotion, to something entirely made up like a "band," is silly and can even be dangerous. I'll always have the comfort and consolation of making music, even if it's just me and a guitar. If it stops feeling okay, I can end it. I *need to* end it.

There are only three people I've committed myself to completely for the rest of my life: Susie, Spencer, and Sammy. My actual family. Everybody else, we'll take it day to day. If we still want to be around one another and play music with one another, let's keep doing it. If not, we can take a break. Life is short and you should wake up in the morning feeling excited about what you do. And if you don't and you can afford to stop, you should stop. Even if it makes some people angry.

THE WAY YANKEE *Hotel Foxtrot* ended up being heard initially as an almost clandestine Internet-only release really ended up being a stroke of luck. Without being dropped by our label, we would have presumably kept our original release date of 9/11/01. Who knows what impact that would have had on how the music was received, especially with the album art featuring two towers? I have a feeling it might have been pulled off of shelves.

Instead, by the time we played Town Hall in New York City a little over two weeks later, our fans had already been listening to the album online for weeks. The common wisdom at the time was that records leaking and being heard well before they were released was just about the worst, stupidest thing you could ever allow to happen. Bands and labels were going to great lengths to prevent the exact same scenario we had just orchestrated and embraced. In some cases they were forcing journalists to listen to advance copies superglued inside CD Discmans to prevent them from being "ripped" and shared online. The Internet was causing hysteria. In hindsight the music industry's growing fear seems warranted, but for our band at that time, it felt like it was our best shot at reaching people without having to be a part of the larger machinery.

AND AFTER THAT, we continued, and continue, to do things with as little input from outside the band as we can manage. We don't make videos anymore unless we want to make them. We might go to the Grammys, but only if we really feel like it. If we do show up and we're walking down the red carpet and somebody tries to get us to pose for the Glam Cam 360, there's a pretty good chance we're going to say, "Fuck no." But if Kermit the Frog and Pepé the King Prawn want to interview us and coax us into singing "Rainbow Connection," we're probably going to sing along, because not singing "Rainbow Connection" with Kermit means you're garbage. We're getting better at recognizing when to say yes and when to say no.

The only Grammy we ever won, for *A Ghost Is Born*, happened in 2005 when we were in Birmingham, Alabama. We got the news, made a little toast, and then we played our show. We opened with "The Late Greats," which expressed our feelings about the Grammys better than anything we could've said in an acceptance speech. We won for Best Alternative Music Album, and then lost in 2008 and 2012 when we were nominated for best "rock" album, because obviously we'd gotten too big for our britches, thinking we weren't alternative anymore and could join the big boys at the "rock" table. Interestingly, both times we lost a Grammy in this category, the award went to the Foo Fighters. Which leads me to only one conclusion. If Wilco is ever going to get the mainstream attention and adoration it deserves, I need to kill, and eat the heart of, Dave Grohl.

9

TOBY IN A
GLASS JAR

"J EFF TWEEDY? LIKE Jeff Tweedy from *Wilco*?"

The kid in rumpled blue scrubs behind the window at the pharmacy drive-through was staring at me. He looked like he was straight out of pharmaceutical college—a big clean-cut kid, but disheveled like a drunk altar boy or someone who just woke up from a nap. I smiled back at him and tried to look like a guy with his shit together.

"I've seen you play a bunch of times, man," he told me, glancing at my prescription again. "My friends . . . we're all fans."

I said, "Thanks," and struggled to make eye contact. "I really appreciate that, yeah."

I never know what to say during encounters like this. I've learned that saying thanks is all that is required, but it never seems like enough.

The guy disappeared into the maze of shelves behind him, and I tapped impatiently on my steering wheel. I was here to get Vicodin, which I had somehow talked my psychiatrist into prescribing for anxiety. I'd been taking opiates on and off for years, but most of my prescriptions had been for migraines. This was the first time I felt like a doctor had gotten tired of me begging and knew he was doing something wrong, but just didn't care. For years, the standard pattern had been to get someone to write me a script when my migraines became unbearable and then stop cold turkey when I ran out of refills, or when I started to panic about all the pills I was taking. Now something different was happening. I was depressed and I had started to only feel normal and human when I had plenty of drugs on hand. Before, I had always needed to be in actual pain to rationalize asking a doctor for painkillers. An air of legitimacy had always propped up my self-esteem; I wasn't a drug addict if my use was sanctioned by a health-care professional. Now those pretenses were disappearing fast.

The pharmacist kid came back and handed me a big bag. It felt heavier than usual.

"I took care of you," he said, giving me a wink.

"I'm sorry?" I asked.

He gestured toward the bag. "I tripled your prescription," he whispered through his teeth, motioning with his eyes to be cool.

I was flustered but grateful. "Oh, well, wow, thanks, you can do that?" I blurted, still not quite comprehending what he was saying. Was I the lucky millionth customer?

"Listen, man, if you ever need anything . . ." He then put his thumb to his ear and mouthed, "Call me" into his pinky.

"No shit? Awesome. Okay," I said. My hands were shaking, and I felt high already. "Thank you again. I don't know what to say."

I drove away slowly, elated and a little scared. Up until that moment, getting large quantities of drugs had been hard. And having it be difficult had created the delusion that I was living safely behind some natural barrier that would, circumstantially and without any willpower expended on my part, protect me from having access to the amount of drugs it would take to be a "real" drug addict. Now it was going to be easy. Even in what felt like a lotto-winning moment of euphoria, I knew that making this connection was one of the worst things that could have happened to me.

I HONESTLY DO NOT remember a time in my life when I didn't have headaches. I think I was six when I learned they were called migraines and that it wasn't something that happened to everybody.

They do run in my family, though. My sister gets them and so did my mother. It's possible that when I was a little kid, migraines felt normal to me because my mom had them and it was a way of feeling close to her. I remember her being knocked out for whole days, and I would make tall glasses of Coca-Cola on ice to bring to her in bed, just like she did for me when I was sick.

Every school year I'd end up missing many, many days because of migraines. In addition to the pain, I'd get sick to my stomach and end up vomiting so much I'd have to sleep by the toilet. Sometimes I'd get so dehydrated I'd end up in the hospital. One year I missed forty consecutive days of school because of my migraines and vomiting. When I came back, I had to remind the other kids who I was.

In the beginning, before we really knew what it was, I went to see a lot of doctors. I remember reading many *Highlights* magazines in doctors' offices, waiting to get shots. When I was eight or nine, they determined my migraines were probably the result of allergies, so they gave me one of those allergy tests where they scratch your back and introduce allergens to every scratch. It turned out I was allergic to everything. Literally. Everything. Which, to me, was the opposite of surprising. Do some people really *not* have a reaction to having their back covered with small wounds and then rubbed with crabmeat, cat dander, and bee venom?

I got allergy shots twice a week after school for years. I got really good at getting shots at a time when most of my peers were deathly afraid of them. We also had to keep my beloved teddy bear, Toby, sealed in a jar, because I was allegedly allergic to house dust. Try to picture something sadder in this world than a teddy bear stuffed inside a glass jar. But the shots and the imprisoned bear never helped the migraines.

My theory, and I don't know if it's born of any kind of scientific research, is that migraines, or at least my migraines, were connected to mood disorders.

I grew up in a house full of caring people—my parents were nurturing and wanted me to be happy and healthy. But it was a different time. If a kid from my generation moped around a lot and was frustratingly inconsolable, my parents' generation's typical response would be "What is wrong with you? You have nothing to cry about. I'll give you something to cry about." I could try to tell them "I just feel sad for no reason" but it was much easier for them to understand if I was visibly in pain. In other words, the migraines were a way of making psychic pain visible to the people around me. It's obvious your kid is hurting when he can't stop vomiting and can hardly open his eyes. And since my mother had migraines herself, she could identify—she knew they were real.

Who knows where the mood disorders ended and the migraines began? They could feed on each other and make everything worse. When I'd have a panic attack, my stress levels would skyrocket for days and even weeks afterward because of the fear of having another attack, and that anxiety would contribute to the next headache, and it would begin a cycle that was hard to stop. When I'd get a migraine at school, they'd always send me home because they didn't know what to do with a kid curled up on the floor and crying. They wouldn't have been as sympathetic, I don't think, if I'd explained that I was having a panic attack because my mom was going to die someday and *then I'll be all alone because I don't think my dad can take care of me!* The migraines were real, and so were the panic attacks. But which came first? And which one needed to be treated?

ASIDE FROM MY mother, sister, and me, nobody else in my extended family (that I know of) suffered from migraines. But there were a lot of diagnosed and undiagnosed mood disorders and the coping was done mostly in the form of alcohol.

My dad's father died before I was born, and I never heard a word about him other than that he died on a barroom floor. My grandfather on my mother's side drove a cab when she was growing up, and apparently, in those days, "cabdriver" also meant "pimp." When I was growing up he lived in a run-down apartment above the tavern where he tended bar. It was one of the countless dives along Main Street whose clientele was limited to ten or twelve regulars who seemed to live there as well. My grandfather had a colossal whiskey nose, like some cauliflower-beetroot hybrid, and he chain-smoked Camel straights right up to the day they killed him. Dropping me off with Grandpa Werkmeister was the absolute last-ditch solution to childcare. My mom hated him for good reason, so I hated him as well and would beg to not be left with him. I never spent any time with him, not one second, when he didn't smell like booze. He'd prop me up on a barstool and serve me chocolate milk in a chipped beer mug and pass on pearls of wisdom like "No bartender is worth their salt unless they can skim a hundred bucks a night." Sometimes he'd pay me in quarters for sweeping up cigarette butts, and I'd feed them into the jukebox or the bowling machine.

My dad was a lifetime drinker. He'd come home from work every day and drink a twelve-pack of beer. That was his standard beer consumption. If it was a day off or a weekend when he wasn't on call, he could down a case of beer. This wasn't just over the course of a rough year or two, this is how he subsisted for the majority of his life. He got sober at eighty-one years old, on the advice of his doctors, and he did it on his own, without rehab or any type of AA support group. He had to stop, so he stopped. Then he started having panic attacks for the first time since he was young.

That's when it became clear to me that he and I shared the same mood disorders and that he had been clumsily, yet semi-effectively, treating depression and anxiety with alcohol since his teens. Everyone identified him as an alcoholic—my mom, his sister, our neighbors, the mailman, everyone. But he somehow avoided the usual

trajectory of alcoholism. He had no progressively worsening conse-
quences. My dad's life never really got worse because of his drinking.
In fact, it seemed to only get better. He moved up the ladder at the
railroad and never missed a day of work. He kept his family even
when it felt like he was putting in the minimum amount of effort. He
was reliably unreliable emotionally, but other than feuds with my
brothers and occasionally embarrassing us at wedding receptions,
his behavior was maddeningly consistent and predictable. He wasn't
going to show up to your Little League game, but you knew where he
was. In a crisis, when something would go terribly wrong, he was
somehow sober and knew exactly what to do. I have a lyric about my
dad's drinking where I sing, "Head for the cooler and drink your fill."
I think it kind of sums up my family's resignation and acceptance of
my dad's relationship with alcohol. It wasn't ideal, but we knew it
could have been worse.

I was always a reluctant drinker. Even when I drank a lot, I could
never quite get over being disappointed in myself that I was letting
my mom down. I had promised her, and myself, that I would never
drink even a drop of alcohol, so I spent a lot of time wallowing in the
guilt of being too weak to resist what felt like destiny, and guilt only
made it easier to keep drinking. I really didn't want to feel like I was
just one more drunk person in her life. It was a vicious cycle, and
when I was able to put it to a stop and quit drinking at the relatively
young age of twenty-three, I was convinced my problems were
solved. As long as I avoided drinking, I was cured. No one in my
family had driven their car off the road on weed, so I smoked weed
until eventually my anxiety disorder began to make every bong hit
result in an almost instantaneous heart-pounding panic attack. For a

while my drugs of choice were mundane and relatively benign—Diet Coke and cigarettes—which would have been a resounding victory for a guy with my DNA if I'd been able to freeze my drug use at that level of potency. Alas, the Diet Coke and cigarettes weren't enough. Nothing relieved the pain or helped me feel relaxed and normal, the way I pictured other people feeling, for very long.

Then we went to Canada.

It was 1997, and we were part of the Tragically Hip's *Another Roadside Attraction* tour with Los Lobos and Sheryl Crow. I didn't know much (or anything) about pills at the time. I'd taken plenty of non-narcotic pain medication in my life, but mostly in suppository form due to my inability to keep solids down during a migraine. What's that? You didn't need to know that? My bad. The point is, I was unfamiliar with pills, okay? Anyway, in Canada it was apparently much easier to find pharmaceuticals than in the States, so Jay Bennett and some of the guys from the other bands were starting to carry stockpiles around that made them sound like maracas when they walked up stairs. I was bored and homesick and they all looked like they were having a blast.

"What should I try?" I asked Jay. I was cautious, but curious. He astutely recommended Valium because, duh. It's what they prescribe for anxiety anyway, isn't it? So technically I wouldn't even be abusing the drug, it was semi-legit. But, meh, the sensation was just . . . okay. I wasn't as anxious about going onstage anymore, but I didn't like how tired it made me. The sedating quality wasn't particularly helpful for someone who already likes to nap 20 percent of the day. So I took a Vicodin—just one, because I was still nervous about it—and within an hour I was like, "Oh yes, okay, there it is, now I see, that's the one. I'll have more of *those*, please."

Not everyone has this reaction, but opiates energized me. The warm maternal sense of well-being that every opiate addict loves was there, too, of course, but for me at least, it was like waking up from the perfect night's sleep. I was alert, motivated, and clearheaded. I felt *normal*. I had never really been attracted to oblivion as a key component of some dunderheaded rock-and-roll mythology. You know, "Sex, drugs, and rock and roll"? I always kind of looked down on championing anything but the rock and roll part. Anyone can do drugs or have sex or do sex-drugs or have drug-sex. To me, rock and roll required more awareness and commitment. I didn't even like the lack of control that came with drinking. I tried to be the guy who could drink too much and never seem drunk. Even slurring my words felt like surrendering too much. But with Vicodin, there was none of that. I thought this was what other people felt like all the time. So why was I not allowed to feel that way, too? I could go for a walk or read a book or write a song and I wouldn't fall into a heap on the floor in a fit of weeping and panic.

When I ran out, I quit, partly because I didn't want to become addicted, but mostly because the pills ran out. But in a few months, I'd get down or I'd have a migraine and it would pop back into my head that I knew of something that would, without a doubt, make me feel normal again. I was never particularly great at making connections with people who had access to illegal substances, but being in my line of work (especially in the nineties) was a good starting point. We'd go to a club, and I'd casually ask anybody who worked there,

"Do you know where we could get some painkillers? I really hurt my back." And within a few hours someone would cough some up. I don't know if this was common at the time, but I remember tattoo parlors being a reliable place to get painkillers. Maybe because they'd give them to people after they got tattoos? I'm sure they couldn't prescribe them legally, but it certainly seemed like something they had access to. I never went to a tattoo parlor in search of pills, but I was at many, many, many rock venues where I'd ask about painkillers and somebody would say, "I'll call over to the tattoo parlor and see what they've got." (By the way, can I just say, I think it's adorable they're still called tattoo *parlors*.)

I'd start, and then stop, and then start taking opiates again, and it never felt like a problem. I thought they were good for me. "How could this be bad?" I'd bargain with my conscience. "I'm not panicking anymore, I'm able to function like an adult, I'm not debilitated by my thoughts." And I was good at quitting them! At least until I started taking them again.

It's impossible to worry that you're making the wrong decisions when everybody around you is treating it like perfectly rational behavior. I didn't feel like some weirdo for liking Vicodin, because *everybody* liked Vicodin. It was like walking into a dinner party and asking the host, "Um . . . I don't know if you're into this, but, uh . . . Do you have any red wine? Maybe something in a California zinfandel?"

I PULLED INTO THE pharmacy drive-through wondering how to ask what I needed to ask.

My guy was there. The big kid with the mussed hair.

"Hi," I said, waving at him and then immediately feeling stupid about waving at a pharmacy employee.

"Hey, Jeff," he said. "What can I do for you?"

"I, uh . . . I can't get a prescription right now, so I was wondering—"

"I've got you," he interrupted me. "I get off at eight. I'll just swing by, okay?"

He came to the Loft with a big ziplock bag full of painkillers in every shape, size, and color: Percocet, Lortab, Norco, tons of Vicodin.

"You don't take more than one at a time, do you?" he asked, looking me in the eye. "You take them as directed, right?"

Then he laughed and tossed me the bag.

"Call me earlier next time. That's all I could grab in one night."

"Aren't you going to get in trouble for this?" I asked.

"No. Why?"

"Isn't anybody going to notice that all these pills are missing? Aren't you worried about getting caught?"

He laughed again. "First of all, *I'm* the guy who counts the pills. And that one pharmacy filled about two hundred and fifty thousand prescriptions for Vicodin this year. Nobody is going to miss a few hundred pills."

"If you say so."

I gave him tickets to Wilco shows, but I never knew if he came. He never asked to go backstage. I only saw him during his visits to the Loft, when he brought bagfuls of pills and we'd talk about how easy it was for him to bring me pills, and then he'd go away. I worried about him sometimes. He was obviously addicted to pills, too. He was always a little sweaty, and over just the few years I knew him, he had started to look like an old baby.

When I went to rehab, many years later, one of my roommates was a former pharmacist who claimed he took eighty Vicodin a day. *Eighty a day!* During his first week there, all he did was sleep. I barely saw his chest rise and fall. When he finally woke up and introduced himself, his skin was yellow. It was a miracle he didn't die, or at least didn't lose his liver.

THE DRUGS COULDN'T keep up. Because of course they couldn't. There were never enough drugs to keep up with keeping me normal.

We were on tour opening for R.E.M. in Milan, Italy. There were seventy thousand people there, just an enormous audience packing an old dusty soccer stadium, and I couldn't stop crying and vomiting long enough to get myself to the stage. I was in terrible shape—for seemingly no reason, the bottom had just dropped out. I was constantly having migraines, which led to panic attacks, which made the migraines worse. Or maybe I was panicking so much I was giving myself migraines, I could never be sure. So I just stayed in the dressing room sitting on a chair in the shower with cold water raining down on my head, because it was the only thing I could do that felt comforting. Our tour manager got the local paramedics to come backstage and take a look at me. At the time I thought they were confused, but now I think they recognized an addict, but had somehow gotten cause and effect reversed. "What did he take?" they kept asking. It was really hard to explain in broken English that I wasn't OD'ing. What I wanted was for them to *give* me narcotics. It was like being seven again, and feeling ashamed at the arched eyebrows of disbelieving adults, who frowned at me and said, "Migraines? Come on. Isn't it all in your head?"

I kept telling myself that I wasn't being weak. "I'm not some junkie who wants to disappear. I have real migraines. I have real panic attacks. And I'm only being responsible by finding a way to control them so I can keep doing my job. I know all about addiction and that is *not* what *this* is."

In November of 2003, we went to New York to record with Jim O'Rourke. Myself, John Stirratt, Glenn Kotche, Leroy Bach (a multi-instrumentalist who'd been with us since *Summerteeth*), and Mikael Jorgensen (who'd helped us integrate the technology we had started using live during the *Yankee* tour and was now joining as a bona fide member on keys) were going to hole ourselves up at Sear Sound in midtown Manhattan and start work on *A Ghost Is Born*. It's also where I was pretty sure I was going to die.

I mean that in all seriousness. I thought I was going to die. Every song we recorded seemed likely to be my last. Every note felt final.

I don't know if anybody else noticed. They were aware that I was unhappy and struggling with depression, but they had no idea how serious my drug use had become. I wasn't staying up all night party-ing or doing anything that would make them say, "Hey, man, you have to cut it out." I tended to keep myself away from people when I was at my worst. They only saw me during the most functional part of my day. Like my dad, I was always able to maintain a work ethic and not shirk responsibilities. I managed to keep creating, I didn't cancel gigs. I wasn't always as spiritually present and mentally alert as I should've been, but my body always showed up.

The worst of it happened when I was alone in my hotel room having panic attacks, taking too many pills and then panicking because I'd taken too many pills. Every night I'd lie in bed—or just as often, in the tub until the bathwater would get cold—telling myself, "If I fall asleep right now, there's a pretty good chance I'm not waking up. People die in this situation all the time." My Internet search history alone was a cry for help; page after page basically asking Google, "Am I going to die?" Looking for reassurances that you're not killing yourself with the narcotics you just ingested is not a job the World Wide Web is cut out for. Sometimes, if I called home, hearing Susie's voice could pull me out of the abyss, but it was more likely she would hear the fear in my voice and get scared, which would make things way worse. It was easier for me to keep her in the dark and feel some comfort imagining her cuddled up on our couch with our boys, unaware that her husband has potentially overdosed.

I think the looming sense of imminent demise came across in the songs. The lyrical elements of *A Ghost Is Born* were originally conceived as a sort of Noah's Ark analogy. That's why it had so many animal songs: "Muzzle of Bees," "Spiders (Kidsmoke)," "Hummingbird," the fly in "Company in My Back," "Panthers" (which never made the album). I had this vague idea that the album was built around, where all of the songs were animals representing the different aspects of my personality worth saving. I don't know, it sounds ridiculous now, but at the time it made perfect sense. The dread I was feeling was profound and definitely biblical in its scope; it felt like a big flood was coming, something no one could survive. So I was saving anything I could, piling it all onto this ark as a way to salvage whatever I could of myself. I was a goner, but I didn't have to lose everything. *A Ghost Is Born* would be a gift to my kids, who could turn to it when they were older and put together the pieces of me a little bit more than I'd been able to put myself together for them in real life. "There will be a new day someday," I thought, and I wanted this record to be an elemental tool for Spencer and Sammy to reconstruct my worldview, to have some deeper connection to the dad they'd lost.

Grim stuff, I know. And more than a little maudlin. Which may've been why I dropped the whole thing. Or maybe I just got tired of writing animal songs. Looking back, I didn't think my kids would be able to reconstruct a surrogate father or that they were going to be parented by an album. I just wanted them to know I cared about them if I wasn't around anymore.

I will say that I can still relate to the overall ark/album analogy though, even without that explicit intention. All of my albums really were the very best I could do at any given time. The fact that I feel that way about them should give anyone interested a fairly detailed set of clues as to how I saw myself when I finished them. Beyond that, I think almost any album by anybody can be a helpful starting point in imagining an artist's future and reverse engineering their past.

Setting all of my grandiose album conceptualizing aside, the hard part was staying functional as a human. When you are an addict, logistics become complex by orders of magnitude. Nothing is easy or simple. It's all quantum mechanics. You're simultaneously there *and* not there! Everything was easier said than done. There was rarely more than a two-hour period in any day that I could guarantee the others I'd be present and capable of making music in a way I felt good about. The rest of the day would be spent trying to time my pill intake, hoping to catch some golden hour of lucidity and alertness in the studio. I'd take a nap in the bathtub until the drugs wore off and my migraine would reappear, hand in hand with another panic attack.

I really tried hard to avoid recording high, so for a lot of the time I spent in the studio, I was in enormous throbbing migraine pain. A lot of material on *A Ghost Is Born* reflects that fact. "Less Than You Think" has an outro built on glacial electronic drones and slowly evolving repetitive mechanical noises arranged to mimic the isolating alien landscapes migraines often induce when the pain wraps itself so tightly around your skull it starts to warp your perception of light and time. I can't remember if that was the original intent during tracking, but that's what my mind was focused on when we were doing the final mix.

"Spiders (Kidsmoke)" is another recording where I feel like you can hear my condition pretty clearly. Because of its length, getting a great full take felt unlikely with the window on my ability to remain upright closing fast. So we restructured the song to be as minimal as possible with the fewest number of chord changes. This allowed me to just recite the lyrics and punctuate them with guitar skronks and scribbles to get through the song without having to concentrate past my headache too much. We attempted two takes and take one is the one on the record. Take two was incomplete.

Things didn't get better when we returned to Chicago. I have vague memories of being awake but not really awake and wandering through my house, going through all the closets and rummaging through the pockets of every coat, because, goddammit, I knew there was some Vicodin in some of those pockets. And then thinking, "What am I doing? I have to stop this!" For weeks and sometimes months, it would be over. And then it would come back.

I've done horrible things that I'd rather forget. My wife, Susie, she remembers when her mother was dying from lung cancer, and she was still living with us, and the morphine that her doctors had prescribed to make her more comfortable in the end started disappearing, and Susie figured out that I was the one stealing it. I barely remember that, and I wish I didn't remember it at all. I want the memory to disappear forever, to be expunged from my permanent record. But there it is.

I had a therapist making everything worse. This guy was a quack, an idiot, and probably criminally negligent, and I was vulnerable and desperate. I was reaching out for help and in no condition to be discerning. He was under the illusion that I was a celebrity client, and that just made him more eager to tell me whatever he thought I wanted to hear. When I told him I was an addict, he disputed it and reassured me that the Vicodin my psychiatrist prescribed me was perfectly okay. He also recommended that I avoid antidepressants because they were blocking my creative energy. I didn't listen to him about the antidepressants (at first), but his advice about the opiates was too alluring to ignore.

"You're an artist, let it fuel your art," he said. "The pain comes from the conflict between enjoying yourself and capping your joy with mood stabilizers."

I bought into it for a while. But then one day he told me he should probably be coming on the road with me and Wilco. That set off alarm bells in my head. "Oh, I get it, this guy is evil," I thought. "He's not trying to cure me. He needs me to need his help. I'm his best customer." I wasn't thinking clearly about a lot of things, but I knew I had to get away from this guy immediately, just sever all ties and never look back. I unloaded on him, called him "the actual devil," and then I asked him to drive me home because I could feel a panic attack coming on. My whole body was vibrating. We drove in silence—he must've realized I'd had a moment of clarity and was onto him, because he wasn't trying to convince me to stay—and when he pulled up to my house, I got out and he sped away almost before I could close the door behind me, squealing his tires as he took off down the street.

I decided to quit cold turkey. Not just the painkillers, which I was pretty sure were killing me. Anything that came in pill form suddenly seemed like poison. I was convinced any medication I had been taking was making me sick, so I threw out everything. It didn't go well. I lost thirty pounds and stopped being able to function. I couldn't play music anymore, couldn't be a father or a husband. During the day I'd stay in bed, but I couldn't really sleep. I was panicking all the time, and I'd spend most of my days walking around the park, because I didn't want to scare my kids. Susie didn't know what to do, and after what had just happened, I was too terrified to trust a doctor. I thought maybe after a few more weeks of panicking and not sleeping and pacing all day in the park, I'd start to come out of it.

Five weeks later—theoretically, I was clean by virtue of the fact that I wasn't on drugs—I suffered a serious mental collapse. My brain chemistry crashed, and my body was revolting against me. I tried taking the antidepressants again, but they couldn't work fast enough. I told Susie, "I know I'm not having a heart attack, but I feel like I'm being chased by a bear." She took me to the emergency room, and they shot me up with a heavy dose of antianxiety medication. That worked for exactly a day, and then the panic returned. We went back to the emergency room the next evening, and I begged them to admit me into the psych ward.

They suggested I go to a dual diagnosis clinic, which is basically a mental hospital that also treats addiction. This was the first I'd heard that such a place existed, and it immediately made sense.

"I need that," I told the ER nurses. "I need that now. Where is it? Can I go there today? Do they have an open bed? Can you call them and tell them I'm on my way?"

"Are you sure you want to go?" Susie asked.

"Yes," I said. "Anything is better than this."

A CONVERSATION BETWEEN SUSIE AND ME ABOUT HOW MUCH OF MY RECOVERY FROM OPIATE ADDICTION I REALLY WANT TO REVEAL IN THIS BOOK

SUSIE: I still can't believe you're including the part about stealing my mom's cancer medication.

JEFF: I think that's important. I don't want to romanticize any of this. It wasn't glamorous or fun. It was awful.

S: And you thought you were getting away with it, that's what I still can't believe.

J: When did you figure it out?

S: It was right after Lounge Ax closed. So, 2000. Ugh, that was just such a shitty, shitty year. My mom died, the club closed, I found out my husband was hooked on Vicodin.

J: Did you find a bunch of hidden pills or something?

S: No, Heather [Whinna, the producer Steve Albini's wife] told me. She was at our house, and you said hello and then walked out, and she turned to me and said, "You know your husband's a drug addict, right?" I was like, "What? No, he's not! He just takes medicine for his migraines," blah blah blah, all the usual excuses. But she insisted. She said she could tell just by looking at you. So then I started paying more attention to what was going on and how many pills you were taking. But there was probably way more going on than I was aware of.

J: Have you read this chapter so far?

S: I skimmed it.

J: Okay. Um . . . You know it's about me, right?

S: Jesus Christ, Jeff, I've been a little busy! I had cancer again, goddammit!

J: Hey, hey, we haven't gotten to that part yet. You're ruining the whole narrative arc.

S: Sorry. What was your question?

J: Have I left anything out? Is there anything I'm glossing over?

S: Well, you forgot to mention that for a while you were asking me to be the giver of drugs for you, to help you monitor how much you were taking and make sure you weren't overdoing it. But it never worked, because you always had a reason why you needed more than what we had decided on. So that really sucked.

J: I'm really sorry about that.

S: It was just not a position that I should have ever been in.

J: You're right, you shouldn't have. What else did I forget to mention?

S: You only included the first time you went to rehab. You tried more than once.

J: Where was the other place?

S: It was in Pennsylvania. Within just a few hours of being there, you freaked out and hated it, and took a hundred-and-fifty-dollar cab ride back to the airport. I had to argue with that place for years because they wanted to charge us for the time there you didn't stay.

J: That wasn't good.

S: And then when we went to the emergency room and they told you about the dual diagnosis facility, you make them sound really helpful and nice, like the ER nurses were all "You should go here, my dear." I don't remember it that way at all.

J: How do you remember it?

S: They were treating you like a shitty drug addict. Like you were wasting their time and they just wanted you out of there. "Why don't you try the mental hospital so we can take care of the *real* patients?" It was awful.

J: Oh wow.

S: And when we went to the rehab place—let me know if I'm not re-membering this right—they thought you were gay?

J: Oh yeah. 'Cause they put me in the Pride Wing.

S: When we first got there, and we were meeting with the doctors, you asked me to leave the room, and I thought that was strange because you never wanted me to leave your side, 'cause you were a basket case. Then I found out later you were in the Pride Wing, and I thought, "Oh, that must have been what you told them. You're gay, and you don't know how to deal with it or tell me."

J: That's why you asked me if I was gay?

S: I tried to be nice about it. "Honey, are you gay?" And you said no, you weren't gay, but they wanted to put you in the gay section 'cause you were so fragile and messed up, and there were some sections in the rehab center that were a little rough. They thought you'd be better off.

J: There were a lot of people there that had come straight from jail.

S: But now that I'm hearing myself say it out loud, that can't be true, can it? A mental hospital and drug treatment center wouldn't have a gay section.

J: It did.

S: It was 2004! No, no, that's stupid, of course there wasn't a gay section. There was probably just a section for patients with more delicate sensibilities. This was not a nice, cushy rehab center. It was very hard-core.

J: Were there bars on the windows? Am I remembering that right?

S: There were absolutely bars on the windows.

J: I thought I was being dramatic.

S: No, the place was mostly people with court orders or Medicaid. Your dickwad therapist wanted you to go to one of those fancy celebrity rehab places.

J: Not on our budget.

S: We didn't have the money. You were just going where you're going.

J: I don't want to oversell this. It's beginning to sound a little *One Flew Over the Cuckoo's Nest*.

S: Well, no, it wasn't that bad.

J: They did save my life. They did something right.

S: So focus on that. Talk about the good stuff that happened there.

J: What about the part about me being in the Pride Wing?

S: There was no gay section!

THERE WERE TWO moments during my stay in rehab that were pivotal for me getting better, or at least feeling like I was on the path toward getting better.

Because this was a very hard-core city hospital in an underserved neighborhood, there were stretches in my monthlong stay where I was the only white person there or the only person who didn't come from a gangbanging background, situations that were much, *much* more serious than mine. So it was never lost on me that I was very fortunate to have a lot of support from a lot of people, including my band and my wife and my manager. I really didn't have anybody in my life I was going to have to cut out to stay sober and get healthy.

I would feel guilty. I'd sit in group sessions and listen to other patients talk about their lives, and what they'd endured was beyond anything I could imagine. They came from homes where they never felt safe; being physically and emotionally abused was just a day-to-day reality. Food was scarce, hope was scarcer, and it was a toss-up whether there was more danger outside or inside. One guy told us about seeing his father murder his mother when he was nine and that he had his first taste of alcohol that night because his father forced him to drink whiskey, thinking it would make him forget what he'd seen. Hearing a story like that made me ashamed of how little I had

had to survive and how much pain I'd derived from so much less actual trauma. What was I gonna say when the group got to me? "Um . . . I cry a lot. I get scared sometimes. I have headaches, and it makes it hard to make music." That was the worst of it. I was out of my league.

One time, after a group session, a few of us were in the smoking room and I confided to them, "I feel like I shouldn't even open my mouth. I don't want anyone to get the idea that I think my situation compares."

This big black guy, who towered over me, turned around and started shouting at me. "What the fuck is that shit? Shut the fuck up! We all suffer the same, motherfucker!"

"I'm sorry," I said, backing away. "I didn't mean—"

"Listen to me, motherfucker, listen." Getting right up in my face. "Mine ain't about yours. And yours ain't about mine. We all suffer the same. You don't get to decide what hurts you. You just hurt. Let me say my shit, and you say your shit, and I'll be there for you. Okay?"

It set me straight. I still think it's one of the wisest things I've ever heard. I was trying to put things in perspective by pretending I had no perspective, by denying my own feelings. It's always going to be important to acknowledge someone else's pain, but denying your own pain doesn't do that. It just makes their pain relative to yours, like a yardstick to measure against. It's a waste of pain. After that I started listening more and I started feeling again.

I'd spent the first few weeks of rehab overanalyzing everything. I wondered, What if getting better meant I'd never play music again? Was I willing to do that? I thought I was, I sincerely felt like anything would be better than what I had been going through. If I could be healthy and able to cope with life and take care of myself and Susie and our kids, what wouldn't I trade for that?

The other big moment for me happened in the laundry room of the halfway house I'd gone to live in, on the hospital's recommendation, after rehab. The rest of the band had been getting together without me to rehearse the *A Ghost Is Born* material in hopes that everything would soon be back to normal and we'd be touring like always. I was sitting by myself in the corner and playing the guitar, just trying to see if I still knew how to do it. I was playing "Muzzle of Bees," softly so I wouldn't disturb anyone. There weren't a lot of private areas in the building, and the laundry room was the least crowded place I could find. A few people wandered in and out, carrying plastic laundry baskets or stuffing bundles of clothes into dryers, but they mostly ignored me. I didn't realize I was being watched until I finished. He was an older guy, probably around my dad's age, gray-haired, wearing what looked like clothes from a vintage shop, but you could be certain he had bought them when they were new.

"You know what, son?" he said to me. "You've got something special. I don't know what it is, but you've got it, and you need to do something with it."

I smiled back at him. "Thanks," I managed.

"The only thing you're lacking is confidence," he continued. "What you need to do is get out there and get in front of some people and play your music for them."

I was really touched by that. He had no idea that this was what I did for a living, that I'd been playing music in front of strangers for practically my entire life, long before I'd learned how to drive a car or had a girlfriend or didn't depend on my parents to feed me. Music had always been the only thing in the world I felt qualified to do. But for a random person to say that, completely unsolicited, when he knew nothing about me, made it feel so much more meaningful. It cut closer to the bone. He had no ulterior motive, other than thinking, "Things have been rough for this kid lately, and I bet he could probably use some encouragement."

I thanked him, and he shuffled off, and I never saw him again. About a month later I was walking downtown and I saw my face on the cover of Chicago's weekly paper, the *Reader*. I'd forgotten I'd even done an interview with them before I'd gone into the hospital. *A Ghost Is Born* was about to be released and the press was starting to come out. Around Chicago, I was starting to see my face more places than ever before. I couldn't help but wonder if that older gentleman had recognized the kid from the laundry room's face on the side of a CTA bus and shook his head in wonder.

10

SUKIERAE

THE DAY AFTER Spencer was born in 1995, when for some reason they trusted us to leave the hospital with our brand-new baby boy, we went straight to Lounge Ax. It just felt normal for us to be there, and when a tiny human being is thrust suddenly into your world, you need to feel normal again. We introduced the baby to everyone (or I guess vice versa). We did the same thing when Sammy was born four years later.

I wasn't ready to be a dad, but that's probably true for anybody. Spencer wasn't planned, and not in the same way my parents claim I wasn't planned, where it's followed by a wink and a nudge from my father. Being parents wasn't a possibility we seriously registered in our brains. Susie was under the impression that she couldn't get pregnant, because as she explained to me, "I had a doctor tell me once that I'd never be able to have kids because I get my period once a year." Turns out, her doctor was wrong. Then, after Spencer was born, she started getting pregnant "like a crazy person" (her words), and for a few years she was "very miscarriage" (also her words). We were unprepared and scared shitless by all of it.

The reality of having Spencer in the world hit me harder than I'd anticipated. It was disorienting. It wasn't just the responsibilities of parenting that caught me by surprise, but having something else in the world that I loved not just as much as but *more* than I loved music. I did not see that coming.

When Spencer and Sammy got older, I wanted to make sure the work I did, and the music I made, was a part of their lives. I knew what my dad did for a living—well, vaguely—but I only visited the railroad one time that I can remember. So I never really developed a clear mental image of where he was or what his work was like. We didn't want our kids to have that same mystery, so Susie and I made sure they came to as many shows as possible. It's why Spencer and Sammy were always at Lounge Ax, and why they were backstage with me whenever I played somewhere a short drive away. I wanted them to know what a backstage looked like, so when we were apart for longer than we wanted to be, they'd at least be able to visualize it. They've traveled with me; they've been on the tour bus, they know what the routine is, what the hotels are like, what my life is like away from them.

I don't believe that your kids should look at you as infallible. They should be able to look at you as a person who is struggling and persevering. They have pretty well-tuned bullshit detectors. I've said to Spencer and Sammy more than a few times, "Listen, guys, I have no idea what I'm supposed to do right now. What do you think?" You can never go wrong with asking questions. Well, maybe you could if you have an especially devious kid who knows how to manipulate you. But even then, if you ask enough questions, you'll eventually get to the right place. It's my same strategy when arguing with some-body about politics. You can't just tell somebody they're wrong. They have to arrive at that conclusion on their own or it's never going to happen. So I keep asking questions, not in a confrontational way, but with sincere curiosity. Give people enough rope, and they'll hang themselves. They'll eventually realize they don't know what the fuck they're talking about.

I just pretend every child is a miniature "staunch conservative" who's pretty sure that I'm an idiot. Let them talk, and keep asking questions, and they'll talk themselves into a corner. "Well, what would *you* do if you were the parent and your kids acted this way?" You need to approach it with enough humility so it's clear that you're being sincere and not just asking loaded questions. "I wish I knew the right answer, maybe you can help me, I don't know." Trust me on this, it drives them crazy. I think they would have usually preferred a time-out.

I know the boys didn't like it when I went on the road and disap-peared. I didn't like it, either. We all dealt with that distance in our own ways. I did it by being really sad and beating myself up emotion-ally. Spencer did it, at least when he was younger, by watching a lot of Wilco videos. We had a VHS tape of Wilco highlights—it was two or three hours of videos and interviews and late-night talk show per-formances and live clips, anything the band did that was recorded in the nineties. Spencer would watch it over and over again while sit-ting on the floor with his mini Les Paul Junior guitar and his tiny amp, and he'd pretend to play along, mouthing the words until he started to commit them to memory. It drove his babysitters insane. Then, when he'd watched the video so many times that even he couldn't sit through the "Outtasite (Outta Mind)" skydiving video again, he'd pack up his guitar and amp and walk to the front door. His babysitter would ask where he was going and he'd say, "I gotta get to the gig."

Very cute, yes. But as a dad, a story like that gave me the bends. Hearing that your four-year-old is having fantasies of hitting the road with a band so that he can be closer to you is almost too much to take.

A Conversation with Spencer about How Much of Our Relationship He Really Wants Me to Reveal in This Book

JEFF: Can you just write this part? I feel like it'd be better if you wrote this part.

SPENCER: I don't think I could do any better. I'm probably more biased.

J: You're just protective.

S: I want this book to be a pure representation of who you are. And I'm not sure if I'm the best person to capture that. This might be typical of a lot of young adults, but I'm trying to figure out to what extent you, my father, are changing and to what extent I'm changing. You know what I mean?

J: You don't feel the same way about me that you did when you were a kid?

S: It evolves and matures. My perception of you has changed a lot even in just the last few years. And not necessarily negatively or positively. When you're growing up, you automatically get confronted with how your idealized version of your parents differs from what they're really like. Both versions are presumably true. So that's what I've been trying to figure out these days—what are the things about you that I haven't noticed until now, or was thinking about in the wrong way? And what are actual instances of you as a person changing? I can't rule out that your behavior is different than it was when I was a little kid.

J: Wow. That's heavy stuff.

S: It's what I've been grappling with.

J: I was hoping that maybe you could just talk about how I sang "Forever Young" at your bar mitzvah and it was really emotional and sweet, and that makes me a good dad.

S: [*Laughs.*] Well, sure, there's that.

J: Even that was entirely Susie's idea. I just managed to pull it off without crying.

S: It's an emotional song.

J: Let's fill this chapter with stories like that. We could talk about how I wrote a song for *The SpongeBob SquarePants Movie,* and I brought you and some of your friends to the studio to do the *na-na-na-na-na*s part.

S: How old was I? Eight? Maybe seven?

J: Eight at the most. And you were so excited to be there, to be recording a real song with me. It was one of my favorite things I've ever gotten to do in a recording studio.

S: Or how about when you brought me onstage at Madison Square Garden on my thirteenth birthday to play drums on "The Late Greats"?

J: Best birthday present ever, right?

S: Definitely the most terrifying.

J: You were so good!

S: Thank you. I was also a thirteen-year-old kid who suddenly had twenty thousand strangers staring at him.

J: Huh. I never thought about it that way.

S: No, no, I don't mean it was bad. It was such a huge deal for me. All I'd wanted for most of my life was to be in a band with you, and here it was finally happening. I just mean, if you want to focus on the things that really define our relationship, I don't know if that's the place to start.

J: Where would you start?

S: Some of my favorite memories are when you'd drive Sammy and me to preschool, and you'd play Captain Beefheart for us. What was the CD you put on all the time? *Safe As Milk*?

J: Whatever has "Electricity" on it.

S: Such a perfect song.

J: It's nonsensical and funny and weird. It seemed like perfect kids' music to me. And then you guys started asking to hear it, and I thought, "I am victorious as a father."

S: I haven't listened to it in a while, but I know when I do, it's going to give me extreme visceral preschool feelings.

J: How old were you when we started jamming?

S: Jamming! That's been a huge part of our relationship for what feels like my whole life. We've been doing that since I was at least six.

J: It was never a planned thing, like a father-son activity that was on our calendar. We'd just be sitting around the house, and there was nothing else to do, and I'd look at you, and we'd both know it was time.

S: It usually started with you saying, "You want to jam?" Like some dads say, "You want to throw the ball around?"

J: And then we'd go down to the basement and start playing.

S: Me on the drums and you with a guitar and amp. We'd improvise without speaking. Now that I'm a grown-up, or a grown-up-ish, I play with other people, and I go to a school with a music conservatory, and I've discovered that the unspoken bond that you and I have when we're making music together—where it feels like we can anticipate each other and know where a song is heading without saying a word—it's not as common as I thought. I took it for granted because that's what we did all the time.

J: We have our disagreements, though.

S: Oh yeah. When we were doing the *Sukierae* record, I remember being horrified that you wanted to put a piano on "High as Hello." It just didn't sound right to me.

J: [*Laughs.*] That's right. You were very upset.

S: But you were calm about it. You told me, "I'm just trying something. Relax." The piano ended up in the final mix, and I like it now. But in the moment, I just couldn't believe you would do that to the song.

J: If that was my worst offense as a dad, I think I did okay.

S: I don't know if I ever told you about this. Sammy and I were at Jewel buying cereal one night.

J: What? Where was I?

S: On tour, I think. It was around nine p.m., and we ran into a teacher from our high school. She looked at us with this really sad, mournful look. Like "Those poor kids."

J: Buying their own cereal. How Dickensian.

S: She walked over to us and gave us both a gentle squeeze on the shoulder.

J: I don't like where this is going.

S: Hold on, it gets better. So she says to us, "I know it's hard with your father never being around."

J: Oh come on!

S: It probably didn't help that we were there with Scott Reilly.

J: Bullethead? He's harmless.

S: Yeah, but a couple of teenagers buying cereal with Mojo Nixon's manager? It didn't look good.

J: I feel like this book just needs to be honest, you know? I don't want to gloss over anything. Even if it doesn't "look good."

S: Okay, how about this? You just come right out with it, say something like "I feel like I was a really bad dad at some moments in my kids' lives. I feel like I really let them down when I was struggling with addiction or on the road too much. But they have since assured me that they really appreciate the . . . blah, blah blah," whatever. You just talk about how you feel you failed, and how your perception didn't always line up with reality.

J: Yeah, but that could come off as a little needy. I know that I *am* needy, but I want to hide that from the public as much as possible.

S: Okay, so maybe you don't talk about it. You show it with stories.

J: Yeah. Let's show something that doesn't seem like a cliché. Everybody knows parenting is hard, and being the son of a musician who travels all the time is hard. But how do we demonstrate the complexities of our relationship? I want to write about it without relying on the same tired father-and-son tropes.

S: Well, here's something. On the *Sukierae* tour, remember the show we played in Austin, Texas? With the lady in the front row taking pictures?

J: Oh yeah. She was the worst. She just walked right up to the stage and stood in front of everybody, snapping photos like we were doing the show just for her.

S: In between songs, you started yelling at her, "You've got to go back to your seat! You're being a dick right now!"

J: She was being a dick.

S: She was furious when you told her that. She came and did something again, and you addressed her again. And then she left. I don't remember if we asked her to be taken out or if she left on her own. But then hours after the show, when we were out in the alley, walking to the tour bus, she found us. She might've been drunk, and she was bawling her eyes out. She was screaming at you, "You're such an asshole! My nephew died! I've been looking forward to this for months! This was my release from that! You're such an asshole! I fucking hate you!"

J: She ambushed us.

S: Well, yeah. But here's the thing. I've been around you enough, and I've seen you be around enough people. When I see you interacting with your peers, I don't see it as peers interacting. I project my own privilege onto it. I assume that everybody you're talking to thinks of you as some rich, exalted celebrity. It's taken me a while to realize that, from your perspective, it doesn't matter who you're talking to. In your mind, you're just talking to another human being. I've even encountered things like that in my own life, where I'm talking to other people and I'm just interacting like we're equals, and I'll realize that other people are witnessing an inequity, like I'm a spoiled rich kid with a rock star dad, or whatever. So I project that when you're talking to other people, especially when it's a fan.

J: You thought I treated her badly?

S: I did at the time, which is why I intervened. But you were just being honest with her, and saying, "No, you were out of line and disrespectful." You were treating her like an adult. And I got in the middle of it. I just wanted you to take it a little easier on her. I felt like, she's so vulnerable, and you're so powerful. She doesn't deserve this. But I was wrong.

J: I don't know. Maybe you weren't wrong.

S: No, I was. Because you don't undermine your own team. It is completely inappropriate and dangerous for me to undermine you when something like that is happening.

J: But maybe I should have been kinder to her.

S: When people have any sort of success, other people tend to perceive them as transformed. But they remain the same in their self-perception, generally speaking. Or maybe not. But that's been my experience watching you, in my limited career as a young person. It seems like, regardless of how much or little creative or commercial success you've had, you feel the same.

J: I do feel the same.

S: And you look at the world the same way that you did when you were eighteen and in Uncle Tupelo. It's everything around you that changes. I think that's been one of the things I've admired most about you, and I've tried to emulate.

J: That I haven't changed much since I was eighteen? [*Laughs.*]

S: Your lack of preciousness. It's like you're floating through life, and I don't mean to say you're being aloof. You just really care about the moment. You don't even write things down too much. You have this kind of intense focus on the moment. I'm really anal in a lot of ways, and I like to make stuff meticulously. I like to cover all my bases and feel like a finished product is the absolute maximum idealized form of something. But working with you, like early on in the *Sukierae* sessions, we would just try stuff, and spend time following things and going down rabbit holes that we knew might not even help. I wanted to hear the finished thing in my head already. But you were like "Relax. We'll get there. Let's just throw some stuff against the wall and see what sticks." That had a big impact on me.

J: I'm glad about that. [*Long pause.*] You want to jam?

S: Absolutely.

SPENCER CAME OF age in the studio, and it was a real revelation. I realized how talented he was while I was working on the second Mavis Staples record. Mavis and I had done some promotional videos where it was just me and her with an acoustic guitar, and she liked the idea of making a whole record like that. We started on that record with that concept, and as the material was coming together, it really felt like it would be better if we could give them a more full arrangement. One song that Mavis said she wanted to cover was "Revolution" by the Beatles, and it felt like it wouldn't feel exciting enough without drums. I asked Spencer, who had been drumming in a band called the Blisters with his friends since he was seven, to come by after school. I said, "You remember that song, right?" And he said, "I think I remember it." Then he came by after school and sat down, and we played it once through, and it sounded exactly like the Beatles record. He played it perfectly. I was stunned. "Did you practice this?"

"No, that's how it goes, right?"

"Yeah, that's really, really good . . ."

Then I sat him down and played him some songs, letting him do some overdub drumming. He was playing to my acoustic guitar, on tape. Things that aren't cut to a click, as they say—with a metronome, basically—tend to be kind of hard to play to for a drummer, because the tempo kind of floats naturally, it slows down and speeds up just enough to be obvious when a steady beat is put next to it. It's really not a fair thing to ask a drummer to do because it usually makes them sound like they have no idea how to play the drums, but Spencer sat down and matched my performances bang on in no more than a couple of takes, like it was my DNA playing the drums with no perceptible speeding up or slowing down. When instruments play together tightly, you don't notice that. You only notice it when one guy takes off and makes everybody sound like they're slowing down, or vice versa. Tom, our engineer, looked at me, and said, "I don't know if he knows what he's doing is really hard."

I thought about that a lot. Basically, we were doing what we'd done his whole life. Playing together is something he enjoyed doing with me, bonding-wise, since he was as little as I can remember. We would get on the floor and play music together. He'd also grown up in a culture of belief. The way that professional baseball players have kids who end up being professional baseball players. The odds of any kid being a professional baseball player are really, really small. And it's not just connections—you have to actually be able to do that. But it's not a thing that they believe they *can't* do, because they have a modeled behavior, and an atmosphere of "Yes, this is something perfectly reasonable to expect out of life."

And I think that's huge for people to be able to live in an environment where they believe that they can accomplish things. That it's not strange to accomplish things. I think that has something to do with it. But Spencer just basically came out of the Mavis sessions thinking, "I really, really enjoy doing that a lot." After we finished that record with Mavis, we kept doing what we'd been doing, having him come by after school and having him play drums on songs I was working on. And that's really what we've been doing ever since. Putting drums on Wilco records—most songs start with Spencer, and then Glenn kind of comes and replaces him with Glenn's style. Almost everything I've recorded in the past seven years or so started with Spencer. When we toured as Tweedy, I looked over a lot of nights and said, "I don't know how I got to be this lucky."

Sammy came around to it a bit later, when he was really young I think he thought of it as more his brother's thing and he wanted his own thing. He fell in love with photography and poetry. Recently he started getting interested in modular synths, so I brought home the refrigerator-size system Jim O'Rourke left at the Loft when he moved to Japan. Within a few days Sammy was hooked on ambient drones and had started making his own patches.

Then, for his senior year project in high school, he got the go-ahead from his adviser to make a record. Susie and I were a little nervous that he might have backed himself into a corner, partially because he had the impression that whipping up a record was pretty easy and normal, and partially because his adviser assumed that having Tweedy as a last name meant you can play an instrument. We were even more nervous when I asked him what kind of record he wanted to make and he informed me that it would be "Kind of like John Fahey with some modular synth but mostly acoustic finger-picking in the American Primitive style." Which was surprising for a lot of reasons but primarily because neither of us had ever even seen him hold a guitar. But he did it! He scheduled some lessons with our friend Jim Becker from Califone and he made a record of fingerpicked acoustic guitar instrumentals and experimental noise collages.

After Spencer heard it he texted me. "How does Sammy feel about you playing guitar all over his record? Wasn't it supposed to be his senior project?" I got a thrill out of getting to be the one to tell him that I hadn't played a note, that it was all Sammy. Spencer was astonished. He'd been away at school and he had only heard the discouraging aftermath of one of Sammy's first lessons. Lately, I've been having Sammy come by after school and double my vocals, and you'd never know it wasn't me if I didn't credit him, except that he maybe sounds a bit skinnier.

Sammy listens to music like it's his fucking job. At eighteen years old, he's almost impossible to stump. I'll put things on in the car and be like, "Do you know what this is?" And he'll be, "Yeah, I think it's Leonard Cohen, *Live at the Isle of Wight 1970*." No, he *knows*. "Okay, tough guy, what's this?" "Um, it's *My Life in the Bush of Ghosts* by Brian Eno and David Byrne. That's a great record." I'll be, "How do you know this?" "I listen to it all the time." He knows *so* much, it's insane.

I love how Sammy is making his own connections, cross-referencing, listening to stuff he likes and then reading about who they like, going back and listening to Kluster and Kraftwerk when LCD Soundsystem talks about them. Listening to Japanese noise, looking at his mother's old schedule for Lounge Ax, realizing, "Oh my god, Merzbow played your club!" But it's not just stuff like that. It's also "What's your favorite Etta James record, Dad?" It's pretty wide ranging. His friends don't understand it. He has a friend who claims to not like guitars, singing, or chord changes in music. He only likes power electronics, like records by the band Whitehouse. That is pretty fascinating in itself. How does that happen? "You know Luke's parents hate Wilco, right?" Well, that explains it. They're noise people or whatever. But he'll put on a John Prine record, and before any delightfully melodic folk storytelling can even begin to unfold, his friends will say, "How can you listen to this? Why would you ever listen to this?"

When Sammy sang with us on our recent Japanese tour, he asked questions like "Does that mean I have to come to soundcheck?" Yes, it means you come to soundcheck. You're not just going to come out and sing it in front of an audience. Finally, he had no place else to go but to soundcheck, so "You want to try 'Thirteen'?" We had been playing it in the dressing room with him for the whole trip. He did a great job, and it was amazing to have him onstage with us.

Now Sammy says that he's ready to devote more of his energy to growing as a musician. I never push him, but I do tell him, "You have a unique advantage over a lot of people making music, in that you're a really good listener. That's almost more important than being a good performer. To be a good writer, to make your own music, you have to be a great listener. To make interesting stuff, you have to be an insightful listener, and you are that already. To me, that's more of a special attribute than having a lightning-fast faculty on the guitar or something like that."

And Sammy has challenged me to grow in ways I could have never predicted when I was his age. Susie is Jewish, and both Spencer and Sammy were bar mitzvahed. So when it was Sammy's turn to start Hebrew school and he began begging to get out of it, I offered to help him by studying with him, and decided I was going to convert. He was bar mitzvahed, and I had a conversion ceremony. It was more involved than I thought it would be on a number of levels, including a level that required a mohel, a storage closet, and a sharp object. You'll be able to read all about it in my follow-up book, *Leave Them Wanting Less*.

"I WANT TO SEE if I can get this out without crying," I told the crowd at Purdue University around midway through our set in 2006. "I lost my mom this week. And she was very, very dear to me. She would have wanted me to be here tonight, even though it's someplace that I really don't want to be, I have to be honest with you. But she would be mad at me for not being here."

I'm still amazed that I made it to the show at all. It was early October of that year. My mom had died on a Friday and Wilco was booked to play in West Lafayette, Indiana, the following Wednesday. I was a wreck. Inconsolable. I don't know if it was the best idea for me to play a gig so soon afterward. I was very raw and emotional. But I believe what I said up there. She would have been angry with me if I'd canceled the show because of her. This was the woman who drove me out to the country to buy a guitar that we'd read about in the paper, who rented the halls I used to play in with the Primitives, who paid for the PAs and passed out flyers and collected the money. She was my biggest fan, and not just in the mom sense. When her doctors discovered that she had blocked arteries in 2002, which caused her EKG reading to flatline and they had to scramble to save her, she walked out of the hospital the next day because she wasn't about to miss Wilco's tour-ending show in St. Louis. Nobody believed in me like she believed in me.

Her death was unexpected. She didn't take great care of her health, but she was happy and vibrant. She had a heart attack while playing cards with friends—the same social circle of women she played cards with once a month for more than forty years. One of them told me, "She went down like a ballerina and she was gone." So I guess it was the kind of death we'd all sign up for. A good death, if there is such a thing. There were no bedroom vigils, no praying for a recovery, no whispered conversations with doctors. Just a bunch of "old broads" (in their words) sitting around card tables, slapping down cards, and eating gooey butter cake, until one of them decided to cut the game short.

Music helped me survive my mom's death like it helped me survive everything else. Music kept me emotionally afloat during those first uncertain years of fatherhood, even as I doubted whether I wanted to play music again. Music kept me alive when I thought the pills might be the thing that finally killed me. And music is what kept me sane when cancer came back for Susie.

The first half of 2014 was torturous in ways I didn't know it was possible to be tortured. We learned in February that there was another tumor growing in Susie's chest, in the very same spot where they'd removed a tumor twenty-two years earlier. But they didn't know exactly what it was, if it was cancer or something else. So they did biopsies, and the doctors kept telling her, "We're not sure yet, we need to run more tests." For four months we waited, trying not to let the worst-case scenarios play out in our heads.

It happened just as I was trying something new, to write and record a solo album. I loved making music with the rest of Wilco, but I wanted to see if I could do it alone. I'm on a need-to-know basis with any instruments besides the bass and guitar. But it makes me think about songwriting in a different way when I can't just say, "Hey, Pat, do you have a piano part to put here?" Or, "Okay, Nels, this is the part of the song where you tear a hole in the space-time continuum." My limitations as a musician make my songs feel different than when I'm relying on other people to go ahead and be great all over them.

Without breaking stride after the Mavis record, Spencer kept coming by the Loft every day, and something was just starting to take shape. It was a thing we were doing because it was exciting and it felt fresh. But it was also a coping mechanism, a way for us to hold on to each other without just hugging all the time. We were hopeful, but also really freaked out. Why can't the doctors tell us what's in Susie's chest? Why is this taking so goddamn long? Just take a fucking X-ray and tell us what's in there! Every day that there was no news, Spencer and I kept working to take our minds off the phone not ringing. Sammy was invested, too. Paying close attention and weighing in on lyrics and arrangements. Thinking and talking about music made our world seem normal. Our family needed music to keep going.

The news, when it came, wasn't good. She had not one but *two* types of cancer—a rare form of non-Hodgkin's lymphoma (primary lymphoma of the bone), and liposarcoma, the same cancer she had twenty-two years ago, which the doctors didn't know was cancer until they'd cut it out of her. She would need six rounds of chemotherapy treatment and a surgery, where they would have to saw her rib cage in half, and then radiation and two more years of maintenance chemo. Unlike the first time Susie got sick, I wanted to know everything. I'd sit at the computer for hours, Googling the minutiae of her cancers. I don't know if it accomplished anything, other than annoying her doctors by me asking too many questions. But I needed some semblance of control. And I needed to be a pillar for her the way she had been for me when I needed her the most. She had driven me to too many hospitals, held my hand when I explained to countless nurses that I thought I was dying. She'd endured living with a drug addict and stayed with me when any reasonable person would have cut and run. The least I could do was have her back when cancer came after her a second time. Being the badass she is, she was facing down the situation in a way that almost made me feel sorry for cancer. But she also got scared, and she started relying on me more than she ever had before. She needed me, and I wasn't going to let her down.

I only showed her the cracks in my seams once, when she was in the hospital for a bone marrow biopsy. The doctor was explaining what they needed to do, and it involved cutting and sawing and drilling and removing part of her spine. He kept using the words "skeletal" and "lesions." It was a lot of information. I tried to do the thing where you're listening but not really listening, where you're just nodding but trying to distract yourself by staring at the ceiling. The next thing I heard was Susie shouting, "Jeff! Jeff!" And then I was out. Next thing I remember I'm in a hospital bed out in the hallway, with a couple of nurses checking my vitals, and I see Susie being wheeled past me on a gurney, rolling her eyes at me on her way to surgery. "Hi," I said, waving at her with a limp hand.

For months and months we went back and forth, to and from the hospital. She had so many treatments and procedures and tests and scans sometimes it was hard for her not to wonder if it was worth it to put her body through so much. In the midst of it all, we made a record—Spencer, Sammy, Susie, and I together. It was our project. Spencer and I played the instruments, but more than any other record I've ever made, it became something the whole family stayed focused on. It needed all of us to keep it going. We would listen to the songs together, hearing arrangements grow and take shape, and it was a warm place for us all to disappear. It became a healthy outlet for our fear and anxiety and sadness. We called the album *Sukierae*, which was a family joke. When Susie was a kid, she had a crush on Peter Noone, the lead singer for Herman's Hermits. She read in some teen magazine that his sister was named Suki, so she started asking all of her friends to start calling her Suki. Just in case she ran into Noone, they'd have that icebreaker—"Your sister's name is Suki? That's *my* name!"—and then they'd fall in love and get married. It was the perfect love story. We added "Rae" because it's her middle name and "Sukierae" is what a handful of her closest friends ended up calling her and still do, to this day.

Susie got better and our lives have all gone back to something resembling how it was before. Like everything that nearly tears you apart, it brought us closer together.

CANCER CREATED ANOTHER detour, this time during the course of writing this book. My dad was diagnosed with stage 4 lung cancer late in the spring of 2017. My father and I had become closer after my mother died. He only fully emerged as a parent when she stopped being around as competition. With her gone, all of a sudden he was warm and affectionate, in ways I didn't realize he was capable of. I would have been happy if it had happened sooner, but I feel lucky we got so close at the very end.

Luckily, my sister and I were both around and free of responsibilities enough to be with him a lot during his final days and months. There wasn't anything anyone could do for him but make him comfortable. So we sang to him at his bedside and got him to tell us what he thought about the whole "living" thing now that he was near the end. "Life is happy and sad and it hurts" is what he told us. Try and sum it up better than that—I can't. About four days before he died we finally managed to get everything set up so that he could receive hospice care at home. The house I grew up in. The mauve one.

We let everyone know it was time. Debbie was already there, and my brother Steve made it back to town. Susie, Spencer, and I were all there, but Sammy had a summer job and we had left him in Chicago. Initially we thought my dad was going to be around for at least a few more weeks, so Sammy had felt like he'd still have a chance to say goodbye when his job ended. But when we finally got my dad settled in the hospital bed we'd had set up in the living room (where my mom and I used to torture him with late-night TV movies), his condition began to deteriorate, fast. It seemed like he'd been holding on just so that he could die at home.

Suddenly, it started to feel like he had hours, not weeks, left. We didn't know what to do about Sammy. It was a tough call, but he told us he needed to be there. So we raced back to Chicago, picked him up, and drove back. A ten-hour round-trip. When we were about an hour outside of Belleville my sister called, sobbing. She didn't think we were going to make it back in time. My dad's breathing had become extremely labored and he was no longer conscious. The hospice nurse had told us that the hearing is the last thing to go, but before we could even suggest to my sister that we say goodbye over the phone, Sammy asked me if he could say goodbye.

My sister held the phone up to my dad's ear and Sammy told him, "Grandpa, it's Sammy. I just want you to know I love you. I'll always love you. You'll always be here in me as a part of me and Spencer. I don't want to say goodbye, but I want you to know I'm going to be all right. Spencer's going to be all right. And my dad's going to be all right. We're going to be all right. So, it's okay to go. You won't ever really leave us. We love you. Goodbye."

It's hard to drive a car safely when you're crying harder than you've ever cried. I was so proud of Sammy. I don't know where he gained the emotional insight that the dying might not want to let go because they're worried about the living, but it was poignant and beautiful. In the end, we were able to make it to his side. Sammy and Spencer and I sang "I Shall Be Released" together, and I tried to sing "Hummingbird," my dad's favorite Wilco song, but I don't think I got very far. My dad died about a half hour after we'd made it back from Chicago, with his girlfriend, Melba, holding his right hand and me and Sammy and Spencer holding his left; family at his side, and a stereo we hadn't even noticed was on, playing Wilco softly in the strange new silence.

11

ON AND ON
AND ON

HAD PUT TOGETHER the band, the Wilco that you see onstage today, right before I went into rehab. Leroy had left the band not long after we finished *A Ghost Is Born*, and it was another one of those moments where bad news became an opportunity. I really love Leroy, and I miss him, but when he left, it was a disappointment, but it didn't destroy our relationship. It was one of those transitions where I got to ask myself, "Wow, who could I get? Who might be interested?" I thought about people I'd seen, musicians I'd been excited about. And I decided, "Let's ask Pat and Nels," and they both said yes.

I realized it would be really helpful to have a lot of hands on deck. When we toured on *Yankee Hotel Foxtrot* we were a smaller band, just a four piece, for a lot of the tour. We were trying to cover a lot of different sounds from the record by triggering samples onstage and trying to use technology in ways that we weren't really adept at or comfortable with. We pulled it off, but that experience made me think that more hands would be better than us triggering things with our feet.

Today, we're a band full of music lifers. It's a little small orchestra put together not just to play *A Ghost Is Born*, but *Yankee Hotel Foxtrot* and everything else we've done. There's John and I, who've been there since the beginning; Glenn, who came in halfway through *Yankee*; Mikael, who started during the hazy post-*Yankee*/pre-*Ghost* period; and Pat Sansone and Nels Cline.

Pat had been playing in a side-project band with John Stirratt for a while and had become friends with all of us over the years. Whenever I would see him and John play and sing together, I would marvel at his mastery of all the great pop and rock guitar and keyboard tones and styles. Just a gifted musician. I can't think of any band on earth that Pat couldn't adapt to and stay afloat in, chops-wise.

And speaking of chops, Nels Cline. I'd first seen Nels when he played with Carla Bozulich in the Geraldine Fibbers. Truly a one-of-a-kind talent. The parts he played in that band were built around pushing the guitar into a purely sonic realm that transcended the traditional roles a guitar would normally play. It was astonishing and unforgettable, but I didn't start daydreaming about making music with Nels until a few years later when I saw him backing up Carla again. They were touring Carla's remake of Willie Nelson's *Red Headed Stranger* album and Nels was playing beautiful and understated lap steel guitar and lovingly skewed country licks all night.

I'm always impressed when I come across a musician who's found the passion to embrace seemingly contradictory approaches to music making, and it was obvious that night that Nels might just be able to play anything. I sent him an advance copy of *A Ghost Is Born* so he could have an idea of where we were at musically, and anxiously waited for him to say yea or nay. Talking on the phone a few days later I began to worry he was turning us down when he kept talking about my guitar playing on the album, how he loved it, and didn't know what he could add to the band. I thought it was a really sweet way to let me down easy. I was wrong, though. It was just Nels being his typical generous and humble self. He wanted in.

One thing I think all of us have in common in our band is gratitude. We all know how hard making a band work really is. When things are going well, and I don't just mean commercially—when you're enjoying it and you can feel everyone is working toward and excited about some common cause—it should never be taken for granted. Almost immediately, this lineup of the band felt whole. By the time I got out of rehab and started practicing with everyone, they had already gelled into a living, breathing rock band, thanks to John's leadership in my absence, his unflagging loyalty to me as a friend, and everyone's belief that Wilco was a cause worth fighting for. As we toured and grew, we just got tighter and tighter. I was worried some of the material from the earlier albums would suffer with this band's strengths being more organized around playing the last two albums, but even those songs sounded better than they ever had to my ears. Aside from being able to nail the current album, *A Ghost Is Born*, the band's takes on the more complicated arrangements from *Summerteeth* and *Yankee Hotel Foxtrot* seemed to add vitality and improve upon the studio-reliant recorded versions. A lot of nights I'd be onstage thinking, "Why didn't we do this sooner?" "Why didn't we put together the right band first and then knock it out live in the studio?" Every song felt so much more immediate and exciting.

So that's where we started on *Sky Blue Sky*. We gave ourselves a few very simple guidelines. Simple songs with highly considered group arrangements built off the ground and performed live in the studio. We did end up allowing an overdub or two per song, but for the most part we stuck to those parameters. I can remember the thinking behind setting some loose boundaries; the obvious one is that it really was a new band and it just felt like the appropriate way to introduce this lineup on a record.

The less obvious reason is that I thought I would lose my mind if I tried to sort through the infinite possibilities this band would have access to in a studio-as-instrument scenario. Nels Cline alone seemed like he could cause permanent damage to my fragile post-hospital psyche just by running through his repertoire of pedal combinations. Playing live forced everyone to be decisive when choosing their parts and sounds and to stay focused on how the band sounded as a collective thing. One sound we were all making together.

The songs themselves were written as an attempt to keep things simpler as well. After a few records of getting more and more comfortable with an abstract and at times cryptic approach to lyric writing, I felt in desperate need of some clarity. Life's complexities had overwhelmed me to the point of hospitalization after our last record, so going into this one, I didn't have much of a taste for pushing myself to any extremes artistically.

By now you're probably beginning to notice two distinct and alternating goals in the way my songwriting has progressed. One seems to stem from an impulsive need to be heard and the other from the conflicting desire to avoid any outright detection of that wish. For most of *Sky Blue Sky* (with some exceptions, like "Impossible Germany") I found myself actively avoiding my instinct to hide. In a lot of ways I can see it now as a fairly typical recovery-themed record. "Either Way" is basically a rewording of the Serenity Prayer, for crying out loud. It's an important record for me in that regard. I think letting down my guard and getting things off my chest in a more humble and plainspoken manner helped me reset an idea of myself as a creative person. Leaving behind as many of the myths surrounding suffering and art as I possibly could was the only path forward.

The fact is, I wasn't sure I still had it in me to write at all. Intellectually, I could point to dozens of authors and musicians who lived lives that bolstered a belief I was fostering that pain and brokenness were inessential and overhyped components of how great art gets made, but the appeal of the tortured artist archetype didn't become ingrained in my imagination overnight so it was unreasonable to expect it to have left my heart so soon. Keeping everything more simple and direct seemed like the perfect place to start over and break free from old habits as a person and a songwriter.

When *Sky Blue Sky* came out, some people seemed disappointed by the simplicity and the overall gentleness of the record, but I was thrilled. It was an amazing feat to me to get six humans, much less musicians, to work that closely together for such long periods without any tumult or dysfunction. It was such a gratifying and triumphant feeling. It was way harder to pull off than a lot of the heavily layered and experimental-sounding arrangements from the previous few albums that people cited as being more complex.

Sky Blue Sky also came at a time in my life where I was still learning how to take care of myself. I had made so much progress by the time we had started. One of the main goals of recovery—and maybe the only essential goal of any kind of psychological intervention, whether it's through meditation or talk therapy or even an AA meeting—is to become aware enough of your thoughts and emotions to see when there is a choice to be made. Addicts are compelled to do things by inner thoughts and feelings that are mostly invisible to them. The subconscious can steer the ship for a long time without your conscious mind ever noticing. It was a revelation when I started to be able to see that there were choices to make, and that it was a hell of a lot easier to do the right thing when you're aware that you *have* a right thing and a wrong thing to choose between. I'm oversimplifying to some degree, but it really works to look at it this way when you have a history of finding yourself dialing the phone to a connection before you even thought about getting high.

This is also the album I was making when my mom died. Everything had been feeling so exciting and perfect, and then I got a call from my dad at 3:00 a.m. saying, "She's gone, boy." So sudden. So unexpected. One of my initial reactions was so selfish, I'm embarrassed to admit it. I felt cheated. Why wasn't I being allowed to enjoy this wonderful period in my life where my band and my mind finally seemed to be working? I felt sorry for myself. "Can't I get through one record without a tragedy?" I felt pathetic.

These are the kind of moments that can be disastrous for people in recovery. But I had a choice, and the choice was easy to make for the first time in my life. I was grieving. People grieve lost loved ones every day. I realized that I wasn't being denied something, I was being given something no one gets to avoid. There wasn't a way back from, or around, the pain of losing my mother. The way out was through it.

I finished the lyrics to *Sky Blue Sky* in this state of mind. "On and On and On" in particular was written for my dad in an effort to console him with some thoughts I wasn't entirely sure I believed but found comforting nonetheless. Do we find each other in some other realm to spend eternity, as promised, in love? My dad thought so. When he was dying and fighting to not die, even when he was unconscious he seemed obstinate, almost stubborn in his refusal to let go of life. His girlfriend, Melba, would get right up to his ear and she'd remind him, "It's okay, honey, you can go. JoAnn is waiting for you."

I might not have mentioned this yet, but my dad was a pretty morbid guy throughout his life. My siblings and I all had moments with him where he would tell us exactly what songs he wanted played at his funeral or what color casket lining he thought wouldn't look cheap. But my sister was the only one who was organized enough and took him seriously enough to write his requests down and file them away on note cards. So when my dad died we knew exactly what to do. There were two things that he had told her that took my breath away. The first: Jeff is not to perform at my funeral (I had tried to play a song at my mother's service at his request and had broken down halfway through and he still felt guilty about it). The second one was: My grave marker should read "On and On and On."

WHILE WE WERE finishing *Wilco (The Album)*, we realized that our record deal was going to be up pretty soon. I was really starting to question the notion of what the record companies were doing for a band like Wilco. I can see what they're doing for a younger band. There is something to be said for not being troubled by the business aspects of any of it for some bands. But as a band, we had already taken on a lot of that work, just out of a desire to have some autonomy and agency in business decisions. It felt like we were already doing a lot of what a traditional record company would do for a band in-house. We had our own publicist and we had a pretty strong Internet presence. A lot of shows would sell out without us having to do much promotion.

It became clear to us that how the financial pie was being divided up wasn't really reflective of how the work was being divided up.

So we presented the label with an idea. We didn't expect them to embrace it, but we thought maybe it would be a good starting point for a negotiation. "We think that maybe you should be getting what we've been getting and maybe we should be getting what you've been getting," in terms of how we divide the profits. And on principle, they said they couldn't do it. That it's a precedent, contractually, that they weren't willing to upend.

We were disappointed, but not surprised. If I were them, I would have had a hard time not laughing us out onto the street. It's the kind of arrogant and cocky shit we always try. Not because we think we're *that* great, but because we think the whole business is *that* lame. That's what led to us starting our own label. So far it's been pretty great. Everyone always asks if we feel like we have more creative freedom, and it's hard to explain that we really don't. For a long time we've been affording ourselves a fair amount of creative freedom, whether we deserved it or not.

The thing that's most positive to us about having a label is that we have more autonomy in how we conduct our business. People get sick of the music business for the same reasons they get sick of any business. It's predictably awful sometimes. Any job, no matter how great it is, can become a job someone hates. I don't know why that is, but it's true. Having more of a hand to play in our own business transactions has taught us that the inverse is true as well. No part of being in a band and making records and putting them out on your own label is so awful that you can't find a way to make it more creative and interesting. I highly recommend it if you have the energy and opportunity to do so.

I DIDN'T WRITE THIS book to give testimonials about the joys of being an entrepreneur, but how drastically owning my own label contrasts with my earliest days of duplicating demo cassettes on my dad's karaoke machine does lead me to reflect on just how much change I've witnessed since I started making music.

Musically, I feel like I've played a part in bridging a few distinct musical generations. I've had the honor of working with Woody Guthrie's words and collaborating with the mighty Mavis Staples, but I've also toured with Sonic Youth and recorded with Vic Mensa. I've cut records to a lathe, recorded to tape, recorded to computers.

I know I'm not the only one who can claim this, but I feel like I'm a part of some connective tissue between two worlds that don't really interact the same way anymore. I feel like I might be a member of the last tribe that made it across the divide before time changed, before people started listening to every era of music all at once because of the Internet. When I first started making records, each new thing was built on the things directly before it. Time was linear. Musical styles would evolve and distort with the passage of time. It was hard to maintain access to bygone generations of music because it would literally disappear. Now time feels almost circular. It still moves in only one direction (unfortunately), but it's all still happening and almost anyone can access any era of music at any time. So instead of being influenced only by the recordings and generations of musicians most accessible and obtainable to study, musicians today can draw upon almost anything ever recorded and track down and share artists and techniques in an instant that would have taken my generation years to piece together.

The most time my kids will have to spend finding a piece of music is ten minutes. On some of the streaming sites they might have to work a little bit to find something rare, maybe it's on YouTube, maybe you have to find the torrent or something. For us, some albums would have had such small initial pressings and have been so scarce that the only way to even know about them was to read about them. We would spend years kind of trying to imagine what Big Star's "Third" sounds like. Based on "It's really tormented, it's got strings on it, it's really tormented."

There's obviously something really nice about the democratization of it, that everybody is able to find everything. There are probably some upsides to that. But we probably benefited from having digestible chunks of music to consume in ways that allowed us to be very familiar with one piece at a time, or even a song or two at a time, in the case of 45s.

I've been lucky enough to meet a lot of my heroes who aren't around anymore. I bought a Minutemen T-shirt directly from D. Boon at a show in St. Louis. One time I had Rick Danko from the Band tell me that I sound desperate when I sing, and that I should never allow myself to *not* sound desperate. I guess the most miraculous encounter of all would be when Uncle Tupelo opened for Johnny Cash at a club in Santa Ana, California, in 1993. We didn't meet him and June Carter before the show, but we could hear them during our set, watching through the curtains on either side of the stage and shouting, "Woo-hoo," between songs. It was startling. There is nothing in this world that can prepare you for Johnny Cash shouting "Woo-hoo" at you while you're trying to remember how to play the bass. Backstage after the show they were so complimentary and sweet. They were impressed we were playing old songs like "Moonshiner" and "No Depression," which was written by June's father, A. P. Carter. I don't know about the other guys, but I don't remember saying much. What was there to say to Johnny Cash? It was like talking to the Empire State Building or a bald eagle.

They invited us to a songwriting barbecue they were hosting in Nashville. I'd never heard of such a thing, but it sounded amazing. June kept saying she just wanted to take us home and give us all baths, and I wasn't sure if that was part of the deal, but it didn't sound the least bit dirty when she said it. The offer seemed so genuine and crazy, we seriously contemplated canceling the rest of our tour so we could drive two days straight through, all the way to Nashville, and be able to say we wrote songs and ate barbecue at Johnny Cash's house. Then the financial impracticality of that plan set in, so we took a rain check and stood dumbstruck in the parking lot behind the club, waving goodbye to their tour bus.

I met Johnny Cash again years later when Wilco played a CMJ showcase in New York City. We'd just finished recording *Being There* and were planning to play our new songs for the first time publicly. Maybe an hour before the show, our dressing room door opened and Johnny Cash wandered in. He was noticeably weaker-looking than the last time I saw him, and his hair had more gray, but his aura was undiminished.

"Where's Jeff?" he asked.

I just about fell out of my chair. He knows my name?! When did I get on a first-name basis with the Man in Black? How?! He told me he wasn't feeling well and asked if it would be okay if we switched slots with him and let him open up the show. I said, yeah, of course, that's no problem. He smiled and kindly patted me on the shoulder with one of his gigantic hands. "Thanks, Jeff. I appreciate it. Good to see you again."

What had just happened didn't fully hit us until several moments after his presence had evaporated from the room. What?! Oh shit. We have to *follow* Johnny Cash?! This is ridiculous. Can't we just leave with everyone else when he's done? No dice, the powers that be told us. We had to play even if it was to the custodial team. In a lot of ways it was freeing. You don't get on a stage after Johnny Cash has left it and feel like you owe anyone a return on their entertainment dollar. The stakes haven't been raised; they've been obliterated. You're like a four-year-old walking out onto Wrigley Field. Nobody's expecting you to hit a home run. It'd be a miracle if you just managed to hold a bat upright. When we played "Misunderstood" and "Sunken Treasure," they sounded awful, we were dissonant and loud and childish in the glee we were getting from not giving anyone what they wanted. We just assumed the audience wasn't into us. And we were right.

Afterward, Joe McEwen, our A&R guy from Reprise, came backstage and asked, "What the hell happened? You guys used to be so good." His outrage was heartwarming. Pissing everybody off in a memorable way was our best-case scenario. Nobody should ever follow Johnny Cash onto a stage. It was never going to be a reasonable way to arrange the universe. We did the best we could do, and the best we could do was fail spectacularly. What were our options, though? Say no to Johnny Cash?

Just a few years ago we were asked to do a summer-length tour opening for Bob Dylan. I'm sort of surprised, writing this, that I haven't talked about him yet. Maybe it's because his importance to me feels like it's too obvious to bring up. Kind of like "Human, you say? Let me guess, you like oxygen?" I write songs, and Dylan is the peak I'm going to keep climbing toward.

There really wasn't a whole lot of interaction with him, but the contact I did have was memorable, including the first day of the tour. In the backstage area, we had all been warned that in the minutes leading up to Dylan's set time, everyone was to stay clear of the route from his dressing room to the stage. We were also told not to gawk or try to talk to him. So we did our best to look casual hanging in the doorway of our own dressing room so as not to miss at least getting a first glimpse up close. Craning my neck out the door, I could see his band walking toward us with Dylan trailing a bit behind. As they got to our door I heard what sounded like a Bob Dylan impression. "Hey, Jeff, how's it going, man? Good to see you!" Bob had spoken to me. Without breaking stride. And I was left in his wake trying to play it cool, but I could feel all of the other folks around us looking at me. It was impossible to play it cool. "Dylan talked to me. Did you guys see that?!" I immediately undid any credibility I had just accrued by being visibly rattled. I had to sit down. Later, when I had collected myself, I called Susie to let her know Bob and I were already best friends.

DOLLY PARTON ONCE said that her advice to anyone wanting to be an artist was to "Find out who you are and then be that on purpose." Or something like that. As I've gotten older, those are the people I find myself drawn to work with and stay close to. People who have figured out who they are and are good at being that on purpose. Like Mavis Staples. Don't get me wrong; I also believe she has a grandiose desire to change the world with her songs. But I've never met anyone with more graceful humility and who is more comfortable in her own skin.

Our first meeting was an arranged marriage. Her management was telling her, "Jeff Tweedy wants to meet you," and my management was telling me, "Mavis wants you to help her make a record." I still don't know who came up with the idea or set the wheels in motion, but however it happened, I'm thankful. We planned a first date; I agreed to meet her for lunch in Hyde Park, on the South Side of Chicago, and we drank iced teas and talked about our families for more than three hours.

I wasn't sure if I'd made any impression on her at all, but she told me later that she was worried I might be another Prince. He had produced two of her records—1989's *Time Waits for No One* and 1993's

The Voice—she adored him, but the process hadn't been easy. He was shy and reclusive, she confided, and she sometimes had to communicate with him by writing letters, because it was the only way to reach him. When I wasn't as immediately outgoing as she'd hoped, the thought went through her head, *Oh Lord, don't send me another Prince!* But then she tested me; she told a joke, and I apparently could laugh freely enough for her to believe I was worth taking a chance on.

Mavis and I have now made three albums together, four, if you count the album Pops Staples left behind when he died, which Spencer and I helped Mavis finish. She treats us like family. She calls Susie her daughter and Spencer and Sammy her grandkids. As for me, she calls me Tweedy; not once has she used the name Jeff. She calls Bob Dylan "Bobby," which makes me a little jealous. But Dylan asked her to marry him in the sixties, and she said no, so they have a history there that's predated me by a half century. In fact, one of my other interactions on tour with Dylan had been him telling me to "Tell Mavis she should have married me!" I told him I would, so I relayed the message to her and she asked me to remind him that she's still available. When I saw him stage-side the next night, I told him what Mavis had said, and he laughed and said, "Yeah? I wish!" Being a literal go-between in a playfully flirtatious conversation between Mavis and Bobby is probably the pinnacle of my career. I should probably hang it up. It's not going to get better than that.

Writing and producing songs for Mavis has given me the courage to take chances I wouldn't normally have tried. A middle-aged white guy from the Midwest should definitely think twice about writing a song like "If All I Was Was Black," and I did. When I first shared the song with Mavis, I admitted my misgivings to her. I wanted to make sure I wasn't putting any words in her mouth she didn't believe or feel accurately described how she feels.

"We can't let anybody know I wrote this," I said. "They'll tear me apart. They'll say, 'Who does this Caucasian think he is?'"

"Tweedy," she told me. "As far as I'm concerned, you *are* black."

I bragged about it later to Susie. "Mavis says I'm black," I said. In any other situation, if I'd claimed to be African American to my wife, she would have mocked me mercilessly, and I would have deserved it. But with Mavis's seal of approval, Susie didn't object. "Well, if Mavis says you're black, you're black," she said.

Working with Mavis made me less cynical. Not that I was an indie rock Ebenezer Scrooge, but there were things about the music industry that I could never bring myself to believe in, like the Grammys. Just to reiterate what I said earlier in the book, I've never dreamed about being nominated, I've never dreamed about winning—it's nice when it happens, but my mind never really goes there. But when our first record together, *You Are Not Alone*, won a Grammy in 2011, it was a big deal for her. She'd been making music for six decades, recorded classics like "Respect Yourself" and "I'll Take You There," and never got so much as a nomination. We weren't there, but Susie and I were watching the live stream on a computer in her office when Mavis walked up and accepted that award, with such sincere gratitude and shock and appreciation, and bursting into tears while telling the crowd, "It's been a long time coming." I couldn't help but get choked up.

Her willingness to take chances and try new things outside of her comfort zone has always been remarkable to me. This was not a person I considered a musical equal, but we'd be recording at the Loft and I'd say to her, "You need to sing this out in the staircase so we can record it with that great natural reverb." "Are you crazy?" she'd fire back. "It's freezing out there." A valid point, because it was December in Chicago and the temperature outside the studio, even in the relatively protected staircase leading down to the street, was maybe twenty degrees at best, and that was only if the sun was out.

But I persisted, saying something insane like "Somebody get Mavis a coat and scarf and let's do this." She agreed to try it, even though a musical icon who's been making music for longer than I've been alive shouldn't have to stand in a hallway in a scarf and jacket to sing a damn song, with temperatures so cold she could see her breath, just because some jackass said he likes the stairwell reverb better than the twenty other reverb sources we have inside the warm studio. But she did it.

When we work together, I give her demos to take home so she can get a general sense of the songs before we record them. I'll sing her vocal parts on the demos, just to give her a rough framework of what I'm thinking. But Mavis is Mavis, and I always assume she'll make the songs her own. *And the same thing happens on each record* her first run-through of the first song of every session. Her voice loses its husky contralto and she sounds more like, well . . . me.

"Um, Mavis," I'll say, stopping her mid-song. "I appreciate what you're doing, but it's sounding a little, um . . . nasally."

"Does it really?" she'll ask.

"You know, you don't have to do it *exactly* like the demo. No one wants to hear Mavis sing like Jeff Tweedy," I say.

"Oh good, good," she says, seeming honestly relieved. "I wasn't sure how close you wanted it to sound to the way you sang it."

I don't think you could find a better example of how we all should be. Mavis sang behind Martin Luther King Jr., she was in *The Last Waltz,* and Bobby Dylan and she smooched (her words) back in the day. If anything, she has earned the right to walk into a studio, barking orders and telling everyone exactly how a damn record is supposed to be made. But instead, she approaches it with humility, assuming she isn't the only talented person in the room, and maybe isn't too old to try something new.

I want to live in a world filled with people like Mavis.

IN 2012, WILCO started putting together our own festival, Solid Sound. At first, we intended to have it every year, but after the first two years we decided every other year would give us more time to plan and save enough energy to make it truly special every time it happens. We invite our favorite bands, all of our side projects and other collaborations we've worked on outside of Wilco perform, and we all contribute and curate installations and activities that we're interested in. The event takes place at MASS MoCA, a contemporary art institution in western Massachusetts, which is housed in a gigantic old textile mill. It's an incredible space and a beautifully curated and unparalleled showcase of living artists from around the world. We feel extremely privileged to be able to use it as Solid Sound's home.

After doing it a few times, I think Solid Sound is maybe the purest expression of what Wilco is to us. Wilco at this point in time is really an art collective, and that's a fact much more evident in our festival than on any one record, or any one show outside of that environment.

Being afforded an opportunity to present ourselves alongside the music we all make outside of Wilco, other musicians and bands we love, beers we like (well, not the beers I like, since I don't drink, but you get the idea), comedians we love, in a brilliantly curated world-class art facility is a dream.

Sort of like a State Fair for a state of mind. It's as close as Wilco can get to being a place, a physical space you can walk around in and explore.

The other thing on display at Solid Sound is our community of fans. It's hard to take too much credit, but it's also impossible to not feel some pride looking at the vibrant, multigenerational and diverse crowd that has gathered around our band. They're generous, thoughtful, and loyal, not just to us but to one another, as well. Without their commitment to the experiment, their willingness to be exposed to new things, and their caring for one another, it would be just another rock festival.

I have had some difficulty understanding our fans over the years. Wilco has always played songs from every era. We've never really shunned any part of our catalog. So there have been times when you could sense different factions in our audiences. Not everyone at our show would be there to see the same band. Our records were very different from one another—drastically so, in some cases—and it used to feel as though specific records had their own fans.

Now it doesn't feel that way. It seems these days that if you like our band, you're ready for changes. I'm glad we went through the more difficult period without ever turning our backs on anyone, though. There's an amazing opportunity that so few people ever have in their lives to fulfill a wish for somebody. It's so rare that such a simple act, like playing a song someone loves, can make someone so happy. If you have that opportunity, that power, to do that for anyone, that's an incredible gift. All songs rely on a collaboration with a listener. Someone other than you has to put the song and its meaning together in their consciousness for it to have any meaning outside of yourself. I think I should always err on the side of acknowledging that fact and honoring it. I don't always feel like playing "Jesus, Etc.," for example, but if doing so can complete that circuit for someone else, what good reason would I have to deny them? I play the song one more time, and I'm always glad I did.

THESE DAYS, I do most of my work at the Loft, the magical recording studio/bunkhouse I'd dreamed about while watching *The Monkees*. I walk there most days—it's just a few miles from my house—and when I get there, it's all about work. I'm not necessarily crafting a new album, but I'm always working on new songs. I have dozens of songs—too many songs, maybe. I make batches of songs and then put them away for later. Maybe I'll release them someday; maybe they'll just stay lost until I die.

I sit up in the Loft with my friend Tom Schick, who's been the full-time engineer there for the last six or seven years. Most days, it's just my buddy Mark, who manages the studio and is my most trusted friend, and Tom and me up there. Sometimes Spencer, if he's off from college and feels like recording. I like working on too many songs at once, because you're never focused on one thing for too long. If a song starts to lose its magic, and I start telling myself, "I don't know what I was thinking. This sucks," we just let it go and move on. What else is there that needs another listen? If I stay away from a song long enough, when I come back to it, it sometimes feels like I'm hearing it for the first time. That's a beautiful place, if you can get to it, where you're mesmerized by the potential in a song you don't remember writing, and you finally have the energy and enthusiasm to finish it. About once a month I cut out early and go see the same doctor who took care of me when I was in the hospital. For fourteen years now, I've been happy to be in his care, and I feel that that consistency gives my life a lot of balance I wouldn't have if I started pretending that I didn't still have room to grow and things to learn about how distorted things can appear to my addict mind.

Back at the Loft, Tom and I know when we've been tweaking a song for too long. He says it's when I start focusing on things that "Will not affect sales." If I'm thinking about what the hi-hat sounds like, it's time to stop. I've gone too far and I've lost my mind. Nobody in the world gives a fuck what a hi-hat sounds like. As long as it doesn't break the spell, nobody cares. If somebody does care about it, then they work in a recording studio and they're already too far up their own asses to ever truly like anyone's record anyway.

Making these songs, arguing over the minutiae with Tom—it's all that matters. Whether any of it comes out or doesn't come out doesn't ultimately concern me. I mean, I'd love to have people hear as much of what I create as possible, but I don't worry about it too much. I think that's the secret to this line of work—you have to be okay with music being a great thing to do, and not rely on it to be the thing that makes you rich or even the thing that pays all of your bills. As long as it's something that makes you feel better and you wake up every morning wanting to get back in the studio to make something else, then there's not much anyone can fucking do to ruin it. You can find an audience. You can take your time. You can find your voice. You can find new ways to express yourself. You can explore it. You can get better at it. If you keep it close, no one can take that from you. It exists. The beautiful part has existed and it will continue to exist.

EPILOGUE

WHEN I WAS growing up, my dad would always say, "Let's go, so we can get back," whenever his presence was required somewhere other than his comfort zone. Sometimes it would be an appropriate response to common and relatable hassles, like a company picnic or the funeral services of a distant relative. But a lot of times he'd say it as we would be leaving to go somewhere or do something that surely even he was looking forward to, like a fishing trip or going to grab an ice-cream cone.

He meant it as a joke, obviously, but it really wasn't. There were times when his "comfort zone" would become so specific and narrowly defined as to be no more than a single chair in our unfinished basement. Even then, his level of ease would additionally require proximity to cold cans, not *bottles*, of whatever niche, subvarietal shitty American beer he was fiercely loyal to that month. Say, Pabst Blue Ribbon Light Select Extra Dry for example. Or maybe Michelob

Silver Ultra-Light. None of us understood what could possibly prompt the dismissal of one brand and the sudden loyalty to another. Sometimes, seemingly overnight, an animus toward one beer manufacturer would appear that had the weight and feel of some real betrayal. And we'd all have to pay attention and stay current so that when our refrigerator would suddenly fill up with a new and unfamiliar can, and we were called upon to fetch we could avoid riling him up with a spurned holdover from the transition.

As we all got older, the phrase started to become less of a joke and more of a succinct and accurate description of the anxiety that permeates my family. I think everyone has their comfort zone that they would prefer not to leave. But not everyone allows that feeling of inconvenience to become a coddled and catered-to dysfunction. Codependence is what they call it, I guess. In our case, there surely was a team effort to keep things nice and bad so as not to make anything worse.

For me personally, I became so adept at "let's go, so we can get back" that I eventually graduated straight to "let's not leave." As you can imagine that's not a tenable situation for someone in a traveling rock band, and it was certainly an unworkable solution to the problems I was facing. I never wanted to leave the comfort of opioids or whatever maladaptive behavior was providing me some safe harbor, and for a while, I had plenty of enablers and facilitators to seal off any challenges to that status quo.

And then I got help. That's maybe the only thing about me that I think is truly unique. It's statistically unlikely for an addict to be successful in their struggle to recover. Beyond that, I saw plenty of substance abuse growing up but I never saw anyone get better, so I had no idea what that transformation looked like. Addiction is a cunning disease, so the odds are always stacked against any addict, but I did it. And I'm doing it.

I'm not trying to pat myself on the back. I'm sincerely appreciative of the fact that a ton of luck was involved in me getting the help I needed. I think that's part of why I wrote this book. I wanted to write about, and understand, and share the part of me that has always been able to be vulnerable. This allowed me get to the place where I was able to ask for help and accept it. Then, eventually, I found the part of me that has been able to stay committed to understanding myself better and to keep working through the things I've struggled with. The changes and the work and the support that have allowed me to have some sense of comfort wherever I am and wherever I go, and the relative ease with which I've been able to live within my own skin these last fourteen years or so—it all seems like something worth sharing. Or at least worth sorting through publicly. In recovery they tell you that sobriety isn't something you keep by keeping it to yourself. Sounds right to me.

That was the one story I knew for certain I had to tell. Beyond that, I wasn't so sure. I'm not naturally nostalgic or prone to reflection. I have terrible biographical memory. At least once every tour, I'll say to someone in Wilco, "Wow, what a beautiful old theater. I wonder if they just renovated it," and they'll say something like "This is the theater where two guys started fighting in the balcony during the quiet part of 'Via Chicago,' and the last time we were here they turned up the lights in the middle of the show so some EMTs could give CPR to this dude, out cold, right in the middle aisle. Remember? We had just played 'Heavy Metal Drummer.' Ended up he was super wasted. I think this is about the eighth time we've played here. Two times ago, Nels's amp blew up but it sounded incredible right before it started smoking. . . . Oh! And then there was the show . . ."

Point is, I can't remember shit and it's never really bothered me that much. But I started writing and I was surprised by all of the vivid, detailed memories this book conjured. Like the fake-stone interior and potted rubber trees in the waiting room at the doctor's office where I used to get my allergy shots twice a week when I was in the fifth grade. Or . . . I'd almost forgotten how my mom would call me "Shicky-poo" when she was in a good mood, and that my dad almost always called me simply "Boy."

The red Naugahyde booths at the lunch counter where my aunt Gail worked came back to me. Along with the rest of the soda fountain fixtures where I'd get a grilled cheese sandwich and a scoop of tapioca almost every day on my way home from grade school. And Bunn's Groceries, the corner store I'd walk to to get penny candy on the street I grew up on. The store part was the ground floor of one side of a duplex. The Bunns lived above their store, and my dad's mother lived in the other side of the duplex with a man who wasn't my grandfather who I called Grampa Oscar. I remember how no one could understand Grampa Oscar because he only had half a tongue or his tongue was paralyzed or some shit . . . and how he seemed to always be watching professional wrestling on a tiny black-and-white TV, hollering at the wrestlers in their pre-spandex unitards. And now I'm remembering his loud, utterly terrifying, brutal, consonant-less emanations. As I write this, I'm realizing that growing up in an old midwestern industrial town in the seventies and eighties has made my memories sound like they were filmed on the set of some fifties sitcom. Soda fountains?! Penny candy?!? Tapioca!!??? Man, oh man. I promise I didn't make any of this up or fill in the gaps in my drug-dimmed memory by watching reruns of Andy Griffith.

I've had more recent recollections, too, like the sweeter memories of being in a band with Jay Farrar, and what a thrill it was discovering so much music together and through each other, and how it changed our lives. I recalled how Joe McEwen, the guy that signed Uncle Tupelo to Sire, had the most perfectly inscrutable A&R-man dance ever devised. Eyes closed as if in reverie, slightly swaying in time with the music, and simultaneously shaking his head side to side, like his body was saying, "Everyone at the label can't wait to work with you," while his head respectfully informs your band that "Warner Bros. is not interested in your demo submission at this time." Writing also brought back all of the long hours in the studio with Jay Bennett, pushing crazy ideas on each other. Like the time he tried to convince me that the expensive recording studio we were renting wouldn't mind if we dropped a twenty-pound weight on their $50,000 piano as long as we covered the lid with a packing blanket, and how that is, in fact, the last sound you hear on *Being There*.

Writing has even helped me take a closer look at some memories that are almost too unbearably bittersweet and poignant to spend much time with under normal circumstances. Like the specific expression of gratitude and relief in Susie's eyes when she finally got to come home from the hospital after cancer surgery and all four of us plopped down on the couch to watch a movie together. And how seeing her smiling with tears in her eyes gave us the first sense that anything was ever going to feel all right in the world again.

I've been doing this—writing and reminiscing and talking with my family and comparing notes—for a couple of years now. Most of their suggestions have made it into this book. With a few notable exceptions: Spencer and Sammy wanted me to tell you about the most punk-rock thing I've ever seen, which is the time Ween opened for Wilco at Lounge Ax, and Gene Ween, their lead singer, smashed his acoustic guitar. During *soundcheck*! The cherry on top of that particular anecdote was the casual way he walked offstage after stomping his guitar into splinters and asked me if he could borrow mine.

During this same period of time that I've spent writing this book and discovering that my walks down memory lane aren't so colorless and nondescript after all, I've kept busy working on a lot of music as well. Wilco made *Schmilco* while I was just getting up the nerve to start writing and beginning to get an idea of the kinds of stories I might have to tell. There are a few songs on that record that are evidence of some mental overlap between the two projects. In particular, the song called "Quarters" wouldn't have the lyrics it does without this book dredging up some of the semi-traumatic memories I have of my maternal grandfather's attempts at the rare combination of barkeeping and babysitting (baby-keeping?). Good times.

Most recently, in the summer of 2018, I finished a solo record, my first of all new material. Writing this book has made those songs some of the most direct, personal, and autobiographical that I've ever written. For a while now, the primary way I've kept my songwriting feeling honest to me is to imagine I'm singing only to myself, pretending no one else is listening.

But the songs that have grown out of the writing of this book are different because I've been thinking about what exactly I would like to say directly to someone. What I would like to say to you. I've imagined you sitting across from me, interested in what I might have to say.

Now I have a whole batch of songs like that, too. Maybe the first songs I've ever written with the intention of telling someone something I want them to know about myself. Things I want you to hear. If you finish reading this book and you listen to the album I just made, which is called *WARM*, it should be fairly easy to recognize what I'm describing.

I think I've finally stopped worrying about getting back from somewhere less comfortable—some place where I'm sure I'm going to be miserable. I believe I'm starting to be "okay" wherever I am. I think I'm ready to just say, "Let's go."

Bombs Above

All my life
I've played a part
In the bombs above
The ones you love
I'm taking a moment to apologize
I should have done more
To stop the war
So I'm sorry

I leave behind
A trail of songs
From the darkest gloom
To the brightest sun
I've lost my way
But it's hard to say
What I've been through
Should matter to you

A man so drunk
He could hardly stand
Told me once
Holding my hand

LET'S GO (SO WE CAN GET BACK)

Suffering is the same
For everyone
He was right
But I was wrong
To agree

DON'T FORGET

Don't forget
Don't forget you've got a key
Yeah a cosmic key
Oh I love you so much

Don't forget
We're all blowing in
The interstellar wind
I'm your little galaxy

Don't forget
Don't forget sometimes
We all
We all think about dying
Don't let it kill you

Don't forget
I won't forget the long drive
We arrived in time to say goodbye
And the way my roses shook
I won't overlook
The willows bending by the graves
The very next day in the shade
Sweating in a new suit

LET'S GO (SO WE CAN GET BACK)

I don't regret
I don't regret sometimes
We all
We all think about dying
Don't let it kill you

Don't forget
Don't forget to brush your teeth
Or you'll have a funny smile
You don't have to smile at me

Don't forget
Don't forget sometimes
We all
We all think about dying
Don't let it kill you
Don't forget
Don't forget sometimes
We all
We all think about dying
Oh

Let's Go Rain

Oh I've heard about Noah's flood
Washed away a world of sin
Some say destruction is an act of love
And think it should happen again

Let's go rain
Let's go rain
Again
Let's go rain
Let's go rain
Again

Once upon a time I was a Christian
I didn't know I didn't need to know
Now when the sky speaks I'm going to listen
And when it's pissing I'll just figure I'm alone

Let's go rain
Let's go rain
Again
C'mon rain
Let's go rain
Again

Oh I should
Build a wooden ark

LET'S GO (SO WE CAN GET BACK)

Wouldn't you rather live
On an ocean of guitars?

Aw c'mon rain
Let's go rain
Again
Let's go rain
Let's go rain
Again

Oooooh, oooh, ooh
Aah, aah, aaah

Maybe you're not a believer
Or maybe you don't have a choice
Or maybe it's a fever that you haven't caught yet
'Cause you haven't met
Scott McCaughey

Let's go rain
Let's go rain
Again
Still no rain
Let's go rain
Again

Having Been Is No Way to Be

Oh I was naive
My shoes were untied
In heaven everything is just fine
But the phones are dead
And so is the light
And so are you
And honey so am I
But the earth still turns
For the unconcerned
Days pass below like train windows
I was a sapling tree
The birds looked like me
So I begged my nerves to kick me something new
From time to time
I'd watch you sleep
I wonder how much freedom we can dream
And I'm sorry when you wake up to me

I just got tired
Shining steady like a spiderweb
Is an empty stage
Now people say
"What drugs did you take?"
And "Why don't you start taking them again?"
But they're not my friends
And if I was dead

What difference would it ever make to them?
If I got high
From time to time
I wonder how much freedom you would need
And I'd be sorry when you wake up to me

I'm reaching out to you
I'm writing all the time
I don't see deep but I see far and wide
I see dead trees
But the roots have leaves
Just because I can't describe it doesn't mean I shouldn't try
To untwist the knife
To unmake my mind
Having been is no way to be alive
And I'm alive
When I watch you sleep
I wonder how much freedom we need
And I'm here
When you wake up to me
I'm still here
When you wake up to me

WARM (WHEN THE SUN HAS DIED)

Please take my advice
Worry into your song
Grow away from your anger
Distance belongs

Oh I don't believe in heaven
I keep some heat inside
Like a red brick in the summer
Warm when the sun has died

ACKNOWLEDGMENTS

M Y EDITOR, Jill Schwartzman, is the least flappable and most positive person I've ever met. Two traits I've undoubtedly challenged during the course of finishing this book. Without her, this book would have been an unreadable mess and very likely would have never existed at all. I am eternally grateful.

I'd like to thank Eric Spitznagel for working so hard on my behalf getting this book off the ground and for helping give it its overall shape.

Tony and Deb, thank you so much for getting this ball in motion and for all the many years of hard work and devotion you both have put in to help me build a life worth writing about.

David Dunton, for being so patient and somehow not losing faith in me or this book, I thank you.

When you write a book about yourself, it's hard to not look around at all of the people who have helped you over the course of your life, and when you've finished, you realize that you owe deep debts of gratitude and appreciation, which have somehow gone unexpressed on its pages. For me these deficits of recognition fall into two categories:

People I wrote about but not nearly enough to convey my indebtedness:

Bob and JoAnn Tweedy	Steve Albini and Heather Whinna
Melba Mueller	Sam Jones
Gail Henties and family	Julia Adams and Patrick Monaghan
Debbie and Jerry Voll and family	Fred Armisen
Steve and Janet Tweedy	Mark Greenberg
Greg and Robin Tweedy and family	Tom Schick
John Stirratt	Mavis Staples
Glenn Kotche	Brian Henneman
Nels Cline	Joe McEwen
Pat Sansone	Peter Buck
Mikael Jorgensen	Jim O'Rourke
Leroy Bach	Brian Paulson
Ken Coomer	Scott Reilly
Jay Bennett	Chuck Wagner
Max Johnston	Debbie Southwood-Smith
Jay Farrar	Peter Miller
Billy Bragg	Paul Kolderie
Nora Guthrie	Sean Slade
Mike Heidorn	Jon and Helen Langford

And people who mean the world to me who somehow didn't end up in the book. To you I'd like to apologize for the omission and offer my warmest and most sincere thanks.

ACKNOWLEDGMENTS

Dr. Martin Paisner

Scott McCaughey

Nick Offerman

George Saunders

John Hodgman

Stephen Colbert

Josh Grier

Jaime Herman

Brandy Breaux

Cherie Breaux

Jonathan Parker

Yvonne Staples

Matt Macnamara

Frankie Montuoro

Nate Murphy

Josh Goldsmith

Jason Tobias

Haydn Johnston

Eric Frankhouser

Stan Doty

Andy Nemcik

Ashley Mogayzel

Lance Powell

Zach Nagy

Jeremy Roth

Jared Dottorelli

Ashwin Deepankar

Crystal Myers

Brandy Breaux

Ryan Marian

Ben Levin

Frank Riley

Dawn Nepp

Emily Rosenblum

Dr. Brian Dickover

Dave Dethrow

Sheba Nemerovski and Billy "John" Biggers

Oona Dicker

Fred Wells

Tavi Gevinson

Danny, Kendall, Leah, and Charles Miller

Ellen Kahn

Bruce Miller

Betsy Hailey

Judy Miller

Paul Karoll, Anita Cullen, and family

Sarah and Doron David and family

Mathew Smith

Nick Sakes

Darin Gray

Jim Elkington

Liam Kazar

Sima Cunningham

Jeanne Roeser

Jeff Garlin

Mark Flanagan

Dave Eggers

Neil, Sharon, Liam, and Elroy Finn

Carrie Brownstein

John "Woody" Woodland

ACKNOWLEDGMENTS

Bob Ludwig

Sheila Sachs

Lawrence Azerrad

Zoran Orlic

Tim and Katie Tuten

Greg Kot

Richard Lloyd

Jennifer Polacheck Goodman and
    family

Ellen and Greg Gartland and family

Dr. Adam Petrich

Thomas Dunning

Kelly Hogan

Nora O'Connor

Margaret and Rudra Banerji

Thom Hale and Sylvia Bicalho

Bob Laskowski and Diana Jackson

The Blister sisters (and misters)

The Brennans

The Katzs

The Van Essens

The Shultzes

The Seebecks

The Wylders

The Soloways

The Staceys

The Lounge Ax family

Emmanuel Congregation

Everyone at Near North
    Montessori

Everyone at Northside
    College Prep

Everyone at XRT

Everyone at Jam Productions

I know I'm forgetting people. I'm sorry. I'm going to remember who you all are eventually and I'll feel awful when I do. So . . . isn't knowing I'm going to feel bad almost better than having your name in my stupid book?